THE VIEW

MIND OVER MATTER, HEART OVER MIND

FROM CONAN DOYLE TO *CONVERSATIONS WITH GOD*

Published for Sir Arthur Conan Doyle's
150th Birth Anniversary

Edited by Dave Patrick

Polair Publishing 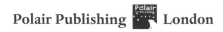 London

First published May 22nd, 2009
by Polair Publishing, P O Box 34886, London W8 6YR

British Library Cataloguing-in-Publication Data
A catalogue record for this book is
available from the British Library

ISBN 978-1-905398-18-8

*The publishers are grateful for permission to publish the extracts from
White Eagle's teaching, along with words of Grace and Ivan Cooke,
which are © White Eagle Publishing Trust, and to the same publisher for
permission to reproduce Simon Bentley's article '2012 and all that', which
first appeared in the White Eagle Lodge journal, Stella Polaris; also to the
publishers of* WORLDSHIFT NOW *for permission to reproduce Ervin Laszlo's
chapter, 'The 2012 Horizon'*

Set in Monotype Dante by the publisher and
printed in Great Britain by Cambridge University Press

THE VIEW

edited by Dave Patrick

Dave Patrick is a writer and Certified Quantum-Touch ® Practitioner and Instructor. Based in the Scottish Highlands, he practices this powerful form of energy healing in Inverness and Nairn; he also runs QT workshops in a variety of locations. For further information visit www.TheHighlandHealer.com.

Dave's writing is now mainly focused on spirituality and the new consciousness. He has long been an admirer of Sir Arthur Conan Doyle's life and works; compiling and editing THE VIEW has provided the opportunity to re-examine Sir Arthur's contribution to humanity's spiritual advancement. Dave hopes thereby to have brought a deeper level of truth and justice to the beliefs Sir Arthur was passionate about, contained in his 'vital message': beliefs he so dearly wished to share with the world. For more information on Dave's writing see www.thevitalmessage.com.

CONTENTS

INTRODUCTION

Dave Patrick

THIS IS a book wanting to be written, of stories longing to be shared and voices seeking to be heard.

Stories written from the heart to connect with the heart. Your heart, but also our heart, for we are all one heart, one consciousness. All one, interconnected.

The journey to this book's publication has been a humbling experience, as well as an amazing one. It has taught that the generosity embedded in the human spirit is infinite. It has shown that the Law of Attraction has nothing to do with money or material wealth, and neither has our happiness, peace of mind or well-being. It has proved that there are only two real emotions—Love and Fear. We may choose to live a life centred on Love, or one haunted by Fear.

Although it is difficult to pinpoint in time exactly when journeys begin and end, the focus for this one has been towards celebrating the 150th Anniversary of Sir Arthur Conan Doyle (ACD), born in Edinburgh on 22 May 22nd, 1859, and died July 7th, 1930.

The idea for the book's theme emerged from ACD's 1919 publication THE VITAL MESSAGE. What a magnificent title! 'Vital', as in 'full of life', and 'Message', as in 'an inspired or significant communication'.

The collective 'View' set down here contains our 'Vital Message' to you.

A Blending of Vision, Insight, Compassion and Storytelling

Having said this is a book wanting to be written, books do not write themselves (even inspirational or automatic writing requires human intervention). This project has been blessed with input from a rich, diverse, mix of contributors; in the main, the overriding message is one of hope and optimism for the future.

There may be one word, one phrase, one sentence, or one paragraph which makes your heart sing. Write it down, cherish it, hold it close to your heart, meditate on it, live it, breathe it. Whatever resonates with your heart, continue to do it. That is what we are here to practise. To experience and learn, recover and move on from past mistakes, patterns and challenges; to transcend them.

Listen to your heart, your inner guidance system, the 'still, small voice within', the source of your inner power.

Life is about choice. Your choice. Choose wisely.

Now let us proceed to the book itself.

I. *Sir Arthur Conan Doyle*

As this book's primary purpose is to mark the 150th Anniversary of the birth of Sir Arthur Conan Doyle, which falls on May 22nd, 2009, the first section has been dedicated to him.

Sir Arthur Conan Doyle is best known as the creator of the fictional master detective Sherlock Holmes, and his colleague Dr Watson. Less well known, and still extremely controversial, was his commitment to promoting Spiritualism.

Included here is an intriguing piece by eminent historian and ACD biographer Owen Dudley Edwards (author of THE QUEST FOR SHERLOCK HOLMES, 1983), entitled 'Arthur Conan Doyle's Spiritual Imagination'. Like Conan Doyle, Owen Dudley Edwards was brought up in the Roman Catholic faith, but has reached very different conclusions about religion and spirituality.

Roger Straughan, retired Reader in Education at the University of Reading, has contributed 'A Study in Survival: Messages, Mediums and Materialism', which sheds some interesting new light on survival after death and the afterlife, based on his personal experience.

The influence of Sir Arthur Conan Doyle in the formation of the White Eagle Lodge in 1936 is described by Colum Hayward, editor of ARTHUR CONAN DOYLE'S BOOK OF THE BEYOND (1994), in 'The Age of the Spirit'. His story is about the power of spirit in our lives.

At the end of this section, a fictional narrative of my own, entitled 'The Mystery of Sir Arthur Conan Doyle's Vital Message' explores the context of ACD's 'message' and what may have happened to it in the ninety years since his book, THE VITAL MESSAGE, was first published in 1919.

II.   *Spirituality*

Although Sir Arthur Conan Doyle was known for his interests in Spiritualism, it is hoped that this book will demonstrate that he was essentially advocating an enhanced perspective of a wider and deeper spirituality. This next section is a natural follow-on.

The 'Conversations With God' series of books has become a bestselling phenomenon since Neale Donald Walsch asked God to give him guidance, at a time when he had hit rock bottom in his life, not knowing which way to go. Here, in his own unique version of 'The Vital Message', Neale provides some piercing insights into how we might navigate successfully through a period of enormous and accelerating change, in a way which is joyful, peaceful and beneficial to all concerned.

Colum Hayward in 'The Age of Brotherhood' talks about the importance of 'brotherhood' as a way of valuing each other as fellow members, men and women, of the human race, in the spirit of kinship. He sees it as the religion of the coming age, in the form of a natural spirituality.

At a time when meditation is becoming increasingly popular, even at the simple level of helping us cope with the strains and stresses of everyday life, Jim Baltzell in 'Making Meditation Mainstream' provides a practical overview about the background and philosophy of meditation, as well as useful tips for anyone starting on this path, or wishing to enhance their meditation practice.

Elyan Stephens has given us 'To All our Relations, The Brotherhood of All Life', a gentle, very personal account of her spiritual journey, from the practical challenges of living on Shetland in the North of Scotland, via encounters with the late Sir George Trevelyan of the Wrekin Trust, to her current work with the White Eagle Lodge in Wales. In her story Elyan quotes Robert Burns—'A Man's a Man for A' That'—perhaps the best encapsulation of our spiritual equality for any generation to consider. (The 250th Anniversary of the birth of Robert Burns, born 1759, also takes place in 2009).

III.   *Empowerment and Health*

This section shows how we each have a 'silent power' within, a direct connection to our Higher Self and the Divine, which can not only help us lead happier, more fulfilling lives, but allows us to take responsibility for our own health and wellbeing.

Writer, spiritual philosopher, scientist and futurist Peter Russell invites us to engage in the process of 'Returning to Natural Mind' and demonstrates how we might achieve that peace of mind we all desire so deeply.

Life coach and soul astrologer Ruth Hadikin has developed 'A Holistic Science for the Soul-Age', where the current scientific paradigm based on separation is replaced by a more comprehensive worldview to incorporate our 'inner knowing'.

Founder of the Conscious Journey Institute, Anya Sophia Mann, shows us the extent to which each day is an opportunity for new beginnings, hope for a fresh start, in 'In the Light of a New Day'.

Gaye Mack, author of IGNITING SOUL FIRE, revisits the world and work of Dr Edward Bach, whose work with the Flower Remedies that bear his name has enabled a whole new subtle science of healing to be born. The more esoteric and mystical undercurrents of Dr Bach's life are explored in 'Visionary Medicine Man for the Aquarian Age'.

Dr Helen Petrow is in the unique position of being a medically trained doctor who has now dedicated her life to Vibrational Medicine and Vibrational Healing, having trained and worked with the late dowser healer Jack Temple. She points out that humanity is rapidly 'Coming of Age' at this present time regarding health and medical matters.

'Renaissance Man' Dale Pond, author of THE PHYSICS OF LOVE and UNIVERSAL LAWS NEVER BEFORE REVEALED', works in the groundbreaking field of Sympathetic Vibratory Physics. He has been instrumental in bringing the work of John Worrell Keely and Nikola Tesla to public attention, and here outlines a framework for 'Creating Our Experiences'.

Finally, a call to action is sounded by Morag Paterson in her essay 'Wake Up! Out of 'The Matrix' … into 'The Divine Matrix'!', where she challenges us to break free from our current, often less than positive, version of reality into a new vision, full of anticipation, vibrancy and fulfilment.

IV.   Nature, Community and Family

From the viewpoint of our individual health and wellbeing concerns, it is a natural step to look at how we engage with the greater world around us, both with nature and in our family and community relationships.

Professors Alexander and Kathia Laszlo in 'Syntony and Flow: The Artscience of Evolutionary Aesthetics' highlight the importance of conscious creation, in order to develop new ways of living, learning and working aligned with social and environmental integrity.

Bryan Harrison provides a real-life case study of living closely in community, which has developed and evolved over several decades, and offering a potentially viable model for sustainable community-based living in the future.

Shirley Kilday, in 'The Journey of the Soul', says we must look at life through the eyes of a child, beyond our normal five senses. She takes us on a magical trip through multi-dimensional reality, encountering Ascended Masters, Angels, Devas and Sacred Geometry on her travels.

Findhorn spiritual community co-founder Dorothy Maclean, in an essay adapted from an opening keynote presentation she made to the Positive Energy Conference hosted at Findhorn in 2008, underlines the importance of co-creating with nature, as well as demonstrating in practical terms how we can each tune in to our inner wisdom.

Focusing on the family, Nikki Mackay, in 'A Father's Place', investigates the underlying causes of problems in society, such as depression, and how these challenges might be addressed by looking more closely at male and female roles within families, family relationships, and the legacies carried down the line from family ancestors.

V.   *Sustainable Business Leadership*

If there is any area which the emerging new consciousness is challenging more than any other, a prime candidate must be the business world. Those engaged in gaining power and status from the excesses of greed and corruption within multinational corporations and banks, until recently acknowledged by many as just 'business as usual', are finding no support among the growing number seeking change towards a more balanced and fairer society.

Drew Pryde, Chairman of the Scottish Institute for Business Leaders (SIBL), takes us through his remarkable healing journey in 'Don't Push The River', and underlines the need for a change in the way business is conducted.

Innovation expert Darrell Mann in 'Embracing Conflict/Transcending Conflict' considers the various scenarios for the future facing us, and gives some interesting insights into the tools available to resolve this conflict dilemma.

Knowledge Management practitioner and author Verna Allee has been pioneering the Value Network approach, helping communities as well as business organizations. Her contribution for this book, 'Letters to a Younger Consultant', highlights the practical difficulties of driving change in organizations.

Jan Stringer, co-author of the book ATTRACTING PERFECT CUSTOMERS, provides a planning template for the creation of a 'Heart-Centred Business', identifying love as the fundamental ingredient around which a business wishing to be successful should be designed.

In 'The Economic Case for Climate Action', Natural Capital President Hunter Lovins points out that shifting towards 'greener' business models is good for business: that the climate crisis can be solved not as a cost but as an investment for the future.

VI.   2012

The year 2012 has become a point of imminent focus and attention, with various theories being expounded about its significance. Exactly what will occur around that date remains open to speculation, although there appears to be a growing consensus that something profound is already taking place.

In 'The 2012 Horizon', Ervin Laszlo, founder of the Club of Budapest, examines some of the deeper trends and indicators concerning what is going on, and the significance of the various cross-impacts being generated. Again, it is a call to action, to prepare for real change.

In 'Driving Your Soul', Scott Fratcher gives a crash course in how to ride through the expected turbulence, advising that we must be able to use our intuition to guide us.

Simon Bentley, in '2012 and All That', provides an overview of the various popular prophecies circulating about the year 2012, but reminds us that the future is uncertain and that we have the power to create what we want.

Errol Weiner is a transpersonal astrologer who looks at significant astrological events leading up to, and through, the year 2012, taking into account the various esoteric teachings for the New Age, in his essay '2012: A Time of Intensified New Beginnings and Old Completions'.

Getting from There to Here

How this book came to be written has been a tale of journeys within journeys, stories within stories.

We are each on our own unique, individual journeys, all spiritual in nature whether acknowledged as such or not; we each encounter the highs and lows of life, moments of great joy mixed with times of unbearable heartache. We somehow get through it all, carrying on with life as best we can.

April 1980 was the lowest point of my life; our first son, Lee, died suddenly at the age of one month from an undiagnosed congenital heart defect. Nothing prepares you for the loss of a child.

Two days later I was walking down Union Street in Aberdeen and passed a 'Save The Children Fund' stall. I tried to engage in conversation but found I couldn't talk past the tears.

The song 'Bright Eyes' by Art Garfunkel was riding high in the music charts at the time, and it seemed that every time I listened to the radio, or heard background music in a store, it would be there, gnawing at my already shredded heartstrings. I can hear it in my head to this day ('How can the light that burned so brightly…'), but the grief associated with it has subsided over time.

There is a poignant synchronicity attached to this book as 'Brighteyes' features in it, albeit in a completely different context.

Despite the enormous sense of loss, anger, bewilderment, and all the other emotions which engulf you in times such as these, I had a deep inner knowing that I would meet Lee again some day. Now I have a better understanding of the truth behind this knowingness; the experience had made me promise myself from then on that I would keep an open mind about all things spiritual.

The Beginnings of the Conan Doyle Connection

Fast forward twenty-five years to the year 2005. A series of major life upheavals led to a move that Spring from Aboyne in Royal Deeside, 30 miles inland from Aberdeen, to Nairn, near the Highland capital of Inverness on the Moray Firth coast.

Sir Arthur Conan Doyle was someone I was aware of, like most people, through his detective fiction writing, featuring Sherlock Holmes and Dr Watson. I had a vague knowledge of his interest in Spiritualism but it was a field I knew very little about.

ACD having passed on in 1930, 2005 marked the 75th anniversary of his passing; several articles appeared in newspapers and magazines to commemorate this. Although naturally paying full attention to the sustaining power and popularity of Sherlock Holmes, these features tended to be dismissive about his involvement in spiritual affairs, as if he had started to lose his senses in the later stages of his life.

This did not sit easily with me, and I started to do some research into this aspect of his life. At around that time I visited a Psychic Fayre at the Nairn Community Centre, where I discovered the event had been organised by the Inverness Spiritualist Church. Although I had never set foot in a Spiritualist Church before, I decided to go along to find out more about Spiritualism, as part of my ongoing journey of spiritual exploration.

This started a remarkable onward leg of the journey. As Spring merged into Summer, I received my first message from a medium at the Church, telling me things known only to myself. I was so intrigued I fixed up a one on one session with the medium, Jean Glen from Stirling, the following day. There she gave me a message from my mother, who had passed away the previous November. On telling her about my interest in Sir Arthur Conan Doyle, she said that he would be there from time to time to help me with my writing.

Over the next nine or ten months I visited not only the Inverness Spiritualist Church but also the Spiritualist groups at Evanton, on the Black Isle above Inverness, and Nairn. Every fortnight, like clockwork, I received a message from different mediums, a total of twenty, and nearly all relating to my writing and healing work.

Healer, Heal Thyself

In the early 1990s, having gone through a marriage breakup and deciding to leave a corporate finance job at Shell, I had an astrological reading from the late Nigel Lucas, a 'metaphysician and astrologer' living in Monymusk, Aberdeenshire.

During the reading he told me I was a 'healer' with considerable healing skills. Having come from a professional career background I had no notion of what this was about. However, in alignment with my willingness to remain open spiritually, I began to study alternative healing approaches, building up a lot of knowledge, none of it experiential.

Around the year 2000 I was recommended a book called HANDS-ON SPIRITUAL HEALING by a New Zealander, Michael Bradford, who had also come from a corporate career background. This book was a good basic introduction into energy healing and contained pictures of hand placement techniques which could be used.

Not long afterwards, I was driving my son Fionn, then aged 19, North from Glasgow to stay with me over the weekend. He'd had lower back problems for over four months, and nothing was helping. I got him to lie down flat on his stomach, used Michael Bradford's techniques from his book, and felt the energy flowing into my hands immediately. Using the heat from my hands, I worked on his back for about an hour, although it was very much a light touch, certainly no manipulation involved. Fionn slept well that night and that was the first inkling for me that energy healing really did work.

From there I became a Silva Method Graduate (including a two-day Ultra Healing component), attained Reiki 1 level, then stumbled upon a new energy healing modality called Quantum-Touch on the Internet. I attended two Quantum-Touch workshops with QT Instructor Di Wilson in Whitby, North Yorkshire, in June and August 2005, around the same time I had started going to the Spiritualist Church in Inverness.

Just before the first QT workshop I met Dr Helen Petrow in Nairn, little realizing at the time how she was going to change my life. She identified and cleared a trauma I had suffered at age 4, which had remained hidden in my system over the years. She has changed so many people's lives for the better, including Drew Pryde's. Both Helen and Drew feature in this book with their inspirational stories.

Alongside my Quantum-Touch training, I also trained with Dr Petrow in Vibrational Healing, to discover and learn what lay behind this amazing healing approach.

Spiritual Development

In 2006 I was invited to join a Spiritual Development Circle at the Inverness Spiritualist Church. Although there are many different types of psychic skills, the four most common ones are healing, clairvoyance, clairaudience and clairsentience.

Clairvoyance is the ability to see, clairaudience to hear, beyond our normal five senses. Clairsentience is 'just knowing'. The Spiritual Development Circle allows members to develop these skills as part of their training to become mediums.

At my one to one session with her in 2005, the medium Jean Glen told me I had the capability to become a medium, with my strongest aspects being healing, clairsentience, and some clairvoyance.

What usually happens with new members of the group is that it is very easy to dismiss psychic experiences as 'just my imagination', and I was no exception. However, as you learn to trust, and also get yourself out the way, surprising things begin to happen. You learn to go with the flow, open to whatever takes place.

It has certainly helped me understand more about Conan Doyle's interest in Spiritualism from a practical perspective, especially having received the twenty messages from other mediums, discussed earlier. To that extent it is very similar to healing; unless and until you have experienced it you are not in a position to discuss it with any depth of credibility.

The Return of Arthur Conan Doyle

The following year, 2007, I was shown a book written by Ivan Cooke, published in 1956, entitled THE RETURN OF ARTHUR CONAN DOYLE. I had neither heard of Ivan Cooke nor the book title previously.

It was only through reading it that I discovered Sir Arthur's inner connection with the formation of the White Eagle Lodge, an organization I knew nothing about, only being vaguely aware at the time of 'White Eagle' as a Native American spirit guide.

This initiated a whole new field of research and study. I had known of Sir Arthur's Spiritualist books written when he was alive; now this latest development had literally opened up a new dimension, as the book contained channelled messages via medium Grace Cooke, Ivan Cooke's wife, recorded during sittings in 1931 and 1932.

As well as aiding my research into the life, and afterlife, of Conan Doyle, I felt drawn towards the White Eagle Lodge, and joined the following year.

The Idea keeps Growing

Early in 2008, just at a time I was preparing to develop my Quantum-Touch practice, I started to develop problems in my lower back area. In February I contracted shingles, which made my left ankle swell up. When the shingles cleared up, I thought my back would improve. Instead it got worse, and I ended up walking with a stick to support me.

I went to see Dr Petrow and she said it was to do with a 'life lesson' I had to learn. Being quite immobilised, I started to meditate on what it might be. 'Writing' kept popping into my mind, but I kept dismissing it.

Eventually I got a journal and just started writing, day after day, about anything.

My back started to improve. Other doors started to open for me. I joined a Creative Writing Group at Findhorn and that helped, too.

Also, throughout 2008 the fact that Sir Arthur Conan Doyle's 150th anniversary was looming large on the horizon meant that if something was going to be done, it would have to be done quickly. An update on THE VITAL MESSAGE seemed like a good theme to plan around, but it wasn't until September 2008 that the idea for a book, with a wide variety of invited contributors, really came to mind.

It turned out to be a challenging month. My father passed on, aged 85, having been quite frail for some time.

One morning after the funeral I switched on the television. A still picture appeared on the screen, a painting of an elegant, elderly lady with grey hair, against a pastel blue background. The sound commentary was from a nature programme, unconnected with the picture. Without thinking, I changed down a channel and then back, to reveal lions and other animals in a wildlife park. The still picture was gone. What was going on?

Speeding Up

By the end of September the idea of writing and compiling a book had taken root.

I was also booked to attend an advanced Quantum-Touch Supercharging Workshop with Mervyn Foster in Bournemouth, on the English South coast, over the weekend of November 8th and 9th, 2008. As Bournemouth is several hundred miles from where I live, I decided to spend a week driving down, and another driving back, stopping off to visit friends and carrying out additional research into Conan Doyle's old haunts such as Crowborough (where he lived 1907–1930) and Minstead (where Sir Arthur and his second wife Lady Jean are buried in the local churchyard).

On Friday October 3rd, 2008, I sat down at my computer, composed a one-page invitation, and started emailing it out among my network. By the following morning I had two positive replies, both from the United States.

Two days later I attended a White Eagle Lodge Retreat Day in Glasgow, led by Colum Hayward, grandson of Grace and Ivan Cooke, Founders of the White Eagle Lodge, and editor of ARTHUR CONAN DOYLE'S BOOK

OF THE BEYOND, which is an updated edition of THE RETURN OF ARTHUR CONAN DOYLE. It was the first time I had met Colum. I told him of the book idea and that I would like him to contribute a chapter, and arranged that we would meet up to discuss further during my trip down to England the following month.

The following day, Monday, October 6th, I drove through to a Scottish Institute for Business Leaders (SIBL) event which I had been invited to attend by SIBL Chairman Drew Pryde, and where the keynote speaker was Neale Donald Walsch. I had already invited Drew to contribute to the book and had intended to ask Drew to invite Neale on my behalf, knowing that it was likely to be a long shot given how busy Neale is with his own writing and events schedule.

As luck would have it, just as I was leaving the event venue to drive home, I glanced to one side and saw Neale sitting alone in a small lounge area. He waved me in to join him, and I chatted about the book idea which I'd just kicked into action. We arranged to keep in contact, although he did say that over the coming months he would be busy writing his own new book, WHEN EVERYTHING CHANGES, CHANGE EVERYTHING. If he had the time, he said he would be delighted to contribute, and would let me know.

By the end of the week I had had enough positive responses from invitees to know that the book concept was a viable one. All I had asked in the original invitation was that in honour of Sir Arthur Conan Doyle's impending 150th anniversary on May 22nd, 2009, the book would be using his 1919 book, THE VITAL MESSAGE, as a central theme. Those invited to contribute were asked to write what they considered to be their 'vital message' for humanity, with no constraints other than it be written from the heart.

On the Road

At the end of October, with a growing number of signed-up contributors to the book, but as yet no publisher (I hadn't even thought of a publisher then), I set off on the long drive down to Bournemouth. First stop-over was with friends in Morpeth, a pretty market town just north of Newcastle, North East England. From there I followed a route taking me to York, Norwich and Watford, before making my way to the East Sussex town of Crowborough, where Sir Arthur Conan Doyle's former home of Windlesham is located.

Although there is a recently-erected statue of Sir Arthur in the centre of Crowborough, not much else appears to have been done to strengthen the connection between the town and the great man. The local library were very helpful, providing me with archive material to sift through; it appears there was a Sherlock Holmes festival initiated in the late 1990s but it fizzled out after a couple of years because funding issues between the organisers and the local council could not be resolved. Windlesham is now a nursing home, not open to the public (although it does have the ubiquitous plaque beside the doorway, saying that Sir Arthur Conan Doyle lived there).*

The next stop was Liss, Hampshire, where I had arranged to meet Colum Hayward at New Lands, adjacent to the magnificent White Eagle Lodge Temple. After spending some time looking round the inside of the temple, I met with Colum in a small, comfortable sitting room in the main New Lands house.

I sat down next to the fire, Colum went off to make coffee, and when he returned we started discussing the book. Not long into our conversation, and having ascertained that Colum was happy to contribute to it, I looked up and saw a picture of a woman on the wall—the same lady I had seen on my television set less than two months before.

I asked Colum who it was. 'That's Minesta, my grandmother Grace Cooke, but it's not a very good likeness', he replied. I told him the story about the television picture and asked him what he made of it. He thought it was quite likely that it was his grandmother coming in from the world of spirit to give her blessing on the book idea. I had learnt from THE RETURN OF ARTHUR CONAN DOYLE that she was frequently known as 'Brighteyes', even by Lady Conan Doyle.

As if this wasn't enough, Colum asked me if I had a publisher. When I replied that I hadn't, that the project was relatively new and my focus had been on getting contributors, he told me he ran a small publishing company in London, Polair Publishing, and would I like him to publish the book!

---

*At Crowborough Brian Pugh, Curator of The Conan Doyle (Crowborough) Establishment was at pains to give me all the help I needed; an article of his, entitled 'Arthur Conan Doyle and Crowborough' appears on our website, www. thevitalmessage.com. As I write, there is an appeal underway to save another of ACD's homes, Undershaw, at Hindhead. For further information see www. sherlock-holmes.org.uk/pdf/undershaw-appeal.pdf

Last Leg of the Journey

From Liss it was a short hop to Minstead, a small village on the edge of the New Forest, where the bodies of Sir Arthur Conan Doyle and his wife Lady Jean were reinterred in the local churchyard in 1955, after Windlesham had been sold (both Sir Arthur, in 1930, and Lady Jean, in 1940, had originally been buried in the garden at Windlesham).

The landlady at the farm in Minstead where I stayed overnight showed me a local newspaper cutting published in the mid-1990s about the reinterment; the article referred to Sherlock Holmes as being the creator of Sir Arthur Conan Doyle, such are the two entangled in the minds of the public!

After the Bournemouth QT workshop it was back North again, meeting up with Colum again in Petersfield to talk further about the book. Then it was Glastonbury, Bristol area, Lake District and home to Scotland.

Now We are Here

This has been one version of the 'getting from there to here' story; there are numerous variations. What I have realized is that my role has been as a channel to gather this information in, and share it out. I have been guided by Spirit, of that I have no doubt.

Being involved in a Spiritual Development Circle has benefited my writing and my healing work. To have received so many messages from mediums, and to have acted as a medium on occasion for others, has shown that the veil between the physical world and the unseen realms is indeed very thin, and appears to be getting thinner all the time.

Over to You

The journey is over, the book has been manifested. This publication has shown that with the power of intention, anything is possible.

Looking back, it is clear that Sir Arthur has guided me down the path of Spiritualism, and from there on to the White Eagle Lodge, in order to give me the insights and experience to write and compile this book.

I hope I have done him, and the book, justice. I will leave it to you, the reader, to decide.

> *If the doors of perception were cleansed, everything*
> *would appear as it is—infinite.*
> William Blake

ARTHUR CONAN DOYLE'S SPIRITUAL IMAGINATION

Owen Dudley Edwards

LIKE Arthur Conan Doyle I was born a Roman Catholic, but unlike him I have remained one. He became quite hostile to Roman Catholicism, especially under the influence of his second wife, Jean Leckie, whose will disinherited any of their children in the event of their turning Catholic. The Spiritualist faith, to which Conan Doyle adhered after World War I, has common ground with Catholicism in some important respects. Conan Doyle liked to point out that Spiritualism was akin to the Roman Catholic idea of the Communion of Saints—those on Earth praying for those in Purgatory, those in Heaven praying for both. Most Protestant non-Spiritualists and still more non-Christian ones seem to view Spiritualism as nonsense. Roman Catholics do not agree: we think Spiritualism is wrong in action rather than wrong in opinion. To borrow a term from Conan Doyle's 'The Horror of the Heights', we assume something of a jungle in the spirit world (though we would not call it that), and in that jungle are dangers—monsters, if you want to use the word—entities hostile to human safety and salvation.

'The Horror of the Heights' (1911) itself is not concerned with Spiritualist or preternatural themes (Conan Doyle wrote one novel, which is THE LAND OF MIST (1926), as are a dozen or so short stories, but several more works are on a preternatural frontier). Its concern is a supposed proliferation of creatures, some harmless, some dangerous, in 'jungles'

Owen Dudley Edwards FRSE is an Honourary Fellow in History at Edinburgh University since his retirement from teaching there in 2005. For many years a broadcaster and journalist as well as an academic, Dublin-born Owen Dudley Edwards is Editor of the Oxford Sherlock Holmes Series, and a biographer of Sir Arthur Conan Doyle, P G Wodehouse and Oscar Wilde.

above 20,000 feet from the ground.

It throws a curious sidelight on Conan Doyle's future Spiritualist crusade. Most students of his life would probably acknowledge now that after
his schoolboy defection from Roman Catholicism some part of his mind
remained unsatisfied by the self-confidence of a secularist Science, and he
was constantly trying to harmonize scientific and spiritual considerations.
Ultimately his adoption of Spiritualism, and experiments to make contact
with dead persons, became a scientific activity: it was as though bombard-
ing the spirit world with séances, etc., he might succeed in proving the
survival of the human spirit. But 'The Horror of the Heights' reminds us
that Conan Doyle was not only scientist and (ultimately) Spiritualist, but
also sportsman. He was proud of his record in Rugby football, cricket,
ski-ing, and boxing. He wrote impressive fictions about several sports (his
great cricket story, 'The Story of Spedegue's Dropper' came out in 1929,
the year before his death). The use of the word 'jungle' hints at sporting
ambitions mixing with scientific, and in fact much exploration in Conan
Doyle's time was carried out by scientist sportsmen from US President
Theodore Roosevelt down. The Sherlock Holmes stories in which we are
always expected to think of the hero as scientist, bristles with sporting
metaphors, whether from Holmes, Watson, or incidental characters. One
of Holmes's supreme adversaries, in THE HOUND OF THE BASKERVILLES (1902),
is the naturalist Stapleton, whose pursuit of butterflies is clearly scientific
and sporting. Sportsmen, whatever their age or activity, are essentially
children. (Let me stress that I, for one, do not regard maintenance of child
qualities as necessarily regrettable: I wish more people gave more celebration to what survives from their childhood.) And scientists, in Conan
Doyle's fiction, display both sportsmanship and childlikeness in profusion.
Professor George E. Challenger and colleagues of THE LOST WORLD (1912)
and its successors constantly delight their readers by the inextricable en-
twining of their learning and their juvenility, above all in their schoolboy
glee in winning psychological advantage. In THE POISON BELT (1913) the
impact of alien atmosphere on them brings them out in bad schoolboy
behaviour. At the same time, the sporting quality of their quests is accen-
tuated by the presence of the non-scientist Lord John Roxton, crack shot,
big game hunter, etc. And in THE LAND OF MIST Roxton takes up Spiritualism in a fine sporting spirit, essentially pursuing this, the latest quest, for
the glory of some equivalent of trophy or record. In fact, Roxton finds a

'Dark Soul' too much for him but one of his companions returns to face the tortured but malignant spirit in question.

Conan Doyle's magnificent confession of literary faith—

I have wrought my simple plan
If I bring an hour of joy
To the boy who is half a man
And the man who is half a boy

—should win our hearts. But simultaneously we have to keep our heads at work. One of the prime tenets of the schoolboy of that era was the heroic but sometimes idiotic readiness to take a dare. Putting that logic into the brain of a scientist takes us into sinister places. It may result in the destruction of the scientist, as in 'The Horror of the Heights'. It may result in the destruction of the planet. The last Challenger story, 'When the World Screamed' (1929), entails the scientific genius being bequeathed a huge sum of money which he expends for the purpose of proving the planet Earth is a sentient being. This he does by the process of driving a mighty needle into the Earth which screams in pain and anger and emits volcanic disasters in retaliation;

> It is of course well known that the effect of the experiment was a world-wide one. It is true that nowhere did the injured planet emit such a howl as at the actual point of penetration, but she showed that she was indeed one entity by her conduct elsewhere. Through every vent and every volcano she voiced her indignation. Hecla bellowed until the Icelanders feared a cataclysm. Vesuvius blew its head off. Etna spewed up a quantity of lava, and a suit of half a million lira damages has been decided against Challenger in the Italian Courts for the destruction of vineyards. Even in Mexico and in the belt of Central America there were signs of intense Plutonic indignation, and the howls of Stromboli filled the whole Eastern Mediterranean. It has been the common ambition of mankind to set the whole world talking. To set the whole world screaming was the privilege of Challenger alone.

The narrator, an engineer named Peerless Jones, is fairly critical of Challenger's more obvious social and civil shortcomings during most of the story, and thus provides objectivity: at the end he is duly impressed by

Challenger's achievement but we are evidently to assume that the financial judgments against Challenger are reported by Peerless Jones with few regrets. The story records the danger in which a scientist with unlimited funds would plunge planet and denizens to prove a scientific point, and does not imply approval—in fact, as the story's close, quoted above, indicates, the reader is given the materials whence to justify disapproval. But it indicates the literally daredevil spirit in which Conan Doyle's own invasion of the spirit world was undertaken.

He had shown himself sensitive enough to such possibilities before formally enlisting in Spiritualist ranks. The *Strand* magazine for March 1900, by now his prime platform, printed his 'Playing With Fire', in which experiment in Spiritualism from enquirers of mixed motivation materialises a unicorn from a painting by the artist who owns the house. The unicorn itself is terrified, breaks furniture and doors, and is briefly alone with the artist's wife, who is then left 'lying senseless, struck down by the sight which she had seen'. Is the reader intended to suspect a sexual allusion? Conan Doyle's stories in the 1920s were more explicit on that head. But the narrator, whatever the unicorn's effects, is contrite:

> It seemed to me that lightly and flippantly we had approached the most real and august of sacraments, that communion with the dead of which the fathers of the Church had spoken.

It also allowed for the human psyche having destructive spiritual effects, the theme of the future film *Forbidden Planet* (1956) directed by Fred M. Wilcox (otherwise known for the *Lassie* films). Cyril Hume's screenplay and accompanying publicity made much of inspiration from Shakespeare's *The Tempest*, but 'Playing with Fire' was either another source or a remarkable coincidence in such lines as:

> 'Do you mean to say that I create a thing which has never existed by merely thinking of it?'
>   'But certainly. It is the fact which lies under all other facts. That is why an evil thought is also a danger.'
> (*The second speaker is French*.)

Some of Conan Doyle's early work played with ghosts as swindles, or with sinister mesmeric and telepathic powers from individuals of erotic ambitions (again necessarily muted in recognition of Victorian convention, although stories like 'John Barrington Cowles' (1884) actually show more freedom than the austerity of the publisher George Newnes (1851–1910) would permit in the *Strand*). Consistently his work, whether 'tales of twilight and the unseen' or otherwise set themselves above the common herd by adroit use of comedic possibilities among scientists (of whom Challenger is only the most explosive example) while the pace needed in fulfilment of sporting metaphor as well as sporting themes distinguished him. If frivolity became less evident, he gave scepticism its fair say however deep his conversion to Spiritualism. The late Sherlock Holmes story 'The Sussex Vampire' (first published in the *Strand*, January 1924) opens on Holmes's scorn at being called in to deal with vampires:

> '... are we to give serious attention to such things? This agency stands flat-footed upon the ground, and there it must remain. The world is big enough for us. No ghosts need apply....'

And the story, vintage Holmes, demolishes the vampire suspicion although uncovering a dark psyche at work elsewhere (a mother and baby endangered by a stepson's hatred). Holmes remains to the end a sceptic born from the afterglow of the enlightenment. But as Professor W. W. Robson of Edinburgh pointed out in his edition of THE HOUND OF THE BASKERVILLES:

> he maintains a Voltairean scepticism about the forces of evil while he is in London, but in Devonshire the sarcastic note drops out of Holmes's conversation and does not return. Holmes's grave agnosticism corresponds as it were musically to the characteristic note of intense disquiet that pervades the novel. Greater dramatic reality accrues to the powers of evil when the character who symbolizes reason comes to take them seriously. At the same time the supernaturalistic view, though taken seriously, is not endorsed by Holmes (or by Watson).

This is to show the harmony of Conan Doyle's driving forces at their most effective. Since his formal conversion to Spiritualism was not until 1918, it's natural for us to see a break there, and we might search his stories for more of the zeal of the convert. Yet, other than in THE LAND OF MIST, we would do so in vain. Challenger in THE LAND OF MIST adopts Spiritualism when the spirit of his wife tells him that the death of a patient was not a youthful medical blunder on his part. Conan Doyle himself hungered for such reassurance (as most conscientious doctors, sooner or later, are likely to do), particularly in the case of a youth whose sister Conan Doyle later married as his first wife. He had been a passionate supporter of the British cause and the British war effort in World War I, and the failure of the better world promised by his propaganda to emerge in its aftermath gave urgency to his embrace of Spiritualism: he needed to talk to the victims of the war whom he had known, headed by his son Kingsley and his brother Innes.

But a literary life in which the spirit world had always been in his authorial equipment kept his future use of it largely within the confines it had previously possessed: to be there when called for, but not at the cost of the story's equipoise (a cost greatly weakening THE LAND OF MIST).

The Spiritualist crusade robbed Conan Doyle of much writing time in the 1920s, but the decade gave him at least one fine ghost story, 'The Bully of Brocas Court' (*Strand*, November 1921).

It involves history, and indeed was set by what was then well in the past, 1878, when Conan Doyle would have been eighteen or nineteen and a medical student at Edinburgh. It was roughly the same date we must assume for his longest boxing story, 'The Croxley Master', which required three instalments in the *Strand*, October to December 1899. In that case Conan Doyle simply posited a medical student like himself working as general practitioner's medical and pharmaceutical assistant, as he himself did more than once when doing his degree. The student is exploited by his snobbish and hypocritical employer and an accident enables him to get his freedom by winning a boxing match whose purse will pay for his resumed studies. The story is set in Yorkshire mining districts. The plot is no great imaginative effort—fairy-tales and folk-tales abound with its variants, although nobody may have previously thought of the boxing-ring as Cinderella's godmother—but what it lacks in strategy it easily gains in tactics, and both the environment and the characterization are eloquent and memorable. What needs noting now is that it is also a story of psychological as well as physical brutality. Of the latter there is no lack, and the contest itself is both breathtaking and scientific, but the former is less usual in fictional sporting contexts:

The door of the gymnasium had opened, and a lad about sixteen, grimy and black with soot and iron, stepped into the yellow glare of the oil lamp.

★ ★ ★

'Well, my lad, what is it?'

'It's aboot t'fight, Mr Wilson, sir. I wanted to tell your mon some-thin' aboot t'Maister.'

'We've no time to listen to gossip, my boy. We know all about the Master.'

'But thou doant, sir. Nobody knows but me and mother, and we thought as we'd like thy man to know, sir, for we want him to fair bray him.'

'Oh, you want the Master fair brayed, do you? So do we. Well, what have you to say?'

'Is this your mon, sir?'

'Well, suppose it is?'

'Then it's him I want to tell aboot it. T' Maister is blind o' the left eye.'

'Nonsense!'

'It's true, sir. Not stone blind, but rarely fogged. He keeps it secret, but mother knows, and so do I. If thou slip him on the left side he can't cop thee. And mark him when he sinks his right. 'Tis his best blow, his right upper-cut, T' Maister's finisher, they ca' it at t'works. It's a turble blow, when it do come home.'

'Thank you, my boy. This is information worth having about his sight,' said Wilson. 'How came you to know so much? Who are you?'

'I'm his son, sir.'

Wilson whistled.

'And who sent you to us?'

'My mother. I maun get back to her again.'

'Take this half-crown.'

'No, sir, I don't seek money in comin' here. I do it—'

'For love?' suggested the publican.

'For hate!' said the boy, and darted off into the darkness.

Wilson, son of the local coal-pit's owner, and Purvis, the local publican, are the medical student's backers and patrons: and the social gradations are virtually dissected by Conan Doyle with surgical accuracy. A good author's main characters will always carry a little of their maker, but the medical student is clearly a self-portrait with some wish-fulfilment; however the son of the champion boxer (the Croxley Master, whom the student is training to defeat) shows ugly signs of some autobiographical traits. Conan Doyle's father when sober was a gentle artist, but when drunk was horribly transformed, sometimes making brutal assaults on his diminutive if strong-minded wife. Fiction has its own work to do, and Arthur Conan Doyle, growing up mostly in boarding school, may have suffered relatively little physical damage from his father: it's clear the Croxley Master has in his time punished his son savagely. We are expected to deduce that one cause of the Master's attacks on his son would have been the boy's protest against his mother's supersession by a red-haired mistress who becomes the Master's sparring-partner and second.

There is no ghost in this story. But 'The Bully of Brocas Court', written twenty years after, has a terrifying link with the Master's son and with his unseen wife, as well as with its main pugilistic context. It begins with just such a patron as Wilson, but this time a baronet captain in 'the South Midland Yeomanry' arranging a contest featuring Alf Stevens of Kentish Town who has to be driven by dog-cart to box Farrier-Sergeant ('Slogger') Burton near Luton, in 1878. On the way they are stopped by two men, the first of whom

> wore a hat low upon his brow, but in spite of its shadow both the Baronet and the pugilist could see enough to shrink from him, for it was an evil face, evil but very formidable, stern, craggy, high-nosed, and fierce, with an inexorable mouth which bespoke a nature which would neither ask for mercy nor grant it. As to his age, one could only say for certain that a man with such a face was young enough to have experienced all the wickedness of life. The cold, savage eyes took a deliberate survey, first of the Baronet and then of the young man beside him.

He insists on a boxing contest with Stevens, who accepts. Conan Doyle had carefully established the time as lying between the decay of the old bareknuckle contests famous earlier in the century and the implementation of the recently-defined Queensberry Rules. Stevens finds his opponent fights by the older method and, despite an evident hideous wound in his head, the challenger is well on the way to defeating the gallant but outclassed Stevens when:

…in their approach to the ring the party had passed through a grove of trees. Out of these there came a peculiar shrill cry, a cry of agony, which might be from a child or from some small woodland creature in distress. It was inarticulate, high-pitched, and inexpressibly melancholy. At the sound the stranger, who had knocked Stevens on to his knees, staggered back and looked round him with an expression of helpless horror upon his face. The smile had left his lips and there only remained the loose-lipped weakness of a man in the last extremity of terror.

'It's after me again, mate!' he cried.

'Stick it out, Tom! You have him nearly beat! It can't hurt you.'

'It can 'urt me! It will 'urt me!' screamed the fighting man. 'My God! I can't face it! Ah, I see it! I see it!'

With a scream of fear he turned and bounded off into the brushwood. His companion, swearing loudly, picked up the pile of clothes and darted after him, the dark shadows swallowing up their flying figures.

Stevens, half-senselessly, had staggered back and lay upon the grassy bank, his head pillowed upon the chest of the young Baronet, who was holding his flask of brandy to his lips. As they sat there they were both aware that the cries had become louder and shriller. Then from among the bushes there ran a small white terrier, nosing about as if following a trail and yelping most piteously. It squattered across the grassy sward, taking no notice of the two young men. Then it also vanished into the shadows. As it did so the two spectators sprang to their feet and ran as hard as they could tear for the grassway and the trap. Terror had seized them—a panic terror far above reason or control. Shivering and shaking, they threw themselves into the dog-cart, and it was not until the willing horses had put two good miles between that ill-omened hollow and themselves that they ventured to speak.

'Did you ever see such a dog?' asked the Baronet.

'No', cried Stevens, 'And, please God, I never may again.'

It turns out that Stevens had been fighting the ghost of Tom Hickman, who (or possibly 'which') has been fighting and beating persons accepting his challenge. Hickman was known as the 'Gasman' perhaps from his ability to floor a man with the speed of one of the gas flares (which illuminated prize-fights) going out. Stevens and patron are told his fate by a friendly innkeeper (or publican):

'Yes, sir, they called him Gas. He won his fights with what they called the 'whisker hit', and no one could stand against him until Neate—him they called the Bristol Bull—brought him down.'

Stevens had risen from the table as white as cheese.

'Let's get out of here, sir. I want fresh air. Let us get on our way.'

The landlord slapped him on the back.

'Cheer up, lad! You've held him off, anyhow, and that's more than anyone else has ever done. Sit down and have another glass of wine, for if a man in England has earned it this night it is you. There's many a debt you would pay if you gave the Gasman a welting, whether dead or alive. Do you know what he did in this very room?'

The two travellers looked round with startled eyes at the lofty room, stone-flagged and oak-panelled, with great open grate at the farther end.

'Yes, in this very room. I had it from old Squire Scotter, who was here that very night. It was the day when Shelton beat Josh Hudson out St Albans way, and Gas had won a pocketful of money on the fight. He and his pal Rowe came in here upon their way, and he was madraging drunk. The folk fairly shrunk into the corners and under the tables, for he was stalkin' round with the great kitchen poker in his hand, and there was murder behind the smile upon his face. He was like that when the drink was in him—cruel, reckless, and a terror to the world. Well, what think you that he did at last with the poker? There was a little dog, a terrier as I've heard, coiled up before the fire, for it was a bitter December night. The Gasman broke its back with one blow of the poker. Then he burst out laughin', flung a curse or two at the folk that shrunk away from him, and so out to his high gig that was waiting outside. The next we heard was that he was carried down to Finchley with his head ground to a jelly by the wagon wheel. Yes, they do say the little dog with its bleeding skin and its broken back has been seen since then, crawlin' and yelpin' about Brocas Corner, as if it were lookin' for the swine that killed it. So you see, Mr Stevens, you were fightin' for more than yourself when you put it across the Gasman.'

'Maybe so', said the young prize-fighter, 'but I want no more fights like that. The Farrier-Sergeant is good enough for me, sir, and if it is the same to you, we'll take a railway train back to town.'

And there it ends, the contest with the Farrier-Sergeant being too clearly anti-climactic to report although we may hope the brave Stevens won it. The symbolism of modern security replacing the peril of old roads, vulnerable transport and fighting ways of the past is neat enough, as is the recognition that Stevens, while wanting no more of it, has proved himself as a prize-fighter as well as being the Queensberry rules man who will face the Sergeant.

The idea of a ghost who can inflict physical damage with his former pugilistic skill is new to me: ghosts normally terrify, leaving it to their vic tims to inflict grievous bodily harm on themselves. On the other hand, Conan Doyle is truly logical. What would be the good of a boxer's ghost if it could not make its victims feel its boxing? Equally, the living boxer and patron are not afraid of ghostly boxing opponents. It is the unknown that terrifies them, innocent though they are of the fate of the little terrier.

Tom Hickman really lived and bested all comers until defeated by Bill Neate in December 1821, reported by William Hazlitt in an essay that probably inspired Conan Doyle in the first place. Hazlitt describes his de-feat in a significant passage:

> I never saw anything more terrific than his aspect before he fell. All traces of life, of natural expression, were gone from him. His face was like a human skull, a death's head, spouting blood. The eyes were filled with blood, the nose streamed with blood, the mouth gaped blood. He was not like an actual man, but like a preternatural spectral appear-ance, or like one of the figures in Dante's Inferno.

Thence may have come the double inspiration, both for the idea of Hickman as ghost, and for his damnation in a Hell which forces him to be driven by his canine victim from a victorious prize-fighting against mortals. Yet Conan Doyle may have been very unfair to the real Hickman. Hazlitt says that Gentleman Jackson collected a purse for the beaten champion, not a likely benefit to be conferred on a bully and sadist. When Hickman was killed two months later by a wagon as described in the story, the boxing ring—patrons and, apparently, contestants—contributed to the support of his bereaved family. Unless Conan Doyle found some source unknown to me, the ugly reputation and the brutal murder of the dog were both figments of his imagination. But the story itself had an origin some forty years earlier. The oldest surviving story by Conan Doyle, 'The Haunted Grange of Goresthorpe', remains among the Blackwood MSS in the National Library of Scotland, Conan Doyle as a youth having sent the story for *Blackwood's Magazine* without the requisite stamped, self-addressed envelope for the editor to return it, if not wanted. It was not wanted—he wrote it in the selfsame 1878 when eighteen at the oldest, and it is painfully evident that its origin lay in schoolboy invention. But it has what Sherlock Holmes would call distinctive features, the most obvious of which is a sceptical narrator ultimately convinced by the expertise of a remarkable friend with whom he investigates a mystery. The friend, unlike Holmes, is a believer in the supernatural insistent on a ghost-hunt. But this duly proves a dismaying experience, when they encounter first the ghost of a murderer, and then see him fleeing in terror from the apparition of the little, vulnerable wife whom he has murdered, whose pursuit terrifies the murderer as nothing else can. That unpublished juvenility had lodged itself in its creator's imagination to re-emerge as Hickman and the terrier, and the derivation from Conan Doyle's own parents is all too clear.

Conan Doyle became a Spiritualist from love, love for the family and friends torn from him by the Great War. But his stories themselves testify (in some cases) to a major motivation for spirits revisiting the world they have left: hatred.

A STUDY IN SURVIVAL:
MESSAGES, MEDIUMS AND MATERIALISM

Roger Straughan

SIR ARTHUR Conan Doyle died on July 7th, 1930. The last fourteen years of his life had been dedicated to bringing what he saw as overwhelming evidence for our survival of physical death to as wide an audience as possible. During this period he lectured in practically every major town and city in the UK—but that was not enough for this man. He felt he had to take his message to every corner of the globe, and so undertook lengthy lecture tours to Australia, New Zealand, North America, South Africa and Scandinavia, taking his whole family with him and producing four fascinating travel books about their adventures. He attracted enormous audiences and enormous controversy, for Spiritualism then as now had its vociferous critics as well as its passionate supporters. Wherever he went he had sittings with mediums and wrote about his findings. He took part in high profile public debates on the subject and wrote extensively about it, including a comprehensive history of Spiritualism. One of his last acts, when critically ill with heart disease, was to travel to London to petition the Home Secretary for a change in the law concerning the prosecution of mediums.

Why did Conan Doyle go to these extreme lengths to spread the message of Spiritualism? The main driving force was a desire to free as many

Roger Straughan's career has been spent in education, culminating in his being Reader in Education at the University of Reading, UK, specializing in the philosophy of education. He has had a lifelong interest in psychical questions and is an active member of a number of societies and organizations concerned with psychical and spiritual matters. His book, A STUDY IN SURVIVAL, which gives a fuller account of the subject-matter of this chapter, will be published in Autumn 2009 by O Books.

people as possible from the fear of death. He had himself after long investigation received what he believed to be conclusive evidence of life after death, of the survival of personality and of the possibility of communication between this world and the next. This he saw as a momentous revelation which everyone should be aware of. Spiritualism could be a great unifying force between religions, Christian and non-Christian, because it rested upon fact and not upon faith. The religious significance of Spiritualism was all-important for Conan Doyle, and he argued that the Bible in general and the New Testament in particular were full of psychical goings-on, most of which had obvious parallels in modern Spiritualism.

If Conan Doyle was right about survival and the possibility of communication between this world and the next, it would be logical to expect him to want to continue his mission after his own death by demonstrating his own survival. He had to 'return'. During his lifetime he had made survival something of a speciality as a writer as well as a Spiritualist. He had written one of the most famous survival stories of all time, bringing back to life probably the best-known character in English fiction—a detective who had by all accounts previously died at the foot of the Reichenbach Falls. So if Conan Doyle wished to persist with his mission—and he was a very persistent man—he would have to follow the example of Sherlock Holmes and 'return'.

Since 1930 there have been many claims that he has done just that. This chapter will look briefly at a few of these and will present fresh evidence for another. The earliest and most publicized example took place only a few days after Conan Doyle's death. On July 13th, 1930, a memorial service was held for him at the Royal Albert Hall in London, reportedly attended by 8000 people. An empty chair was placed on the stage between his wife and his elder son. Tributes were paid by many of his friends, and a well-known medium, Estelle Roberts, attempted to establish contact. In her autobiography she wrote:

> I kept looking about me, hoping he would appear. It was not until the audience stood for two minutes' silence as a tribute to him, that I suddenly became aware he was standing beside me. With this realization I became momentarily flustered. He saw it at once and quickly calmed me. 'Carry on with your work. Go on, child', he said reassuringly. Then he went and sat in the 'empty' chair by his wife.

I carried on transmitting spirit messages until Sir Arthur got to his feet and came over to my side. Slowly and deliberately he gave me a test message for Lady Doyle. It was an intimate one concerning another member of the family and referred to an event which had occurred only that morning. It convinced Lady Doyle that it must have come from her husband, as only she and the other member of the family were aware that the small incident described had happened.

FORTY YEARS A MEDIUM, p. 145

Conan Doyle had been Spiritualism's best-known convert and campaigner, and it was only to be expected that there would be many reports of messages and other psychical phenomena emanating from him after his death. His daughter, Dame Jean Conan Doyle, told me herself, when we corresponded shortly before her death in 1997, that many such messages had been received by the family, 90% of which they judged to be rubbish, while the remainder had convinced them each individually that he was indeed in contact with them. Over the years, there have been many claims of mediumistic communications, psychic photographs and physical phenomena, including (improbably?) the malfunctioning of a lift in a London building once occupied by Conan Doyle, and (more interestingly) a friendly apparition at his house in the New Forest, which I have personally done some research into.

But how can we even start to evaluate such claims? The most rational approach one can adopt here is to avoid an uncritical attitude of either wholesale acceptance or wholesale rejection, but to judge each case strictly on its merits. We cannot conduct scientific laboratory tests or expect scientific 'proof' in this area (many philosophers would argue that infallible 'proof' is probably not possible in any area), but that does not mean that rational judgments cannot be made on the basis of the available evidence. That evidence can consist of a variety of considerations, including such things as consistency, the reliability of witnesses, the forming and testing of theories, the following of clues and the drawing of deductions—exactly the kind of methodology employed by Sherlock Holmes!

The rest of this chapter will be devoted to exploring how this approach could be applied to the best known example of alleged communications from the discarnate Conan Doyle—the 'message' received by the medium, Grace Cooke, which has been so crucial in the development of the White

Eagle Lodge. This exploration will also describe some of my own personal experiences, which are highly relevant to the question of Conan Doyle's possible 'return'.

The Grace Cooke 'message' is dealt with elsewhere in this book and it is up to the reader to form his or her own balanced judgment as to its authenticity. For myself, I remained undecided until the further evidence to be presented later in this chapter was offered to me. The story of how the messages originated and of the various personalities involved is too complicated to be summarized here.

Did this material, or at least some of it, really come from Conan Doyle after his death? The sceptical view of such 'communications' is usually that they may be a product of the medium's own subconscious, without him or her being aware of this—Grace Cooke in fact delivered the messages while in a state of trance. This explanation could well account for some of the descriptions of the afterlife which mediums have given, particularly where the content of the 'communication' is a predictable reflection of Spiritualist philosophy. In this case, however, there were several intriguing features to the messages, which raised doubts about the sceptical position.

Grace Cooke had never met Conan Doyle and had apparently read only one of his books. Yet many of the messages are expressed in a style which is often strongly reminiscent of his writing and lectures, in terms of its power, vividness and simplicity, together with his usual humorous touches of self-deprecation. Would a medium unacquainted with Conan Doyle and his writing, and of no literary ability herself, have been able to reproduce his style in this way, together with many of his mannerisms?

The messages were also at times somewhat critical of the current state of Spiritualism, arguing that too much emphasis was being placed upon simply trying to prove personal survival of death, and too little upon our spiritual development before and after death. Wasn't it unlikely that Grace Cooke, who had devoted many years of her life to traditional Spiritualism, would consciously or unconsciously manufacture such criticisms, or imagine that Conan Doyle would produce them?

Finally, the messages had been accompanied by several pieces of factual evidence, including an alleged psychic photograph. The communicator claiming to be Conan Doyle announced to one of the sitters, 'I am to endeavour to give you this material proof on a photographic plate'. This sitter, who had never met Conan Doyle when he was alive, approached a well-known photographic medium who knew nothing of the matter. A striking picture was produced showing the face of Conan Doyle above the head of the sitter, which cannot be identified with any existing photograph.

All of these points impressed me, but I was not wholly convinced (just as Lady Conan Doyle seems not to have been.) The style in which the messages were conveyed was not consistent, and one of the sitters in the group significantly wrote, 'I think Sir Arthur must have been helped a great deal and at times I think influenced'. (ARTHUR CONAN DOYLE'S BOOK OF THE BEYOND, p. 26) So my initial reading of the messages many years ago left me open-minded as to whether the discarnate Conan Doyle had been responsible for at least some of the material.

More recently, however, I realized that I might have the means at my disposal to throw fresh light upon the matter. To explain this further I shall have to strain the reader's credulity by briefly describing an ongoing series of extraordinary personal experiences and experiments which have occurred over the past fifteen years. A short summary cannot carry the conviction that a full account is able to, and such an account will soon be published in a book entitled A STUDY IN SURVIVAL: CONAN DOYLE SOLVES THE FINAL PROBLEM (O Books, 2009). For the purpose of this chapter, however, the essential point is that a completely unexpected chain of apparent 'coincidences' led me gradually and rather reluctantly (because of my ingrained scepticism as a professional philosopher) to the conclusion that communication was possible with the discarnate Conan Doyle many years after his death on a wide variety of subjects.

The simple method of communication which developed involved Conan Doyle's own writings, of which I already had a considerable collection, having enjoyed his books ever since my teens, and which I have continued to add to. As is described in A STUDY IN SURVIVAL, the whole saga began with what Sherlock Holmes would have called 'the curious incident of the dog in the night-time', when a much-loved dog of mine died one evening at my home.

To take my mind off worries that he might have suffered at the end, I casually opened the first book lying on my bedside table. This happened to be a thick volume of collected short stories by Sir Arthur Conan Doyle, which I had had for years but only occasionally dipped into, THE CONAN DOYLE STORIES. The book runs to well over 1000 pages, and with my thoughts elsewhere, still firmly fixed on the dog, I opened it completely at random and glanced at the page. The first words my eyes fell upon were: 'his exit was as speedy and painless as could be desired'. (p. 1054) I didn't remember anything about that particular story, 'The Surgeon Talks', but to my amazement I found that the reference was to the death of a dog— 'the poor little doggie'. In a daze, I turned back to the page before (p. 1053), and at once a sentence seemed to stand out as if highlighted. It read: 'A more malignant case I have never seen'. What was this case? I wondered. The answer appeared a couple of lines earlier—the case in question was 'a frightful sarcoma'. My vet had diagnosed that my dog was suffering from a malignant sarcoma.

Was all this an amazing 'coincidence'? To test this I began experimenting with a more deliberate and 'interactive' approach. Instead of just opening a book at random, I would sometimes deliberately formulate a particular question or concern, either in my mind or out loud, and then close my eyes to make a completely blind selection from the long shelf of Conan Doyle volumes that I now possessed. Without looking at the title, I would then open the book completely at random and focus on the first words my eyes fell upon. This method produced and has continued to produce remarkable results, and I now have records of many hundreds of such 'readings'. These cover an extensive range of topics. In the search for evidence that the discarnate Conan Doyle was orchestrating these 'readings', I posed mental questions or invited comments on subjects in which he might reasonably be expected to have a special interest or particular expertise. These included medical matters, sporting events, military and political affairs, cryptic puzzles and religious topics.

The results went way beyond what could be expected by way of chance, often involving amazingly specific detail relevant to the issue in question. Many of these are fully described in A STUDY IN SURVIVAL, and this chapter is not the place for a lengthy account, so a couple of typical examples must suffice. Current news items proved to be a rich source of material, which was consistent with Conan Doyle's intense interest in current affairs. Stunned like everyone else by the 9/11 attack on the World Trade Centre in New York, I that evening asked for a comment. My eyes fastened at once on six extraordinary words in the middle of the top line of the page: 'IN NEW YORK, IN THE CENTRE' (THE EDGE OF THE UNKNOWN, p.186).

Again, while actually watching live coverage on TV of the scene at the underground station following the London terrorist bombings, I wondered if a comment on such a momentous event might be forthcoming and made the usual completely blind selection of book from my shelf. It fell open at a Sherlock Holmes short story which deals with a death on the London Underground system. I read: ' 'We will begin our investigation by a visit to ALDGATE STATION.... An hour later Holmes, Lestrade and I stood upon the underground railroad at the point where it emerges from the tunnel immediately before Aldgate Station''. ('The Bruce-Partington Plans' in THE COMPLETE SHERLOCK HOLMES SHORT STORIES, p. 978). The bomb had exploded just outside Aldgate Station.

Another dramatic piece of evidence was provided by Conan Doyle's own daughter, Dame Jean Conan Doyle, his last surviving direct descendent. I contacted this lady in 1997 and told her of my experiences. She replied that she and her family had received lots of claims about her father's communications after his death, most of which were highly dubious. In such cases she had a 'test question' which she asked to establish her father's identity. I did not ask her directly what this was, but we continued to correspond until she became terminally ill. At that point I reported to her a 'reading' which, it transpired, had successfully answered her 'test question' without my attempting to do so, providing information which she said no other living person would have known and which had never previously been given to her.

All this was not, of course, 100% guaranteed 'proof', but it was certainly very strong evidence that there was a personal, purposeful intelligence directing these readings, and that the source of that intelligence was a man who had 'died' nearly seventy years earlier. So when I found myself reconsidering the Grace Cooke messages one day, I realized that there could be a means at my disposal which might give me a unique opportunity of throwing more light on them. Why not ask the man himself? If Conan Doyle was behind my readings, he might be expected to have some revealing comments to make about the alleged messages which had been attributed to him.

Accordingly I mentally framed a question as to whether the messages (or some of them) had indeed been a genuine communication from Conan Doyle himself, and then made for the bookshelf. My hand alighted upon a book in which no one could have anticipated finding convincing answers to psychical questions—a collection of light-hearted Napoleonic tales about Brigadier Gerard. Yet ... 'Never had I burned so brilliantly as at that supreme moment when the darkness fell', was the first line I read. (ADVENTURES OF GERARD, p. 223)

That sounded highly promising. Was this a direct account of Conan Doyle's experiences immediately after his death– the very issue I was asking about? 'That supreme moment when the darkness fell' could hardly have been clearer, though in the story it did not refer to the moment of death—another example of the ingenuity which seemed such a feature of the readings. But this did not unambiguously answer the question about whether Conan Doyle had been the communicator of the alleged messages in the 1930s, so I tried again, asking for clarification on that particular point. The same book opened at a different page. 'But soon I understood that my task was not so simple as had appeared', I read. (p. 126)

This sentence, on the face of it not very remarkable, was actually a perfect answer to my question. A recurrent theme in the alleged Conan Doyle messages had been his emphasis upon the unexpected difficulties he had encountered in trying to communicate from the next world. At the very first sitting, almost the first words spoken through the medium were: 'It is difficult—yes, I have heard you calling me. At such times I have been close, and yet there has been some barrier'. (THE RETURN OF ARTHUR CONAN DOYLE, p. 54) At the next sitting, the difficulties of communication were again stressed: ' I have been trying for days to come through…. Be patient! I shall get stronger—I shall never give up—I shall stick to it, and this is what you too must do—stick to our task…. You do not understand the difficulties we have in coming through'. (p. 63) Yet again at a later sitting the same point was stressed: 'Before my passing I had little understanding of the many difficulties holding up communication with the spirit world'. (pp. 80–81)

These comments, recorded at sittings in the 1930s, made the apparently unexciting reading obtained in response to my question about the authenticity of those sittings highly significant—the same point was being made in almost the same words. Surely this was confirmation of the identity of the 1930s communicator? My scepticism was not giving up without a struggle, however, so with the book still open at the same page I asked, 'So you needed help with this difficult task?' and immediately glanced down at the very bottom of that page, where I read the words: 'And then suddenly I had that flash of light which comes to the brave man who refuses to despair'. (ADVENTURES OF GERARD, pp. 126–7)

My scepticism admitted defeat. One or even two directly relevant read-

ings in answer to my specific questions might conceivably have been coincidences, but this third response settled the matter. Again one had to know
something about the original messages before the full significance of this
third reading could be appreciated. In one of the sittings the communicator
described the difficulties he encountered immediately after death in free-
ing himself from 'the entanglements of earth' because of the 'denseness'
around him—a common feature of many apparent attempts by communi-
cators to describe their immediate post-mortem experiences. He went on:
'And then I seemed to be picked up, as it were, by a ray of light. A power
unknown came to my aid, giving me understanding of my true state…. It
proved of inestimable value to me and brought a clear vision of the actual
state of life which exists immediately after death'. (THE RETURN OF ARTHUR
CONAN DOYLE, p. 106)

By this time I was feeling like Sherlock Holmes on one of his most
tortuous trails, finding the final piece of the jigsaw puzzle. In my quest to
investigate whether Conan Doyle had indeed been the instigator of at least
some of the messages relayed by Grace Cooke soon after his death, I had
now obtained three readings in quick succession which appeared to be direct responses to my queries, and which made perfect sense when taken in
conjunction with the original messages. That last reading about the sudden
flash of light coming to the brave man who refuses to despair was particularly uncanny in the way that it echoed the description of being 'picked up,
as it were, by a ray of light'. It appeared that I had been enabled to confirm
the identity of the 1930s communicator seventy years after the event.

There is, then, strong evidence that Conan Doyle has continued his
mission in the years since his physical death. My own experiences, as described in A STUDY IN SURVIVAL, I would interpret as merely the latest chapter
in this ongoing saga, but the originality of the means of communication
and the cumulative weight of the evidence provided forced me, almost
against my will, to commit my story to print and so allow Conan Doyle's
message that death is not the end to receive further publicity. As one distinguished psychical researcher commented on reading my account, 'I think
Doyle has set you up as his secretary!'

But why go to these lengths to present evidence for survival? Is our survival of physical death really so important? Is survival enough? Isn't it the
conditions in which survival takes place and to which it may lead which
really matter most? We do not normally use the word 'survival' to imply

that it is particularly valuable or desirable for its own sake. Surviving to an extremely old age, for example, is not in itself usually seen as something to be longed for; it is 'quality of life' which is normally thought to determine whether survival to a great age is a blessing or a curse. How we survive and what we do with our survival is surely more important than the mere act of surviving.

Both the Christian and the Spiritualist view of life after death are to some extent in broad agreement that 'mere survival' is not enough, and that much more needs to be said about the quality of that survival, what determines it and what it may lead to. Survival is not enough for the orthodox Christian, because it stops far short of 'rebirth', 'redemption' and 'resurrection', which are necessary if spiritual growth is to take place and lead to the gift from God of 'everlasting life'. The Spiritualist view also looks beyond mere survival, emphasizing growing awareness, continuing spiritual progression and the possibility of getting 'stuck' for a time at the lowest levels, if one's concerns and attachments are too 'earthbound'. Some alleged accounts of the afterlife (including the 1930s 'message' of Conan Doyle) have spoken of a 'Second Death', at which we voluntarily cast off and let go some aspects of our 'personal self' or 'soul'.

'Mere survival' is not enough, then, for those who already hold certain religious or philosophical beliefs, and evidence for survival may even be thought by them to be unnecessary, unspiritual or even dangerous. Yet large numbers of people today do not hold firm beliefs of this kind. The fundamental choice for them is not between one religion and another, or one church and another. It is between a materialistic, atheistic view of life and one which allows for the possibility of some form of spiritual dimension beyond the limits of the physical world in which we live our everyday lives. That choice is a stark one. Are we simply a random cocktail of chemicals and atoms, destined inevitably to disintegrate when the cells of our bodies and brains die? If so, it must follow that when you're dead you're dead, and that is all there is to it. Or might we be something more permanent than that, part of a bigger picture which we can at present get only brief and disjointed glimpses of? Which of these two options we choose to accept cannot help but form part of our whole view of the world, including our attitude towards others and ourselves; it will shape the kind of person we become and the ways we behave. That is why the evidence for survival matters hugely.

The importance of the survival question in this conflict between the materialist and non-materialist viewpoints was crucial also for Conan Doyle and his support of Spiritualism was closely linked with his opposition to materialism. 'The differences between various sects are a very small thing as compared to the great eternal duel between materialism and the spiritual view of the Universe', he wrote. 'That is the real fight.' (THE VITAL MESSAGE, p. 98) He threw himself into this fight because of his overriding concern for the ordinary man or woman in the street and the bleak prospect that materialism offered them. If there were strong grounds for believing that materialism was plain wrong, this meant that we were not, as Professor Challenger in THE LAND OF MIST had memorably put it, just 'four buckets of water and a bagful of salts'. The anti-materialist message needed to be presented forcefully and effectively to the general public across the globe, and for Conan Doyle there could be no more noble or worthwhile mission to devote all his energies to. This was precisely what he did for the rest of his earthly life—and the evidence presented in this chapter suggests that he has continued to do so.

References
Conan Doyle, Sir Arthur. ADVENTURES OF GERARD. London: Gryphon Books (1949).

—, THE COMPLETE SHERLOCK HOLMES SHORT STORIES. London: John Murray (1928)

—, THE CONAN DOYLE STORIES. London: John Murray (1929).

—, THE EDGE OF THE UNKNOWN. New York: Putnam's Sons (1930)

—, THE LAND OF MIST in THE PROFESSOR CHALLENGER STORIES. London: John Murray (1952)

—, THE VITAL MESSAGE. London: Psychic Book Club (1938).

Cooke, Ivan (ed). THE RETURN OF ARTHUR CONAN DOYLE. Liss, Hants.: White Eagle Publishing Trust (1963).

Hayward, Colum (ed). ARTHUR CONAN DOYLE'S BOOK OF THE BEYOND. Liss, Hants.: White Eagle Publishing Trust (1994).

Roberts, Estelle. FORTY YEARS A MEDIUM. London: Herbert Jenkins (1959).

Straughan, Roger. A STUDY IN SURVIVAL: CONAN DOYLE SOLVES THE FINAL PROBLEM. Ropley, Hants.: O Books (2009, forthcoming)

THE AGE OF THE SPIRIT:
SIR ARTHUR, THE POLAIRE CONNECTION,
AND THE WHITE BROTHERHOOD

Colum Hayward

AS CHANCE would have it, I am writing this chapter not far from the little village of Lordat, high up above the valley of the Ariège in Southern France, and set among the foothills of the Pyrenees. Lordat has a special fascination for me. My grandmother, Grace Cooke, travelled there in July 1931 with a small party composed of members of the Polaire Brotherhood, a group that was active in Paris from around 1929. She was a Spiritualist medium of some renown, and her spirit guide is still well-known today. His name is 'White Eagle'. Just after Sir Arthur Conan Doyle's death, a series of messages were channelled through her that took our collective awareness of the spirit life onto a whole new level.

How she came to be with the Polaires is a matter interwoven with the overall subject of this book, which is how the life and death of Sir Arthur marks the beginning of a new consciousness, one that is still evolving today. It is a complex but deeply touching story. In June 1930 Grace Cooke was the guest of another noted Spiritualist, Mabel Beatty, along with Mary Conan Doyle, the writer's daughter, at a holiday cottage near Barmouth in Wales. During this visit White Eagle spoke, predicting the wars and disasters of the 1930s, saying that they would be followed by a new age of the spirit. The message was relayed to Sir Arthur by his daughter, and this is the limit of the connection my grandmother had with Sir Arthur during his life, for although a weekend visit to the Conan Doyle family home at

---

Colum Hayward is the author of EYES OF THE SPIRIT: WORKING WITH A SPIRITUAL TEACHER and has been resident at the London branch of the White Eagle Lodge since 1978. The Conan Doyle/Polaire material began to fascinate him many years ago and in 1994 he contributed a fifty-page update on the story when he re-edited the Conan Doyle message for ARTHUR CONAN DOYLE'S BOOK OF THE BEYOND. He has also been principal editor of the White Eagle teaching for many years.

Crowborough was planned, he died before it could happen, on July 7th that same year (pp. 19–20).* He was exhausted, not with writing about detectives, chivalry and eccentric professors, but with promoting the cause of Spiritualism. In the public eye he was its leader.

Seventy-nine years later and particularly in the present context, it is good to recall that message and know that one of the last communications he had from spirit promised a new age for humanity. After their hero died, thousands of Spiritualists gathered in the Royal Albert Hall to celebrate his life and consider the future. A fund was launched to create a lasting Conan Doyle Memorial. The memorial was seen as something material; his widow described it as 'the big Centre' in letters to my grandmother. White Eagle, quite early on, insisted that the Conan Doyle memorial 'must be used, not for the furtherance of a personality but, as his life was spent, for the establishment of truth and justice. Thus will his name, after the death of the body, bring to the brothers the power they need to build on earth a temple of the spirit'. Powerful words. Among those involved, agreement on the form the memorial should take was difficult to achieve, and the response to the appeal, despite the enormous impact Conan Doyle had had on thousands or even millions of lives, as Spiritualist every bit as much as novelist, was a mere two thousand pounds. The material memorial was quietly abandoned (pp. 85–6, 22, 81–4). Today we may ask if there has ever been a proper monument to the great champion of spirit, or is it something we attempt anew with this book?

The answer to that question may depend on the reader's reaction to the next few pages. They make some ambitious claims. First, inevitably, is the veracity of the Spiritualist message itself. A second is that the destiny of the human race is carefully watched and even guided by a group of discarnate souls known commonly as the White Brotherhood. Grace Cooke's friend Mabel Beatty published three books said to contain messages 'from the White Brotherhood', and when Mrs Cooke was invited to

*Unless otherwise noted, any page references given in this chapter are to the 2006 edition of ARTHUR CONAN DOYLE'S BOOK OF THE BEYOND, published by the White Eagle Publishing Trust, Liss, Hampshire. The Conan Doyle messages which comprise most of the text were first published as THY KINGDOM COME in December 1933, and reissued as THE RETURN OF ARTHUR CONAN DOYLE in 1956. The messages have thus been continuously in print for over seventy-five years.

join her circle, it felt exactly right to do so because White Eagle had been speaking about just such a group ever since 1926, urging his hearers to be aware of the spirit brothers (p. 20). Sometimes he referred to them as the sages in the East, sometimes as the Masters. He was not, however, alone in this.

While White Eagle's messages involved trance mediumship, the French brotherhood of whom I have already spoken, the Polaires, had a different means of communication with a higher source. Their secret was possession of a mathematical oracle given to their founder as a child and explored by him and a small group of friends as he reached adulthood. The donor was a mysterious sage known as Father Julian (Padre Giuliano), whose passing onward into the light seems to have occurred shortly before Sir Arthur's, in April 1930. The Oracle de Force Astrale, as it was known, was a coding and decoding device that took a question and translated it into numerical sequences which, when processed, produced answers that frequently astounded the questioner. Such was its reputation that when the small group went 'public' with their oracle in 1929, their tiny organization swelled until it had some ten thousand followers, in a space of months rather than years. The Polaires also had a symbol that rallied people to the cause they led, which was an open six-pointed star, normally shown in silver, or else against a blue background.

What is intriguing is that at just the same time as White Eagle was speaking through his medium about the White Brotherhood, the Oracle was apparently giving just the same information, even though the Cooke family and the Polaires were completely unknown to one another. Intriguingly, too, White Eagle was increasingly referring not just to the Brotherhood, but to the same symbol, the six-pointed star. This strange coincidence was to develop further.

We take up the main story again. Immediately after Sir Arthur died, Grace Cooke made a number of connections with Lady Conan Doyle, the most notable being a visit to her at her New Forest home, Bignell Wood. At sittings and meetings she gave his widow good evidence of Conan Doyle's survival, but the details were circumstantial rather than profound (pp. 21, 83). What is much more extraordinary is that in November 1930, out of the blue as it were, the Polaires in Paris started to receive messages about Sir Arthur from the Oracle. Their content is described by Grace Cooke's husband Ivan,

'Since his arrival in the spirit land he had found that much of what he had previously thought true about Spiritualism ... and of the conditions of the next life needed revision. He desired to correct any errors which he had sponsored. At the moment he was not in a position to do this, as certain ties still held his soul to earth. His passionate desire was to make these corrections....' (p. 79)

One of the Polaires was to come to England and make contact with Sir Arthur's widow. Lady Conan Doyle would then introduce him to the channel that spirit had prepared. He would recognize the person at once.

White Eagle's intimations were ahead of the Polaires at this point (p. 21). Just a few weeks earlier, on October 7th, he had told the little Cooke family that a messenger was coming from a society in France. This message was repeated, and in the Mabel Beatty circle on January 9th, 1931, White Eagle said that the messenger was near. On January 27th, two converging parties, blind to each other's identity up to that point, were in one another's company.

The place was the library in Westminster continued in memory of the crusading journalist W. T. Stead and known as the Stead Borderland Library. Under the care of his daughter Estelle Stead, it served as a Spiritualist information centre. Before the meeting, Lady Conan Doyle had received a letter from a Monsieur Zam Bhotiva so unusual that she had put it in a sealed envelope and had had Grace Cooke psychometrize it. The latter reported that the writer was 'one who has been sent to her by us.... You will be asked to take on some special work. We wish you to accept, although you at present know nothing about this—you must do it when you are asked' (p. 23). White Eagle was, for the first time and without mentioning the Polaires, acknowledging that his own guides and theirs were the same.

When Grace Cooke arrived at the Library the Conan Doyle party, including the French visitor, were already present. In referring to her, Ivan Cooke uses the name Minesta, by which she was often known by White Eagle (to the Polaires and to Lady Conan Doyle, she was known by another name White Eagle had given her, 'Brighteyes').

Minesta entered, crossed the room and seated herself. At once M. Bhotiva rose and crossed over to her. (Neither had met before.) He said:

'Yes, I know you. We have worked together long, long ago—that was in former lives in ancient Egypt. See—I have brought you this little star. It has been sent to you by the wise ones for you to wear.' He pinned it onto her dress, made a gesture of blessing and protection, and returned to his seat. (p. 86)

As the meeting continued, White Eagle spoke at considerable length to Lady Conan Doyle and her sons. Later Minesta rose, still under control.

The medium stopped at last in front of our brother [the account is from the Polaire Bulletin, translated], held out her hand, and a joyful, manly 'I am glad to meet you!' rang through the small room. A long and low-pitched conversation then took place between the 'dead' and the 'living'. Conan Doyle made himself known to Zam Bhotiva as 'Brother', and then, speaking again to those present, spoke of the Polaires as 'a group destined to help in the moulding of the future of the world.... For the times are near'. He then said, turning towards Zam Bhotiva, 'I must speak with you alone in six days. I have some important communications for you; the work, to which I can set no limit, begins. (p. 90)

So began one of the most remarkable series of messages ever received from spirit. The further unfoldment of the story needs greater space than this chapter to tell it, and those interested should go to the book from which most of this information is taken, ARTHUR CONAN DOYLE'S BOOK OF THE BEYOND. We shall shortly turn instead to the messages and their content. Two things however stand out from this end of the story. One is that Minesta, somewhat unnerved by the intensity of all that had gone on, tuned in to White Eagle's guidance on her return home, and received a reassuring message from him, including the words, 'This messenger is sent because of instruction from Tibet, and [he who sent the message] knows of you from there'. Ivan Cooke was to comment on the great sense of responsibility he and Minesta both felt (p. 92).

The other is the identity of the one who sent both messenger and message. Strangely, the confirmation of that came best from Minesta herself. We follow the Polaire account again.

When she awoke from trance she told M Bhotiva that she saw a lofty mountain and a man with a luminous dark face and great dark eyes who held out to her a six-pointed star. Here was the proof for which we waited. (p. 92)

There was no doubt in the minds of any Polaires, when Bhotiva returned home, that the one she described was the Master in Tibet who particularly guided their work, and whom they knew as the *Chevalier Sage*, the Wise Knight. To the Polaires, to White Eagle, and thus to Minesta and her family, it was henceforth absolutely clear that they were joined in work to be done, and that it was directed by the great Brotherhood who manifested in the Himalayas.*

Arthur Conan Doyle's message through Grace Cooke, his own vital message after death, thus cannot be separated from the context of the Brotherhood in the Beyond, or from the work of the Polaires and their six-pointed Star symbol. Here is White Eagle's own description of what that symbol means:

> The six-pointed Star under which you work is the symbol of the perfectly balanced life, the symbol of the Christ-man, the Christ-woman, and the Christ in you. It is the great symbol of perfect being and it forms the foundation of matter as well as the expression of spirit.
>
> White Eagle, PRACTISING PEACE, p. 74

On another occasion he answered:

> What is the Star? We could never define it if we talked the whole length of an incarnation, but to sum up we would say that the Star is God's plan for humanity. The Star is the Creator's plan for the liberation of humanity. It is the symbol of creation; and in the very centre of the Star you will find eternity.
>
> White Eagle, PRAYER, MINDFULNESS AND INNER CHANGE, p. 52

In yoga, an open six-pointed star (as opposed to the interlocked

---

*This identification with the Masters in the East ties in closely with Theosophical teaching.

triangles of the Star of David) is the symbol of the heart chakra; it has a long tradition in esotericism, and it seems to have been a task given to the Polaires and to the White Eagle Lodge, created in 1936 on the foundations of this contact between the several parties, incarnate and discarnate, to make the power of that Star known throughout the world.*

Who were the Polaires? Semi-secret at first in Paris, they rose to great prominence in the early 1930s among esoteric societies, but their very success also led them away from their simple devotion to the teaching given by the Oracle. The original group, who knew of themselves as 'La Racine', the root, and were generally five in number—La Racine was the root of the five-petalled rose—almost certainly withdrew. At any rate, the messages from the Oracle ceased. They had made contact with the group in England, and the White Eagle Lodge was to use their symbol of the Star as a way of focusing the power of the light into dark places throughout the coming war, and has been using it ever since for individual and world healing.† Their direct devotion to the Masters in the East leads us into Theosophy and earlier roots in the Hyperborean myth.

As to their purpose, it is well described in ARTHUR CONAN DOYLE'S BOOK OF THE BEYOND. For instance, they regarded the Star as a 'symbol of the brotherhood which is trying to bring a little solace to suffering souls, which is trying to unite diverse opinions, different faiths, different people, and guide them towards a goal of Light' (p. 18).

The Polaire Brotherhood at its prime formed a body of men and wom-

---

*Despite the long tradition mentioned, a star much more frequently regarded as part of esotericism was the five-pointed one adopted, for instance, as its symbol by the Order of the Star in the East (led by J. Krishnamurti until he dissolved it in August 1929) and by the Bulgarian teacher Peter Deunov when he established a White Brotherhood in his homeland around the beginning of the Twentieth Century. The five- and six-pointed stars do relate to one another, rather as the rose (which is a five-petalled flower) was often seen in complement to the six-pointed Star by the early Polaires, a connection continued by White Eagle in his teaching. I have been quoted elsewhere as saying that I detected a link between the Order of the Star in the East and the six-pointed Star work, but there is no evidence I know of for this beyond what I say here.

†The subject is touched on time and time again in the White Eagle books; for a personal account of the specific wartime work see FAR OUT: THE DAWNING OF NEW AGE BRITAIN, based on a Channel Four TV series of the same name in 1999.

en strongly linked to a great Source of spiritual power, and with each Brother attuned or linked to the other, by a method unpractised since early Egypt. (p. 56*)

Polaire aims included abandonment of all forms of egotism; they also rejected any sort of force in getting their ideas across. Ivan Cooke writes, 'The Polaires were forbidden by their Chiefs to constrain or overrule the freewill of any man…. No pains were spared to make this crystal clear to every Polaire'. Mario Fille, the one to whom (as a boy) the Oracle had been entrusted, at one stage found that he had to reiterate, 'La Fraternité Polaire doit être au-dessus des opinions particulières': 'the Brotherhood should be beyond opinion' (p. 92, 35n). The White Eagle Brotherhood to this day is apolitical, for in that way it can do its work better. Ivan Cooke adds, speaking of the Polaires: 'They did not make great mental efforts to project the light; theirs was rather a relaxing, an opening of themselves to receive the Master's ray so that it might flow through them….

'Part of the Polaire 'charge' or 'obligation' was that the Polaires must strive to remove the mad fear of death which haunts the brain of man' (p. 78). That charge has been fully taken up by the White Eagle Lodge too, but through meditation and counselling work, not just through mediumship. Death is a glorious moving forward, an emergence into the light, White Eagle would say.

A further keynote of the Polaire Brotherhood's work was to utilize the power of thinking positively. Once, we were schooled by the New Thought movement and exponents of it such as Henry Thomas Hamblin and Joel Goldsmith to use positive thought and creative visualization. To-day, 'the law of attraction' has gone so far as to spawn such ideas as Cosmic Ordering; it is interesting how far this must create karma, for good or ill. White Eagle has a deeper reason for wishing us to use positive thought, as he explained in a talk, later in the 1930s, to the English Brotherhood that developed out of the earlier meeting with the French:

There is great turmoil in the world. Do not participate in the destructive thoughts of those brethren unable to see with a clear vision. Be

---

*The words, from a manuscript history of the English Brotherhood, are almost certainly Ivan Cooke's, though they have never been confirmed as such.

constructive in your thoughts. The forces for good are strong; but for the
sake of the lesser brethren we need all the help we can get from you.
(White Eagle, with Ivan Cooke, THE WHITE BROTHERHOOD, p. 132)

'One of the first things that a man is faced with on his escape from
earth life is the world of his own thought', said Arthur Conan Doyle (p.
107). In the messages, we hear how after death he met thought-forms he
had created on earth, and how what he discovered released him could be
condensed into the single phrase, 'personal responsibility and the redeeming power of love' (pp. 51, 105*). Throughout his teaching, White Eagle
has said that the origin of karma is thought rather than action.

Thought-power, though, is more than just right thought. We have just
heard how the Polaires let the light of the Master flow through them, and
of the English brotherhood's projection of the light throughout the Second World War; we have also heard how the Polaire brothers were able to
link with one another, 'by a method unpractised since early Egypt'. In the
messages, Conan Doyle twice mentions how, when he felt bound and limited in the planes beyond death, 'a power unknown came to my aid, giving
me a vision of my true state'. It was 'a ray of light … a projection of love
and power from the Polaires Brotherhood' (pp. 31, 48).† Thought-power,
in other words, can reach right up into different planes of life.

The concept of planes of life is one that had already been taught by
Theosophical writers. Yet the account of the planes of existence given by
Conan Doyle is remarkable for its comprehensiveness, and has the benefit
of being a description at first hand. Above ours, he says, there are various
astral planes, and at one moment he goes so far as to say there are seven

---

*Compare also Dave Patrick's contribution to this book, especially pp. 71–2.
In describing the revelation as Sir Arthur's, we take a certain risk. Lady Conan
Doyle, who never lost faith in or affection for, Grace Cooke, was nonetheless
anxious that the messages should have a validity independent of her husband's
name. The problem that Ivan Cooke faced in preparing the original edition of
them (see note on p. 45, above) was that there is so much self-reference in them
that not to call them Sir Arthur's would render many references nonsensical.
The problem remains, and it needs to be said that Lady Conan Doyle's point
was not to question their authenticity, but their presentation. In this respect, the
evidence in Roger Straughan's chapter in this book (pp. 33–43) is most timely.

†For this intervention, see also Roger Straughan's article, p. 40–1

of them. Some of them are quite dark, but they lead up into the Summer-
land of the Spiritualists. Next there are three mental planes, planes first of
intellectual realization, then of intuition and thought-creation, and lastly
a 'waiting hall of meditation'. Above the mental planes, three in number,
there are three celestial planes that lead to the universal sphere of at-one-
ment (pp. 46–7 and 158–77).

Yoga philosophy, and the Vedic and Upanishadic wisdom behind it,
may seem far from Conan Doyle's messages, but in fact yoga philosophy
perfectly bears out a scheme remarkably like Sir Arthur's. According to
the early yoga writers, the spirit or atman, after it first separates from the
one, takes on a series of veils, or sheathes of illusion, the *maya kosas*. The
ananda maya kosa is the first of these: the bliss sheath, roughly what Sir
Arthur and White Eagle call the celestial body. Next it creates *vijnana may
kosa*, the knowledge body, and then *mano maya kosa*, the mental body. After
that there grows *prana maya kosa*, the breath body, roughly what Sir Arthur
and White Eagle both call the etheric. Last of the bodies in the yoga tradi
tion is the physical, *ana maya kosa*.

White Eagle in his teaching holds a concept of 'the Ancient Wisdom': in
this respect Sir Arthur's message is reassuring not because it is novel, but because of the way in which, in examples such as the list of bodies and planes
of being, it actually accords with, re-emphasizes, age-old truth. But there is
another point to be made. Knowledge of the planes of existence is pretty
much only theory to us, so long as they remain only after-death states of
awareness. Sir Arthur is quite clear, however, that they are not just that:

> It is unnecessary for man to pass through physical death to contact all
> the planes of the spirit life. Mortal man can and indeed does contact
> and responds to the influence of all planes of spiritual being, the dif-
> ference being that when the soul is released, spiritual life gains a sweet
> intensity: the soul having lost a physical body, all the more surely does
> the soul-experience afford greater reality. (p. 177)

This is one of the moments when the Conan Doyle message sends
waves right through all the years since, as these words validate so much
meditation experience, so much awareness in moments of heightened
perception. Indeed, it offers the basis for a technique of meditation that
involves ascending through all the planes of life to the universal level, what

he calls the Christ-sphere, one that has been adopted in the White Eagle
Lodge since its creation.

Conan Doyle also implies in his messages that through our earthly
schooling we may also ourselves reach the level of the Masters who stand
at the gate of the Christ sphere, beyond the wheel of karma.

> In this condition of life dwell those beings who, freed from rebirth to a
> physical plane of existence, are now concerned not only with the earth
> but with the cosmic life of the universe. From this plane go forth cre-
> ative Masters, responsible for the life of the soul on other planets and
> in other spiritual spheres of existence.
>
> Thousands of years must elapse, of course, before the ego attains
> to full expression and development, and only after gaining all knowl-
> edge possible through physical existence does it pass onward, beyond
> the halls of waiting, onward beyond even the celestial, into a still high-
> er plane. (p. 176)

Grace and Ivan Cooke were fortunate at some point in their lives to
meet an Indian professor with great spiritual knowledge, someone who
seemed genuine in his claim to have met a living Master. When they asked
what the Master was like, the reply came back, 'He is all love' (p. 76).* Maybe this gives some background to another passage that has always struck
me. When editing ARTHUR CONAN DOYLE'S BOOK OF THE BEYOND for publication
in 1994, I found that with this passage I wanted to go to the transcript
the Polaires published at the time, even though I had to retranslate it into
English, for I was not sure that vital words had not been lost in the English
transcript. Thus my version reads:

> And I must conclude my message by speaking to you of this love, not
> confined to a personal, individual form, but under the greater form of
> a love beyond the personal, of a love for all human beings.
>
> Love, the great need!
> Love, the Master! (p. 52†)

*My grandmother referred to the same incident in her book THE SHINING
PRESENCE, p. 27–8
†With a new translation from the French of the full quotation

One of the things Conan Doyle's messages do for me is to make real what the deepest love actually feels like; they are at times quite ecstatic about it. 'The redeeming power of love' is not just a theology, it is an actual experience for Conan Doyle. That freshness, that sense of an immediate report of sensation and impression, is one of the things that make the messages special. As to what and how Sir Arthur's soul encountered in that context of absolute love, it seems to be redemptive love, rescuing us from the prisons we create for ourselves; love of souls one for another; and a sense of divine warmth, sometimes bordering on ecstasy. For me, there is verity even in the very passion of them.

A religion of love is something to be achieved by universal human love, the second of these, and I will suggest in a second chapter that the right word for this 'religion' is Brotherhood. Grace Cooke herself made a very radical suggestion about individual responsibility being the salvation of humanity, rather than the person of Christ.

> It is not the man, the Master Jesus, whom the Christian world worships as the saviour and vicarious redeemer of the world; it is the teaching of the Christ spirit or the love and brotherhood, the divine light in the heart of every man, which is the saviour of [hu]mankind. It is this little spark of divine life which the White Brotherhood endeavours to fan into a glowing flame so that it can absorb into itself and feel what its brother feels. This light, this truth is the vicarious at-one-ment—the essence of the teaching of the White Brotherhood.
>
> Grace Cooke, THE SHINING PRESENCE, pp. 35–6

Conan Doyle and White Eagle both saw, coming, a universal religion of love. It was a religion not based on priesthood but upon the connections human beings could make one with another. In another chapter I shall make it clear how much I echo this concept.

> Of universal brotherhood much is said, yet few indeed understand the meaning of the word; for all are taught from childhood to fight for themselves, to assert themselves at the expense of others. Erroneously man has thought the object of life to be enhancement of his personality. At all costs he must become a man superior—that is, if he desires to equal or master his brother man. This sins against the cosmic law of brotherhood. The man searching and seeking only for himself breaks

every law, and while humanity thus continues can result only disease, chaos, and war.

The truly great is he who recognizes, not his own desires, but the infinite and eternal power of love. Each must lose himself to find himself. No man will ever find God whilst encompassed by the error that power and accomplishment come by and through himself. The greatest test through which a soul must eventually pass when it has arisen and thrown off its grave-clothes is to let all sense of self and personality fall away. That soul must then face an abyss of darkness and extinction, so it would seem. One desire only sustains the fainting soul—to yield, to surrender, to be bared utterly of self, to sacrifice every vestige ere the soul can merge into the infinite and eternal love-God.

Such is not extinction; it is expansion. If he reach the point where his love of God become so great, so overwhelming that he desires nothing but to be with God, then his love may enfold even God; then every man to him becomes Godlike, and God dwells in every man....

The man who would understand universal brotherhood must indeed *Leave all and follow Me*.

He must render up—must efface himself, must lose self to find the universal selfless: God! In this supreme moment that man becomes at one, not only with God, but with each and every man.

Such is the meaning of the Brotherhood of Man. (pp. 238–9)

In a quite different book, THE LIGHT BRINGER, White Eagle takes up this theme again. Here, he shows how the coming age will also be one of the development of spiritual powers, and that the one who takes us on from the teaching of Jesus, the one who best enables us to understand the Christian teaching, is John—John the Beloved of Christ.

Jesus came to teach the people how to live the life [of simple love one of another] on the physical plane within their communities. But John began to teach people the purpose of Jesus' teaching, because it is only when men and women can live the life of love and brotherhood towards each other that they can then begin to develop those soul powers of which we speak, those heavenly powers with which God … has endowed them. The new age then is of John—the Age of Brotherhood.

White Eagle, THE LIGHT BRINGER, p. 22

*

I began by saying that I was near Lordat when I began this chapter, in the Pyrenean part of Cathar country. Lordat is indeed a Cathar chateau, not far from Montségur and en route for anyone who might have escaped from there into the Pyrenees. Some eight hundred years after the final massacre of the Cathars there, alongside her husband, Ivan, and led by the Polaires after initiation into their brotherhood, she assisted mediumistically in a search for buried treasure of some kind. It was never found there, but what she did have was a quite extraordinary meditation in which she was deeply aware of a Cathar brother, somehow linked to St John, 'the disciple Jesus loved'. The figure that she encountered was indeed one of indescribable beauty and love. 'After the visitor had withdrawn into the inner world from which he had come, Mrs Cooke 'seemed to live in a haze of happiness for days'.... 'Words could not describe, she says, the sweet and wonderful love of this simple Brother'.'

This link with St John was to prove increasingly profound to her. White Eagle's animal symbol is said to be the eagle, which is also the symbol of John, and the second most significant series of messages ever given through her is probably those given by White Eagle about St John's Gospel. They are reproduced in the White Eagle book, THE LIVING WORD OF ST JOHN.

What is most abundantly clear from the Conan Doyle messages is that as we move forward into the Aquarian Age and through the tipping point of 2012, one of the things we can most expect is an extraordinary outpouring of love from spirit. While we shall need to guard against Aquarian intellectualism and independence, it truly will be an age of the spirit, and one of increasing brotherhood and connection among human beings.

At Lordat, sitting just outside the gate of the chateau,* and in drizzling rain that would later turn to snow, I sat for a while, generously left to meditate there by my travelling companion. Once I had succeeded in getting quiet, my meditation took a very deep turn. I was aware of White Eagle, and aware of Sir Arthur, and of some Cathar connection that linked them. Then the figures gave way to a new one. I saw him slightly at first, but became progressively aware of a most youthful countenance, curly

---

*Today, the chateau, which for many years was completely open, is run as an eagle sanctuary. There may be a nice appropriateness in that, but it means that the castle is inaccessible to visitors between All Saints and Easter.

hair and blue eyes. The smile I saw absolutely radiated love, but a love that was not for me only but for all humankind. In my own small way I believe I was shown a figure that, in the same manner, represented John and whose countenance showed all the beauty, and love, that the disciple had seen in the eyes of his own Master, Jesus. That love, I know, will sustain humanity in its new age.

References

Akhtar, Miriam, and Humphries, Steve, FAR OUT: THE DAWNING OF NEW AGE BRITAIN. Bristol: Sansom & Co. (1999)

Cooke, Grace, PLUMED SERPENT. London: Psychic Book Club (1942)

—, THE SHINING PRESENCE. London, White Eagle Lodge (1946)

Cooke, Ivan (ed). THY KINGDOM COME. London: Wright & Brown (1933).

—. THE RETURN OF ARTHUR CONAN DOYLE. Liss, Hants.: White Eagle Publishing Trust (1963).

Hayward, Colum (ed). ARTHUR CONAN DOYLE'S *BOOK OF THE BEYOND*. Liss, Hants.: White Eagle Publishing Trust (1994).

White Eagle, THE LIGHT BRINGER. Liss, Hants: White Eagle Publishing Trust (2001)

—, THE LIVING WORD OF ST JOHN. Liss, Hants: White Eagle Publishing Trust (1979)

—, PRACTISING PEACE. Liss, Hants: White Eagle Publishing Trust (2007)

—, PRAYER, MINDFULNESS AND INNER CHANGE. Liss, Hants: White Eagle Publishing Trust (2003)

—, with Ivan Cooke, THE WHITE BROTHERHOOD. Liss, Hants: White Eagle Lodge (1939)

THE MYSTERY OF SIR ARTHUR CONAN DOYLE'S *VITAL MESSAGE*

Dave Patrick

SIR ARTHUR Conan Doyle's book, THE VITAL MESSAGE, published in 1919, together with THE NEW REVELATION (1918), represented his first unequivocal proclamations concerning what he referred to as 'the psychic matter', and the question of survival of life after death. But what was this revelation, why was the message so vital, and what has happened to it in the intervening ninety years?

From these innocent questions a mystery began to unfold, the solving of which would surely have taxed the mind and patience of Conan Doyle's master detective Sherlock Holmes himself. What was this mystery?

Sherlock Holmes Takes Up The Case

'Look here, Watson!'

'What is it Holmes?' I replied, startled by my friend's sudden outburst.

'I've been asked to investigate a mystery, regarding the disappearance of THE VITAL MESSAGE, contained in a book written by Sir Arthur Conan Doyle.'

'Who made this request?'

'Why, none other than our great creator and benefactor—Sir Arthur Conan Doyle himself!', beamed Holmes.

I was puzzled by this declaration as, upon reuniting in the afterlife, Holmes had averred that our earthbound exploits were behind us.

Holmes had already read my thoughts. 'My dear fellow, Sir Arthur informs me that humanity has failed to hear the message, and he wants us to go back to find out why, and what might be done about it. This appears to

For a biography of Dave Patrick, see opening page and Introduction.

be a matter of the utmost importance. We cannot let Sir Arthur down!'

He then proceeded to show me copies of THE VITAL MESSAGE and its companion volume THE NEW REVELATION, each concise in content. 'I want you to read these, Watson, and distil the essence of Sir Arthur's view. That will give us a firm foundation for our investigation.'

I proceeded to pore over these books for the next couple of days, pencilling comments into my notebook as I went along. Presently I returned to confront Holmes with my findings.

'Well, Watson, what have you uncovered?'

'This has made the most interesting reading, Holmes,' I replied.

'Pray continue,' said Holmes.

'THE NEW REVELATION begins with this acknowledgement: 'To all the brave men and women, humble or learned, who have the moral courage during seventy years to face ridicule or worldly disadvantage in order to testify to an all-important truth.''

'Yes, Watson, people, especially those of closed minds, have always been quick to attack those in opposition to the prevailing worldview. Consider how long it took before it was accepted that the Sun did not rotate around the Earth, and that the Earth was not flat.'

'The seventy years refers to the period since the start of the modern Spiritualist Movement, which began with the "rappings' episode at the Fox sisters' house in Hydesville, New York State, in 1848', I replied.

'Quite so,' replied Holmes. 'A not inconsiderable period over which to conduct scientific investigations and experiments into these psychic phenomena, wouldn't you agree?'

'Absolutely, Holmes! And what Sir Arthur reveals in THE NEW REVELATION is that significant scientific research was undertaken during that time, often by the brightest scientific minds in the land.'

'Go on, Watson, what else did you uncover?'

'Interestingly, Sir Arthur makes an important statement in the opening chapter.' I pointed to the page, and read out these words to Holmes: 'The subject of psychical research is one upon which I have thought more, and about which I have been slower to form my opinion, than upon any other subject whatever.'

'Hardly the words of an impulsive man, Watson! What else does he say?'

'He refers to his column in the Spiritualist magazine *Light* in 1887, which he uses to emphasize the serious and scientific nature of his research into Spiritualism and psychic phenomena over a thirty year period,' I answered. I then read out to Holmes the following quotation: 'Thus it is manifest that my interest in the subject is of some standing, and also, since it is only within the last year or two that I have finally declared myself to be satisfied with the evidence, that I have not been hasty in forming my opinion.'

'Excellent, Watson!' exploded Holmes. 'We now have the foundations of a strong case. Let us build on this early success. Anything else?'

I flicked quickly through the pages of my notebook, Holmes' increasing enthusiasm now starting to rub off on me. 'Ah, here we are. It appears from what he says next that he was initially sceptical about this field of enquiry. Listen to this.'

I read out the following extracted quotations from my notebook:

But when it came to a question of our little personalities surviving death, it seemed to me that the whole analogy of Nature was against it. When the candle burns out the light disappears… When the body dissolves there is an end of the matter… It seemed to be a delusion, and I was convinced that death did indeed end all, though I saw no reason why that should affect our duty towards humanity during our transitory existence. This was my frame of mind when Spiritual phenomena first came before my notice. I had always regarded the subject as the greatest nonsense upon earth, and I had read of the conviction of fraudulent mediums and wondered how any sane man could believe such things.

'Very good, Watson. With such views most people would dismiss the whole notion of psychic experience as being preposterous. Why do you think Sir Arthur continued to forge ahead with his quest?'

'Perhaps this next segment provides a possible rationale,' said I. Holmes languidly waved his pointed finger in my direction, indicating that I should continue reading extracts of Sir Arthur's narrative from my notebook.

As I read the following words aloud I could almost feel the power of Sir Arthur's passion rise within me.

I was sufficiently interested to continue to read such literature as came in my way. I was amazed to find what a number of great men—men whose names were to the fore in science—thoroughly believed that spirit was independent of matter and could survive it. When I regarded Spiritualism as a vulgar delusion of the uneducated, I could afford to look down upon it; but when it was endorsed by men like Crookes, whom I knew to be the most rising British chemist, by Wallace, who was the rival of Darwin, and by Flammarion, the best known of astronomers, I could not afford to dismiss it.

'Our case gets stronger by the minute!' laughed Sherlock Holmes, trying not to look prematurely triumphal.

I rifled through the notebook to pick out the next useful piece of information. '...the results of psychical research, the deductions which we may draw, and the lessons we may learn, teach us of the continued life of the soul, of the nature of that life, and of how it is influenced by our conduct here.... The question which faces us, then, is how will this influence bear upon the older organised religions and philosophies which have influenced the actions of men.'

'And women...', interjected Holmes.

I continued to divulge the contents of my notebook to my colleague.

The answer is, that to only one of these religions or philosophies is this new revelation absolutely fatal. That is to Materialism. I do not say this in any spirit of hostility to Materialists, who, so far as they are an organised body, are, I think, as earnest and moral as any other class. But the fact is manifest that if spirit can live without matter, then the foundation of Materialism is gone, and the whole scheme of thought crashes to the ground.

Holmes' expression now revealed a darkness that I had not seen for some time. His light-heartedness of a moment before had gone. 'I fear, Watson, that I am beginning to understand why Sir Arthur found such obstacles in his path when trying to convey his message of hope to humanity. What does he say on the subject of religion?'

'He appears to have gone out of his way not to be controversial,' I replied, 'and especially not to the Christian religion. If anything he believes

genuinely that this revelation, backed up by scientific evidence, would enhance Christianity, if I have understood this next section correctly.'

As to other creeds, it must be admitted that an acceptance of the teaching brought to us from beyond would deeply modify conventional
Christianity. But these modifications would be rather in the direction
of explanation and development than of contradiction. It would set
right grave misunderstandings which have always offended the reason
of every thoughtful man, but it would also confirm and make absolutely certain the fact of life after death, the base of all religion.

Holmes sat motionless for several moments.
'I believe we have done with THE NEW REVELATION for now. Let us prog-
ress to THE VITAL MESSAGE. What new light does Sir Arthur shine on the
matter?'
I lifted my notebook and turned to the next section. 'Sir Arthur opens
THE VITAL MESSAGE by reflecting back to THE NEW REVELATION where

...the first dawn of the coming change has been described. In THE VITAL
MESSAGE the sun has risen higher, and one sees more clearly and broadly
what our new relations with the Unseen may be. As I look into the
future of the human race I am reminded of how once, from amid the
bleak chaos of rock and snow at the head of an Alpine pass, I looked
down upon the far stretching view of Lombardy, shimmering in the
sunshine and extending in one splendid panorama of blue lakes and
green rolling hills until it melted into the golden haze which draped the
far horizon. Such a promised land is at our very feet which, when we
attain it, will make our present civilization seem barren and uncouth.
Already our vanguard is well over the pass. Nothing can now prevent
us from reaching that wonderful land which stretches so clearly before
those eyes which are opened to see it.'

'An optimistic view,' ventured Holmes. 'Does he have anything to add
to this vision?'
'Indeed he does,' I replied, the words I was relating to Holmes almost
coming alive on the page.

That stimulating writer, V. C. Desertis, has remarked that the Second Coming, which has always been timed to follow Armageddon, may be fulfilled not by a descent of the spiritual to us, but by the ascent of our material plane to the spiritual, and the blending of the two phases of existence. It is, at least, a fascinating speculation. But without so complete an overthrow of the partition walls as this would imply we know enough already to assure ourselves of such a close approximation as will surely deeply modify all our views of science, of religion and of life. What form these changes may take and what the evidence is upon which they will be founded are briefly set forth in this volume.

'Note the uplifting tone of these opening sentences, Watson. As far as Sir Arthur was concerned the case for Spiritualism had already been proven scientifically, and in his opinion the imperative had shifted towards getting his message out as a wake-up call to the public.'

'But you have already identified major obstacles put in place to prevent this message being spread.'

'Quite so, Watson. Although in many ways Sir Arthur was a man of his times, well-connected in Victorian and post-Victorian society, knighted in 1902 for his work in promoting the British cause during the Boer War in South Africa, he was probably a little naïve and unaware of the forces arrayed against him. To him the message was potentially liberating to humanity, removing the fear of death, but to various vested interests the threat posed by his scientific evidence was all too real—both to materialism and institutionalized religions, mechanisms used for eons to control the masses—and had to be opposed at all costs.'

Holmes continued with his diatribe. 'In essence Sir Arthur was providing a wake-up call for humanity to regain its sense of spiritual reality, something which he believed the traditional religious institutions had failed to deal with effectively, along with a plea for humanity to learn from the carnage of World War I, only just ended the year before the book's publication. There is no doubt that he was particularly sensitive to the latter point, having lost his brother, Innes, and son, Kingsley, to the flu epidemic of 1918.'

'He was very bitter about the impact of that war', said I, glancing down at my notebook to see what points I had recorded on the topic. 'He says that the causes of the war, which caused such devastation and loss of life, were essentially religious, not political, and that the decadent Christianity of the times must be reformed, to be simplified, purified and reinforced by what he calls 'the facts of spirit communion and the clear knowledge of what lies beyond the exit-door of death.'

I continued to read extracts from Sir Arthur's narrative:

What is, however, both new and vital are those fresh developments which will now be discussed...With the actual certainty of a definite life after death, and a sure sense of responsibility for our own spiritual development, a responsibility which cannot be put upon any other shoulders, however exalted, but must be borne by each individual for himself, there will come the greatest reinforcement of morality which the human race has ever known. We are on the verge of it now, but our descendants will look upon the past century as the culmination of the dark ages when man lost his trust in God, and was so engrossed in his temporary earth life that he lost all sense of spiritual reality.

The physical basis of all psychic belief is that the soul is a complete duplicate of the body, resembling it in the smallest particular, although constructed in some far more tenuous material. In ordinary conditions these two bodies are intermingled so that the identity of the finer one is entirely obscured. At death, however, and under certain conditions in the course of life, the two divide and can be seen separately. Death differs from the conditions of separation before death in that there is a complete break between the two bodies, and life is carried on entirely by the lighter of the two....

Holmes rose from his chair and walked to the window, a faraway look in his eyes. He was evidently deep in thought.

'Watson, we have sufficient evidence at this stage showing that Sir Arthur had put his argument on solid ground. Unfortunately, he had simultaneously identified the forces which would prevent his message getting out.'

'What do you make of it all, Holmes?' I ventured.

'Thus far we have set down Sir Arthur's position, but it has all been from his own written material. Find out what else of relevance he has written which strengthens our position. However, if we are to build a successful case, we must search for corroborating information. Watson, I would like you to do more research.'

I set about the next stage of my mission with relish. The following days were filled with intensive periods of investigation, using all the research resources at my disposal, the most helpful being the Internet, something unheard of during the period of Holmes' greatest adventures of a century before.

The first pressing task was to exhaust Sir Arthur's own sources. During the 1920s he travelled extensively, to America and Australia, giving lectures to people eager to listen to him, and wrote several more books on the subject of Spiritualism, notably THE HISTORY OF SPIRITUALISM, published in two volumes in 1926. His lectures and books were popular with those already immersed in the subject, either through direct experience, or through scientific study, in similar vein to Sir Arthur's own introduction to psychic matters.

In that same year THE LAND OF MIST was published, a novel featuring the great scientist Professor Challenger, the central character in Conan Doyle's science fiction epic THE LOST WORLD. THE LAND OF MIST contains a passage where a sceptical Challenger is informed through a mediumistic healer, '...you are a man of character and learning, but you are clearly embedded in that materialism which is the special curse of your age. Let me assure you that the medical profession, which is supreme upon earth for the disinterested work of its members, has yielded too much to the dogmatism of such men as you, and has unduly neglected that spiritual element in man which is far more important than your herbs and your minerals. There is a life-force, sir, and it is in the control of this life force that the medicine of the future lies. If you shut your mind to it, it can only mean that the confidence of the public will turn to those who are ready to adopt every means of cure, whether they have the approval of your authorities or not.'

It was clear that Sir Arthur was also using fictional opportunities to get his message about psychic reality out into the world. Another of the Professor Challenger stories, 'The Day The World Screamed', showed that Sir Arthur had, at least in his imagination, thought of the Earth as a living entity, well before the Gaia hypothesis had come into public awareness.

From this point on, I did what Holmes had requested me to do, to find corroborating evidence. I studied the work of the great scientists in the field, men such as Wallace, Flammarion, Crookes, Lodge and Barrett, all those who had been spoken of in THE NEW REVELATION and THE VITAL MESSAGE.

My early efforts in this direction were encouraging. As I followed in the footsteps of Sir Arthur, digging ever deeper into the works of these eminent scientists, I very quickly satisfied myself that the disappearance of his message had not stemmed in any way from lack of solid scientific evidence.

I took the fruits of my research to Holmes.

'Splendid, Watson!' he exclaimed. 'At least we know that Sir Arthur had done his homework. He has demonstrated a keen scientific mind himself in investigating the evidence.'

'What else should we have expected, especially since he was a trained medical doctor?' I replied. 'Not only that, he did invent your character, which he couldn't have done without himself having that scientific and investigative turn of mind, with which your persona has been imbued!'

'Good point, my dear fellow,' said Holmes. 'And the same applies regarding your excellent qualities as a narrator!

'We have completed the first stage towards solving the mystery, Watson, the validation of the scientific evidence,' continued Holmes. 'I suspect that the next step will be more challenging, the pathway to truth more arduous.'

With that parting comment Holmes waved me away to continue my research.

Sir Arthur Speaks

I am here, putting pen to paper. What a joy to rediscover the art of writing! On passing into the afterlife realm I discovered all communication here is telepathic.

It delights me that Sherlock Holmes has taken on my case, and doing a fine job. Holmes has proved himself a man of powerful presence and persistence.

Connecting with you now rekindles happy memories. I recall my interview with Movietone News in my garden, October 1928. Contented then, I little realized my life would end within two years. Yet life goes on, there is no death.

I spoke about the two things uppermost in people's minds. The first concerned how I came to write the Sherlock Holmes stories. The second was about psychic matters, and why I became a passionate advocate for Spiritualism.

Regarding the Sherlock Holmes question, it started when, as a young doctor, I read detective novels. The plots were invariably disappointing, with results often achieved by chance or fluke, unsatisfying to my scientifically trained mind.

During my medical training at Edinburgh University, Professor Joseph Bell became my mentor. Renowned for his extraordinarily rapid deductive skills in diagnosing patients, using his highly-developed powers of observation, Bell's attention to detail impressed me. I began to wonder how his scientific 'method' could be translated into detective fiction.

The idea of creating a 'scientific' consulting detective emerged. This detective became Sherlock Holmes, who solved his cases using superior powers of deduction. Holmes became so popular that many thought he was a real person!

The 'psychic question' first began to absorb me, initially as a complete sceptic, around 1886 and 1887, a period coinciding with the formation of the Sherlock Holmes character.

What convinced me was the integrity and credibility of eminent scientists pioneering in the field, distinguished men like Sir William Crookes and Sir Oliver Lodge. Their research conclusions were undeniable, and the evidence for the afterlife was demonstrated on numerous occasions, as Holmes and Watson have verified through their own meticulous research.

Indeed, if there were no afterlife I would not be conversing with you here!

Watching that interview now, my words take on fresh resonance:

When I talk on this subject, I am not talking about what I believe, I am not talking about what I think, I am talking about what I know. There's an enormous difference, believe me, between believing a thing and knowing a thing. I'm talking about things that I've handled, that I've seen, that I've heard with my own ears, and always, mind you, in the presence of witnesses.

Here, I am not just talking about what I know, I am talking about what I KNOW, an enormous difference!*

*The interview referred to, on which the whole of this section, 'Sir Arthur Speaks', is based, is the Movietone newsreel mentioned on the previous page and still accessible online at http://www.youtube.com/watch?v=qcr6DTwzayQ.

Sherlock Holmes Returns to the Matter at Hand

'Watson!'

'Yes, Holmes?'

'How is your research proceeding?'

'Very well,' said I, offering across my now-full notebook.

Holmes took it and started leafing through the freshly written pages. 'Good work!' he cried, enthusiastically. 'Tell me more.'

'It appears that Sir Arthur did not rest long after his passing in July 1930. He channelled an updated series of messages through a medium, Grace Cooke, during 1931 and 1932. I found three versions of the book containing these messages, and the story behind them.'

I handed Holmes the three books—THY KINGDOM COME, by Ivan Cooke, Grace Cooke's husband, published in December 1933, THE RETURN OF AR-THUR CONAN DOYLE, also by Ivan Cooke (1956), and their grandson Colum Hayward's latest version, ARTHUR CONAN DOYLE'S BOOK OF THE BEYOND (1994). Within each I had placed a series of annotated cards marking the most important sections for Holmes' closer inspection.

'These books contain Sir Arthur's enhanced message from the after-life,' I informed Holmes.

Holmes arranged the three copies neatly on the table before him. The table was clear, save for a package wrapped in shining gold foil, which he moved carefully to one side.

The next hour was spent in a frenzy of activity, my friend scanning each edition from cover to cover, cross-referencing again and again as he progressed. I had often seen Holmes shut himself off during periods of high concentration. Now he had taken on the mantle of a man possessed.

Presently he beckoned me. 'I had not expected that the trail would lead us in this direction. It is most interesting. These books shed valuable light on the matter, impossible to ignore.'

Holmes picked up the middle book, THE RETURN OF ARTHUR CONAN DOYLE, and read from Ivan Cooke's Preface:

This book contains the new revelation of Spiritualism that he made. His message, however, far exceeded the bounds of Spiritualism; what came through was more in the nature of a religion common to all men.... The message dealt with man's life after death perhaps more incisively than ever before, making clear how life here and life after death are inextricably interwoven, the one being complementary to the other. It then dealt with man's eternal progress beyond death. It answered the question of Freewill versus Destiny, and gave a solution to the Problem of Evil. It outlined a scheme for the healing of all disease. It formed, in fact, a comprehensive view of all life, its meaning and goal.

'Quite an accomplishment, eh, Watson?' said Holmes.

We discussed the books' contents well into the evening. At breakfast the following morning, our conversation about the previous day's events resumed.

'These books clear up part of the mystery,' said Holmes. 'We know that these channelled sessions had an important influence on the formation of the White Eagle Lodge in 1936. White Eagle was the name of Grace Cooke's spirit guide, who bestowed on her the spiritual name 'Minesta'. She was also given another name, 'Brighteyes', by the Polaire Brotherhood, a group originating in France. The Polaires were instrumental in helping Sir Arthur get his message across via Grace Cooke.'

'You mean, this proves that Sir Arthur's message did survive, through the publication of these books?'

'Precisely, Watson. Members of the White Eagle Lodge and those who know about its roots have access to this information,' said Holmes. 'But it remains generally hidden to the wider view, because knowledge of its existence is limited.'

'At least this is encouraging,' I offered. 'The message has not been completely lost, and we have now discovered it has been improved upon. The most recent edition, ARTHUR CONAN DOYLE'S BOOK OF THE BEYOND, is freely available.'

'I agree. Now, pray, let us extract the key elements of Sir Arthur's message.'

I thumbed through the copy of THY KINGDOM COME until I alighted on a page which had been previously bookmarked.

'Here is Sir Arthur speaking through Grace Cooke,' said I, and read aloud the following section:

I have passed through what you know as the 'astral life', and have been freed from the condition which has been hampering my work. To clear the astral vibrations was not altogether an easy matter, but do not be misguided with regard to this state: It is a necessary evil. To be loosed from astral ties does not sever one from his loved ones. It frees the spirit of man and allows him to enter into the full realization of his own nature. You do not yet one another as you will when you pass into the illimitable consciousness of God, and those same ties which bind you here on earth will bind still when you leave your earth condition until you wake to the glory of God's Love.

In other words, we mean this: a loosening of the personal and entering the impersonal consciousness of the creative essence called God, and in that consciousness realizing the 'perfectness' of all you love.

I must work—I must work. I must go forward. For it is shown to me the mission which we have to fulfil. I see so clearly now, whereas before I saw through a glass darkly; and now I see you and all men face to face. Most of all I see myself.

I thank God for the many opportunities he gave me to help my fellow men.

I see certain things in which I was mistaken. No man can have the entire truth. In some respects I was misled. I had before had my suspicions regarding astral memories, and I knew that a certain amount of spiritualistic phenomena was attributable to these memories. But I do not believe that all communications are of such cause; nor are they! I tell you definitely, that it is possible for the spirit, the real man, if he has a definite mission to perform for the good of humanity, to come back and execute that mission and help forward the evolution of the race.

Survival is a proven fact; is unquestionable. But the world is waiting for a greater demonstration and a clearer proof of this mighty truth. Humanity must realize that communication with the astral memory and with the real man are vastly different. It is necessary for the spirit of the loved one on earth to be raised to the consciousness of spiritual reality, ere he can hold true Communication with his beloved in spirit.

So much is futile in the movement to-day; but the glorious truth of survival must be given to humanity in clear and perfect form.

Personal responsibility and the redeeming power of love: Personal responsibility is irrefutable. I find it is not only a man's actions that count, but man's inmost thought. The spirit world is a world of thought, an internal state rather than an external condition of life… Thought promotes action; the actions of an individual again promote thought in his fellows. Thus we return again to the thought world. Truly it is said that: 'as a man sows so he shall surely reap.'

In the broad sense the seeds he sows are interpreted as actions; but I find thought to be actually more powerful than action, since one of the first things that a man is faced with on his escape from earth life, is the world of his own thought.

Let us pass from this condition to the next. It is not always pleasant to be isolated with all the thoughts one has projected during a life-time—but God is Love, Wisdom, Justice. I would not have it other-wise, for it has been revealed to me in a most marvellous way how the love of God manifests in the deepest heart of his children.

Personal responsibility and the redeeming power of Love—this one great lesson I have learned, and I pass it on to you all. No man lives or dies apart from God.... God-Christ-Love ... call it what you will. Earth has seen a supreme manifestation of that great power of Love,—in One—in several personalities.

Upon finishing this reading I was astonished to see the usually inscru-table Sherlock Holmes appear to wipe a tear from the corner of his eye.

'Let me see that book,' said Holmes, and I passed it to him.

Holmes flicked over the next few pages until he located the next marked section. It was Holmes' turn to read to me:

[The new teaching] lies in these words: 'The Kingdom of Heaven is Within'.... I see the need of a Master. In Christ you have all. In His teaching rests the secrets of Life and Death. Man must take up his cross and follow the Light of Love. The Cross symbolises the crucifixion of all selfish aims and desires—the complete submission of the personal to the impersonal love of God—the Creator of all. This is the secret of life both here and hereafter. Man must not live for himself, nor for his good name, for personal power or prosperity, his own success, but to contribute to the common good. Giving all, he receives all. Thus, and thus only will he enter into his Kingdom of Heaven.

Truly it is said 'Man must be born again'—not of the flesh but of the Spirit. Every man incarnate or discarnate must eventually pass through death of himself, and awaken again into new life, into fuller consciousness of the one All-Loving God. Thus only will he find himself and all those whom he loves. From this sphere of Christ conscious-ness descend those whom you love, in Spirit, so until you can attune yourself to their light, your communication must lack something most beautiful and pure.

Consider the gulf fixed between the rich man and Lazarus,—the bridgeless gulf, yet of man's own creation. Still there is a Way... the Way of LOVE. But not, mark you, the personal or possessive love, but rather the impersonal love of self-giving, self-forgetting, and self-sacrifice.

'Unless a man is born again of Spirit he can in no wise enter the Kingdom of Heaven'. True indeed; yet there remain some bound to earth, who seek to contact earth through channels provided by me-diumship. They too need teaching. The veil between this world and yours is thin indeed, compared to the severance between the earthly man discarnate and the man of heaven.

As he finished reading that final sentence he put the book down and looked over at me, his face a picture of serenity.

'You see what the essence of Sir Arthur's message is, Watson, he is showing us the way. It is the 'Way of LOVE'. What greater message, what greater legacy, could he leave for humanity?'

'So those seeds he began planting in 1918 and 1919 haven't fallen on stony ground after all,' said I.

Holmes lifted the gold-wrapped package from the table. 'Open it, Wat-son,' said Holmes. 'It proves that Sir Arthur's message of Love has survived to the present day and is in good hands. Its future looks assured.'

I carefully unwrapped the item. It was another book.

The title shone back at me. It read simply: 'The View'.

THE VITAL MESSAGE

Neale Donald Walsch

THERE IS a vital message right now that humanity would benefit enormously from hearing and embracing. It is a multi-part message, and it has to do with the extraordinary times into which we are moving.

Here is the message I believe humanity most needs to hear right now:

1. The planet earth and all her people will be moving through a period of enormous and paradigm-shattering change in the months and years just ahead. There is no reason for any degree of upset over this, as these changes will open the human race to the most wonderful spiritual, emotional, and physical advances of the past five thousand years.
2. It is possible to move through these changes in a joyful, peaceful, and beneficial way we must know and accept that God is on our side and that the Universe is conspiring in our favour. To do *this* we must use all the mental and spiritual tools at our disposal.

That is why I produced a book focusing its attention directly on this phenomenon and offering nine specific suggestions on how to deal with change as it manifests in our lives.

The book is entitled WHEN EVERYTHING CHANGES, CHANGE EVERYTHING, and in it I point to the fact that we have actually already started moving through

Neale Donald Walsch is the author of twenty-two books, including the 'Conversations with God' series. His writings have been translated into thirty-seven languages, with six of his titles making the *New York Times* bestsellers list. His newest book is WHEN EVERYTHING CHANGES, CHANGE EVERYTHING (2009), from which some of the words here were extracted. He may be reached at www.nealedonaldwalsch.com. Em Claire travels the world presenting her poetry as gifts for the soul. Her additional works will be found at www.emclairepoet.com.

what anthropologist and social scientist Jean Houston calls 'jump time' in her remarkable book by that title.

Jump time, Jean says, is a moment in the eternal cycle of life when we monumentally shift every aspect of our experience, much as humanity did during the three hundred years of the Renaissance (a blink of an eye on the Clock of Eternity), when everything from art to politics to culture to governance to commerce to education to religion to human sexual experience to partnerships and parenting to how to eat, drink, and *talk*, for heaven's sake, changed so fundamentally that nothing—literally *nothing*—was ever the same again.

The heart-stopping characteristic of this, our new Renaissance, is that it is not taking place over three hundred years, but thirty. Yes, I said *thirty years*. This owes to a breathtaking tenfold increase in the width, breadth, scope, and speed of global inter-cultural communication that has taken place on this planet.

We are already living on the edge of what I call *The Time of Instaparency*, when everything is instantly known, transparently. Such moment-to-moment awareness of all that's going on everywhere produces alterations in perspective that start dominoes falling all over the place.

Someone noted a few years ago that it was possible for my great-grandfather to live an entire lifetime without having anything come along that seriously challenged his worldview, because very little happened that he heard about that altered his understanding of how things were.

My grandfather had a different experience. He was able to live thirty or forty years, but not much longer, before some new piece of information was unveiled that seriously confronted his notion of the world. Perhaps half a dozen times during his life such a major event or development occurred that he heard about.

In my father's day that window of change dropped to only fifteen or twenty years. That's about as long as my dad could hold onto his ideas about life and how it works and what is true about everything. Sooner or later something would happen to disrupt his whole mental construction and require him to alter his thoughts and concepts.

In my own lifespan that time has been reduced to just five to eight years.

In the lifetime of my children it will be reduced to something like two years—and possibly less. And in the lifetime of *their* children it could be reduced to thirty or forty *weeks*.

This is no exaggeration. You can see the trend. Social scientists say that the rate of change is increasing exponentially. In the time of my great-grandchildren the period of time between changes will be reduced to days. And then, perhaps even hours.

In truth, we are already there—and have *always* been there. For in actuality, nothing has ever remained the same for even a moment. Everything is in motion, and if we define change as the altering of configurations, we see that change is the natural order of things. So we've been living in a constant swirl of change from the beginning.

What is different now is the amount of time that it takes for us to notice the changes that are always occurring. Our ability to communicate globally about everything within seconds is what has changed the way we experience change. The speed of our communications is catching up with the speed of our alterations. This condition in itself sponsors an increase in the rate of change.

Today our languages and expressions change overnight, our customs and styles change by the season, our beliefs and understandings and even some of our most deeply-held convictions change not with, but *within*, each generation.

The nine changes that I recommend will not stop change or even slow the rate of change (both are impossible). What they *will* do is help us all make a quantum leap in our *approach* to change, in our ways of *dealing* with it—and in our ways of *creating* it.

The first of those changes is our decision to 'go it alone'. We live in a separation society—a culture that imagines its members to be separate from God and separate from each other. There is no single idea currently held by the human race that is more dangerous, in my view, than the idea of separation.

The vital message of the first quarter of the Twenty-First Century is that we are not separate from each other, nor from the earth, nor from Divinity itself. I know that most human theologies tell us differently, but I respectfully suggest that those theologies may be sharing and spreading incredibly inaccurate information on the single most important aspect of life.

Do you think about God? If you do, what thoughts do you think? Do you think that there is a God? If you do, what do you think that God is? A friend in the sky? A loving but stern parent? Someone to fear? Someone to love? Both?

Whatever you think, if you think that there is a God at all, I'm going to wager that there is one thought you hold in common with billions of other people. I could be wrong, you could be one of the few exceptions that prove the rule, but if you are not, if you embrace the view of the vast majority, the thought that you hold in common with billions of others is this: God is separate from us.

Most of the world's people adhere to what I have come to call Separation Theology. I have named the God of this theology *Iohayot*. That sounds a bit like a Native American word, but it is not. It's an acronym for I'm Over Here And You're Over There.

This is as valid a name as any of the others that humanity has come up with, including Allah, Brahmin, God, Jehovah, Krishna, or Yahweh, and it's far more descriptive of the actual concept of God held by most humans. Religion is not noted for producing widespread agreement among people, yet whatever else the fervently religious may disagree on, most concur that God says: 'I'm Over Here And You're Over There.'

God then adds, 'You may come over here if you wish, but there are certain things that you have to do.' God then gives us the list of what that is. This list has been read by many people in many different ways, and those different ways are sometimes called religions.

There is only One List, each of our religions assert, and we must not be confused into thinking that there are many, nor so perplexed or seduced by the False Lists put out by others that we pick the wrong one.

This description of human theologies is simplistic in the extreme, yet it is not that far from being an accurate, if very basic, summary of our beliefs. And these beliefs are killing us.

Separation Theology—worship of the God *Iohayot*—will, if it continues much longer on our planet, bring an end to life as we know it on the earth. It has already begun to do so.

Many people believe that this is because while God is, indeed, 'over there' and we are 'over here,' God has to sometimes come 'over here' to teach us a lesson. And so God comes down to punish us for our sins, make us pay for our offences, or do whatever else is necessary to reestablish the natural order of things and bring Right into proper balance with that which is Not Right.

Under this philosophy the AIDS epidemic, the increasing violence on the earth, the degradation of our social systems, the erosion and destruction of our collective morals, the pestilence and rampant poverty afflicting millions, are all signs of God's anger, punishments from on high brought on by humanity's increasingly evil behaviour.

This belief in a God who is 'over there' and who wants and needs or desires or demands something from those of us 'over here' is what allows humans to grant themselves the moral authority to inflict punishments of their own upon those who ignore God's Word and disobey God's Commandments. We imagine and understand and declare ourselves to be *acting in God's name* as we throw the switch on the electric chair, or throw people behind bars for twenty years, or throw our weight around in whatever other way we have bestowed it upon ourselves to do in retribution for the sins that others have committed.

This idea is what allows humans to fly aeroplanes into buildings, killing thousands of innocent civilians all the while shouting about how great our creator is. It is what allows humans to preemptively strike a nation that they imagine is going to strike them if they don't do it first, killing thousands of innocent civilians with bombs paid for by coins on which it is written, 'In God We Trust.'

If we thought we were doing these things to God, we would, of course, never do them. Yet there is nothing could make us think that we are doing these things to God except the thought that We And God Are One, and that is a thought a majority of us have summarily rejected.

Separation Theology produces a Separation Psychology. That is, an idea held deep in the human psyche that says we are all alone, separated from our Creator, working and hoping to find a way back Home. Separation Psychology produces a Separation Cosmology. That is, a cosmological way of looking at all of Life which holds that everything is separate from everything else. Separation Cosmology produces a Separation Sociology. That is, a way of socializing the human species that separates every person from every other person by declaring their interests to be separate. Separation Sociology produces a Separation Pathology. That is, pathological behaviors of self-destruction—evidenced everywhere on the face of the earth.

So … during this time when everything is changing, we must change everything—and most especially, this decision we have made to define ourselves as separate from God and each other and our earth.

Then we need to change our ideas about change itself, how it comes about, who creates it, and how we can *produce* change rather than *endure* it.

We need to understand two enormous truths.

1.   Everything changes for the better. Nothing changes for the worse.
2.   Change happens because we want it to happen.

We have been seeing change as a disruption, as a break in the flow, as a shift in direction, as an alteration in the condition or circumstance of our lives. Especially with regard to what we view as unwelcome change, this has been our truth.

Yet change is not a *dis*ruption, but an *e*ruption. It is life erupting into fuller bloom. Change is not a break in the flow, it IS the flow. Change is not a shift in direction, it is the direction itself in which all life moves. Change is not an alteration in the condition and circumstance of our lives, it IS the condition and circumstance of our lives.

In our expanded awareness we observe that without change, life itself would not be, for life is movement, and movement is change, by *definition*.

Life is a *self-sustaining* system. It never ends, but sustains itself eternally. How? By *adapting*. Why? So that it can remain forever *functional*. When it can no longer function in a particular way, it adapts. By its adaptation does it render itself sustainable.

Life is making its adaptations in every moment. It is always changing. The question is not whether life is always changing, but why? Life is always changing in order to remain always sustainable. Thus, every change that ever occurs is *change for the better*.

This new idea about change that I'm inviting you to embrace, when put on a more personal level, reads like this: *All change is for your own good.*

Most of us experience this—after the fact.

Most of us have experienced events which we have called, when they were happening, the worst moments of our lives, only to find, as time went by, that what occurred was *one of the best things that ever happened to us*.

The fact is that this is true of *everything* that has ever happened to us, but we do not know this, we cannot accept this, because some things *have* turned out for the worst—*according to our definition*. Yet our definition is warped, constrained as it is by the mind *and its inherent limitations*.

The mind may very know all about what has gone before, but is does not know *why*. The mind may very well hold all of life's Past Data, but it does not hold all of life's information (which is another thing altogether). The mind may very well contain knowledge, but it does not contain wisdom.

Wisdom lies outside the mind. Wisdom resides within the soul. And within our soul we find our connection with an eternally loving, caring, compassionate and creative God, who moves us all through the process of our soul's evolution, through the events of our lives.

The mind cannot grasp the process of evolution in fullness, because the mind deals principally in fact, and not in awareness. Of course, 'fact' and 'awareness' are not the same thing. We can know all the facts about gravity, but if we do not have an awareness of why gravity works, *we know nothing*. We can know all the facts about electricity, and we can even use electricity, but if we have no awareness of what electricity *is* and of *why* it works, *we know nothing*. We can know all the facts about light, and we can even use light, but if we have no awareness of what light *is* and of *why* it works, we know nothing.

Likewise, we can know all the facts about change, but if we have no awareness of what change *is* and of *why* it occurs, *we know nothing*.

For instance, we may not know that….

Nothing changes for the worse. Everything only changes for the better.

That's a pretty big statement, and I understand if it's hard for you to believe. Yet it is true. Let's step back a little from this enormous idea and give it some basis in *physics*. Yes, I said physics.

All of *life* is a mechanism, and like all mechanisms, life operates on energy. Unlike most other mechanisms, life is the energy on which life operates. That is, it feeds on itself.

And so, stars implode and entire star systems disappear into black holes; and so, earthquakes and tornadoes and hurricanes ravage the earth; and so, big fish consume little fish; and so, humans are born, live their lives, and die—ashes to ashes, dust to dust. Yet the energy of none of this—*none of it*—disappears, but merely changes form. Energy is never, and can never be, lost, it can only be transformed.

Life is always in formation. It is forever forming itself into something it was not before it became what it is. It is through the becoming that life breathes life into Life Itself. In simple terms, this is called change.

Yes, there's that word again … *change*.

That is what life is all about. Life nourishes life through the process of life itself, in which life changes its form a hundred million times in the blink of an eye, a *million* million times in seconds, a *billion* million times in a minute, and more times than Time Itself can count in the time that has passed since counting began.

Change for the *worse* is literally impossible within the expression of energy that we call Life. That's because Life Itself can fundamentally alter itself in only one direction: the direction that evolution requires; the direction that expansion demands, the direction that keeps it flourishing. Things can only change for the better, things can only improve, because 'improvement' is the *only Nature of God.*

Put another way, God has no intention of doing Itself in. Life is God's way of proving Itself to Itself. The process by which It does this is called *Improvement.*

And that is where you come in!

'Yes,' you might say, 'but what can I do? What can one person do to 'improve life'?' I am familiar with that question. It is the exact question I asked when I had my conversation with God. Here was God's response:

Bring peace to the Earth by bringing peace to all those whose lives you touch.

Be peace.

Feel and express in every moment your Divine Connection with the All, and with every person, place, and thing.

Embrace every circumstance, own every fault, share every joy, contemplate every mystery, walk in every man's shoes, forgive every offence (including your own), heal every heart, honour every person's truth, adore every person's God, protect every person's rights, preserve every person's dignity, promote every person's interests, provide every person's needs, presume every person's holiness, present every person's greatest gifts, produce every person's blessing, and pronounce every person's future secure in the assured love of God.

Be a living, breathing example of the Highest Truth that resides within you.

Speak humbly of yourself, lest some one mistake your Highest Truth for a boast.

Speak softly, lest someone think you are merely calling for attention.

Speak gently, that all might know of Love.

Speak openly, lest anyone think you have something to hide.

Speak candidly, so you cannot be mistaken.

Speak often, so that your word may truly go forth.

Speak respectfully, that no one be dishonoured.

Speak lovingly, that every syllable may heal.

Speak of Me with every utterance.

Make of your life a gift. Remember always, you are the gift!

Be a gift to everyone who enters your life, and to everyone whose life you enter.

Be careful not to enter another's life if you cannot be a gift (You can always be a gift, because you always are the gift—yet sometimes you don't let yourself know that.)

When someone enters your life unexpectedly, look for the gift that person has come to receive from you.

I am clear if I did these things that my personal world would change. So, of course, would the world around me. I know it. I just know it. In my heart I understand that I have the ability to impact everyone whose lives I touch—and, by extension, the World Entire.

Should you and I choose to embrace God's invitation I know that we will be able to make huge changes in the way we move through life. Specifically, I believe we will be able to change Fear into Excitement, Worry into Wonder, Expectation into Anticipation, Resistance into Acceptance, Disappointment into Detachment, Enragement into Engagement, Addiction into Preference, Requirement into Contentment, Judgment into Observation, Sadness into Happiness, Thought into Presence, Reaction into Response, and a Time of Turmoil into a Time of Peace.

All of this seems almost too good to be true, I know. But it *is* true, and it *can* happen, and it can happen in our lives right now. But we must be willing to change *everything*. Even our dreams. For it is as God said to me in our conversation....

Remember always that yours is a world of Illusion, that nothing you see is real, and that you may use The Illusion to bring you a grand experience of the Ultimate Reality. Indeed, that is what you have come here to do.

You are living in a dream of your own creation. Let it be the dream of a lifetime, for that is exactly what it is.

Dream of a world in which the God and Goddess in you is never denied, and in which you never again deny the God and the Goddess in another. Let your greeting, both now and forevermore, be *Namasté*.

Dream of a world in which love is the answer to every question, the solution to every problem, the response to every situation, the experience in every moment.

Dream of a world in which Life, and that which supports Life, is the highest value, receives the highest honour, and has its highest expression.

Dream of a world in which freedom becomes the highest expression of life, in which no one who claims to love another seeks to restrict another, and in which all are allowed to express the glory of their being in measure full and true.

Dream of a world in which equal opportunity is granted to all, and equal resources are available to all, and equal dignity is accorded to all, so that all may experience equally the unequalled wonder of Life.

Dream of a world in which judgment is never again visited by one upon another, in which conditions are never again laid down before love is offered, and in which fear is never again seen as a means of respect.

Dream of a world in which differences do not produce divisions, individual expression does not produce separation, and the greatness of The Whole is reflected in the greatness of Its parts.

Dream of a world in which there is always enough, in which the simple gift of sharing leads to that awareness—and creates it, and in which every action supports it.

Dream of a world in which suffering is never again ignored, in which intolerance is never again expressed, and in which hatred is never again experienced by anyone.

Dream of a world in which ego is relinquished, in which superiority is abolished, and in which ignorance is eliminated from everyone's reality, reduced to the Illusion that it is.

Dream of a world in which mistakes lead not to shame, regrets lead not to guilt, and judgment leads not to condemnation.

Dream of these things, and more.

Do you choose them?

Then dream them into being.

With the might of your dreams end the nightmare of your imagined reality.

You can choose this. Or, you can choose The Illusion.

I have said to you before, through the words of poets and leaders and philosophers:

There are those who see things as they are and say, 'Why?' And there are those who dream of things that never were and say, 'Why not?'

What do *you* say?

This is the key question. Really, it is the only question. Yet to answer this question grandly, we must all see life differently. We must see it at philosophers and poets see it. And so, I close with this—a look at life through the eyes of a poet....

Please do not regret
all those moments that have brought you
Here.
If you are reading this,
then your perseverance has been answered,
and a Grace is coming.
So for now, hold on loosely to where you are.
And like knots on a rope that mark your reaching,
hand over hand
you will continue to climb --
sometimes through ecstasy,
sometimes through white agony,
higher
into evermore light.
This same formula over
and over again.
Until that day you find yourself
just a beacon;
only flame.
In a place
where even Love Itself has come undone.*

THE AGE OF BROTHERHOOD

Colum Hayward

THE AGE of mass religion is all but over. The age that is before us is one of personal spiritual experience, but unless we are to be in a state of perpetual competition one with another, it has to be an age in which personal spiritual experience can be validated in the realm of human contact, and in which human caring, one for another, and uniting in shared ideals, becomes the norm. It needs the very light that comes from true spiritual experience. It also has to be one in which atheism, agnosticism and faith can sit alongside, for the only real division is between those who take time to think, to live and to experience, and those whom life simply rules, those who are to some extent unconscious. Mindfulness is spiritual life, and prayer is spiritual life, but simply to live with passionate commitment to important values and yet see them objectively is also to be in touch with one's own spirituality. None of this means that established belief systems are invalid; it simply means that we have reached the point in our history where outward enforcement of a system of belief gives way to utter respect for one another.

'As a man and as a brother' was the rallying cry of the nineteenth-century abolitionists of slavery, claiming respect as well as rights. The doubled value is deeply significant. To recognize one another as members of the same species is merely intellectual. It does not protect us from genocide, persecution, or even elitism. 'As a brother' implies that we recognize actual kinship, in the emotional and value-rich sense. We do not simply acknowledge one another, we value one another. The moment of human brotherhood is already, if falteringly, upon us.

Espousal of the values of brotherhood does not dismiss the values of the Creator, for the value we recognize in one another, if it is to be of full quantity, has to accept in some way—however we prefer to articulate it—that we are of one unity, parts of the same organism. Nor does it mean that we need overthrow our teachers, in the style of the Cultural Revolution, for there is endless learning to be had in the path of brotherhood. But there are still ways in which it is revolutionary, because it comes from within, not from without. The path of brotherhood is here to stay. In many ways it is the religion of the coming age.

Brotherhood has had a bad press over the years. For instance, it has been saddled with an association with human perfectibility that has interfered with religious pessimism and been taken over by all the wrong ideologies in history. 'The Perfectibility of Man. Ah, heaven, what a dreary theme!', said D. H. Lawrence. But we are an evolutionist generation, and we must accept at the very least that perpetual betterment is not only to be wished, but is already scripted. Betterment may not happen without upheaval, but it is normal.

The word 'brotherhood' also sounds sexist. It of course is not intended to be, at least by me. My problem is that 'brother–sisterhood' is better in a real sense, but not a good enough sense. True brotherhood cannot be species-ist any more than it can be sexist. Brotherhood needs to be with all life, if it is not to be exploitative. 'Dominion over all life', a concept we took from the Book of Genesis, just will not do in the Age of Brotherhood. Brother–sisterhood implies a spurious completeness—as though the job were done, simply by including women. I cannot myself find an adequate word to replace 'brotherhood', and so I would sooner explain an inadequate word than use one that does seem to need explanation, and therefore perpetuates incomplete meaning. Language is full of words we have to explain, sometimes because of dual meanings that confuse, at others because of a precise meaning that is vital but impossible to convey by use of a more familiar word, and so on. So until a better word comes along, let's take 'brotherhood' but with a footnote every time.

I wonder what word we shall eventually go for? 'Community' is a good word, not without a moral resonance, but a limited one. 'Kinship' is nice, but narrowed by association with family. The nice thing about 'brotherhood with a footnote' is that (as I hope I have shown) there is a huge system of values already attached to the word: not only values, but ideals and a standard of behaviour. Maybe oddly, were I to coin a word myself, it might be one that would feature the central quality demanded of us in order to participate. Thus 'respecthood' could mean all the created things that we respect. Better still, 'joyhood' would include those things that we take joy in, and it would arise from natural passion in living. I like that, although I accept that 'joyhood' would quickly exclude those things we do not easily enjoy. There might become an 'unjoyhood' overnight.

The problem with any moral system—and even 'brotherhood' might be seen as demanding a standard of behaviour that to fall from would involve delegation, even exclusion—is that it puts an onus on the individual which damaged psychology, illness and disadvantage make it immensely difficult to fulfil. Possession of a damaged psychology is not our individual fault, even if as a culture we may decide that to seek healing is a moral prerequisite. My own teacher, White Eagle, has a phrase I greatly admire:

'Be strong in the self, but be stronger in the selfless.'

In other words, selflessness arises not out of self-abnegation but an overflowing of self. Selfishness is fear, and needs to be treated with a caring intelligence by those whose psychologies are more healed. To be selfless is actually to be passionate about life: passionate not about personal interest, but passionate about life as a whole. Brotherhood is a natural overflow of our passion for living. For me, brotherhood arises not out of a denial of self-interest, but out of such a rich concept of life that self-interest is a mere tool, a reference point which helps us avoid rash stupidity. Self-interest is even a mirror, in which to look before selflessness becomes self-abandonment. To an extent, selflessness will always imply self-interest, because we are part of the whole and to deny self is to deny part of the whole.

The writer and activist Satish Kumar coined the phrase, 'You are, therefore I am', which perfectly expresses the relationship we have with one another, and the need we have of others before we can explore our self-identity. How do we get on with establishing brotherhood in a visibly imperfect world? Satish Kumar might say, 'by studying the interdependence of things in nature'. Then it would proceed from our studies. I would add that we begin with self-healing—the healing of our own psychologies, not for narrow self-interest but for effectiveness in society. Another spiritual teacher was asked a question such as, 'Emmanuel, tell us about personal power and its benefits'. He answered—if I remember the words correctly, and may be permitted to italicize the words I recall he stressed:

'Personal power? Ah, it can be used for such good, such healing—*after the healing of self.*'

We are relatively dangerous until we are healed, and we need to get on with that healing. Many people come to the White Eagle Lodge, my own place of work, for physical healing and for the healing of past pain. What I like to believe the Lodge offers beyond that is a safe place for the self to grow strong, so that we can be effective world-healers.

World healers? Quite a strong concept, and certainly one that demands optimism about human progress and the powers available to humanity. My case would be that we need to establish brotherhood first in relative safety, and then let that brotherliness spill over into the greater environment. Thus an organization such as the White Eagle Lodge (but there are many) offers a chance to enter into a small Brotherhood—by initiation, based on personal work done, and thus by qualification, so that membership of the Brotherhood implies safety within the group: lack of exposure to extremes of behaviour, so that we can get on with developing personal behaviours that are respectful, at the same time as gently exploring each other's boundaries. The limitations of such a Brotherhood always need to be recognized, and the need of our brotherly action to spill over into all aspects of daily life, otherwise we risk the negative (sometimes terribly negative) aspects of narrow brotherhood: virtual nepotism, narrow identification of race or ideology, and so on. Our Brotherhood needs to be open to all, so long as the candidate is prepared to accept the disciplines of brotherhood, which begin with absolute respect for others in the group. Absolute respect, not outward respect and inner disapproval.

In another chapter of this book I have written about one such Brotherhood—the Polaires—that existed for only a few years (in any outwardly-known sense) between 'going public', whereon it became so infiltrated by members who did not share the original discipline that it sank, visibly and fast. To practise brotherhood became impossible. The French writer Maurice Magre, for instance, is credited with leaving this group, the Polaires, because he could not live with the political direction the Brotherhood was taking. Several of his closest brethren (for he was with them from an early stage) had left, or become invisible within the Brotherhood, much earlier. Otto Rahn was deceived into flirting with Nazism; the discovery of his mistake, and recantation, cost him his life. Brotherhood is, sometimes, a life-and-death matter.

For something I believe the early Polaires had, a quality I have already commended but have rarely been called upon to show, was passion. Brotherhood mattered to each Polaire as much as his or her life; it should do to all of us. Not to be consciously part of the Brotherhood of all Life is in our new age not to live. Here are some of the Polaire aims and objectives (the full list is a fraction more diverse, and I have taken them from slightly different sources):

• 'The principal aim of the Polaires is to light the Light and to carry the flame wherever shadows exist'

• '...to study, to work, to carry truth into wherever there is charlatanism'

• '...to combat egotism, the source of all our ills, of all catastrophe'

• '...to use the 'White Magic' in those cases where the sadness that torments men can drive them to despair'

• '...to protect and give help to children deprived of tender loving care'

• '...to bring help and assistance to poor animals who are in agony—to the poor animals who have no personal aim to follow but who are full of loyalty right up to their last breath.'*

The White Eagle Brotherhood, originally set up very much in imitation of the Polaire one (and as the one known as 'Brighteyes' conceived it), has a similar set of objectives and ideals that are not formally defined. Some, such as the injunction 'to help humankind overcome the mad fear of death that haunts the mind of man' are taken over verbatim. So is the injunction to refrain from any sort of cruelty to the animal kingdom. If I may suddenly take the language much deeper, here are views on Brotherhood expressed by its founder:

> Is not the way of true brotherhood the inner meaning of Christ's teaching which has been misinterpreted by the church in the doctrine of vicarious atonement? When the soul passes through the ceremony of initiation into the temple of universal brotherhood it realizes the inner meaning of 'atonement' for it finds itself irrevocably attached to its brothers and companions in spirit—to such a degree that it suffers with the suffering of its brothers and rejoices in its brothers' happiness. In this sense it is the Christ light in the heart which takes or absorbs into its own heart the sins or sufferings of [hu]mankind.†

I quoted from the same source in my other chapter in this book, and the paragraph I there quoted very much tied in the concept of brother-

---

*Bulletin des Polaires, 9 May 1930, and other sources

†Grace Cooke, THE SHINING PRESENCE, pp. 35–6. These words follow on from the passage quoted in my other chapter in this book, p. 55

hood with that of a supportive and watching brotherhood in spirit: 'It is this little spark of divine life which the White Brotherhood endeavours to fan into a glowing flame so that it can absorb into itself and feel what its brother feels'. Brotherhood relies on a development of the feelings, leading to increased imagination about our fellow men and women, and the rest of life too.

As such, it certainly does not demand that to explore brotherhood we all have to become part of an initiatory brotherhood. That path may be unattractive, even distasteful, to us as individuals. In this case, the healing of self and the development of true imagination about the needs of all others, human and non-human, is still the way. The Buddha taught only that we should be 'awake'. I believe he may have been referring to the same consciousness.

Here is the Dalai Lama speaking, to give another example.

As human beings, we are all the same. So there is no need to build some kind of artificial barrier between us. At least my own experience is that if you have this kind of attitude, there is no barrier. Whatever I feel, I can express; I can call you 'my old friend'. There is nothing to hide, and no need to say things in a way that is not straightforward. So this gives me a kind of space in my mind, with the result that I do not have to be suspicious of others all the time. And this really gives me inner satisfaction, and inner peace.

So I call this feeling a 'genuine realization of the oneness of the whole of humanity'. We are all members of one human family. I think that this understanding is very important, especially now that the world is becoming smaller and smaller.... Consequently it is worthwhile taking every crisis as a global one. Here barriers such as 'this nation' or 'that nation', 'this continent', or 'that continent' are simply obstacles. Therefore today, for the future of the human race, it is more important than ever before that we develop a genuine sense of brotherhood and sisterhood. I usually call this a sense of 'universal responsibility'.*

Responsibility, sharing, imagination about our brother. White Eagle says, 'It is important for all to realize that we contact the spirit of our brother only through our own spirit. Brotherhood, then, is the essence of spiritual life'.

*From DZOGCHEN: THE HEART ESSENCE OF THE GREAT PERFECTION

The aspiration to brotherhood is quite natural for a herding animal like the human. Today, the choice of brotherhood or not brotherhood is fundamental. The time has come. Yet as the Dalai Lama says, Brotherhood is not about national boundaries, about any barriers and divisions at all. It demands mutual respect from and towards all (the quality I mentioned from the beginning), rejection of generalizations and assumptions, self-discipline, commitment, interpersonal support, the sharing of loads, understanding, a heightened sense of values, and the passionate involvement in living that makes every moment conscious and special. It demands a new recognition of self, and a new discovery of the natural spirituality everyone possesses—and shows each time they remember that they love life. That's my 'vital message' for this present moment.

References
Bulletin des Polaires. Paris, 9 May 1930
Cooke, Grace, THE SHINING PRESENCE. London, White Eagle Lodge (1946)
Fourteenth Dalai Lama, the, DZOGCHEN: THE HEART ESSENCE OF THE GREAT PERFECTION, translated by Thupten Jinpa and Richard Barron, ed. Patrick Gaffney. Ithaca, NY: Snow Lion Publications

MAKING MEDITATION MAINSTREAM

James Baltzell, MD

THROUGH the centuries, meditation was poorly understood by the masses. The teaching of meditation was mostly limited to monks and shamans: to monasteries and some other religious organizations. But the Buddhists, yogis and other mystics were and still are famous meditators. There was mystery surrounding meditation. It was thought that only adepts could meditate. Different words were used for meditation that caused confusion and mystery. Some churches in the West condemned meditation, as it allowed direct communication with God without an intercessory priest.

All this changed in the early Twentieth Century.

Meditation began to be taught outside of a restricted formal setting, and new books were written about meditation allowing anyone who was motivated learn how to meditate. At the same time meditation teachers began teaching meditation in small groups. Grace Cooke of the White Eagle Lodge was one such pioneer in meditation teaching. At first, knowledge about meditation started slowly—but more and more people discovered its effectiveness and began to meditate. It is now commonplace, with news articles about meditation present daily in the popular press.

Later in the Twentieth Century, teachers from the East—many of them yogis from India—came to the West and popularized meditation and yoga. However, they initially retained the mystery and secrecy about meditation. It was thought that only a special few had the ability to meditate. In some groups it was thought necessary to have a special mantra to be able

James W. Baltzell, MD, retired Assistant Professor of Radiology at the University of Minnesota, has taught and practised meditation for over twenty-five years. He co-owned an alternative medicine centre with his wife Karin B Baltzell, PhD. His book WHY MEDITATION WORKS (Polair) is being republished in the USA as MEDITATION FOR THE REST OF US by Fairview University Press in July 2009.

to meditate. Some teachers even charged money for classes that led to the secret presentation to the person his or her own special mantra.

This all changed when it became possible to explore meditation scientifically. Herbert Benson, MD, of Harvard University was able to have students in his classes successfully meditate when they repeated a word such as 'love' or 'One'. A secret mantra was not necessary. The mystery was broken, and broken in a scientific manner. At last, it was proven that anyone could meditate. Dr Benson went on to write a significant book, THE RELAXATION RESPONSE, which further clarified the subject. Since that time the effects of meditation have been examined by modern testing such as MRI and PET scans. Different types of meditation have been shown to be equally effective. Meditation has been shown scientifically to be very healing (see below).

Because meditation works so well and is non-toxic, non-addictive, and free, it is now being used in varying forms throughout everyday society, particularly in stress reduction, medicine, and spiritual study. Many people, including myself, meditate daily and find that their lives are enriched by meditation. The black-and-white world is now seen in Technicolor. Meditation allows the practitioner to work with the body and the autonomic nervous system. Meditation can have a direct effect on the functioning of the body. It also allows inspection of our thoughts and mental processes. It is therefore a tool to allow working with the mind and the body in a beneficial manner.

The challenge with meditation is that it takes practice. It is not hard to meditate with practice, but requires some early dedication until the reward from meditating inspires the meditator to continue. It is easiest to learn with a teacher. It also helps to have a simple understanding of the process.

★ ★ ★

Discussion about meditation has historically been difficult, owing to lack of a common language. Each practitioner has used words from their own language and culture for different types of meditation. Many meditation schools use eastern names which are confusing to western students. For the purposes of this article the following is a definition of meditation that is simple, for a simple definition helps to remove the mystery and confusion around meditation.

Meditation is a state of consciousness in which the individual eliminates environmental stimuli from awareness so that the mind can focus on a single thing, producing a state of relaxation and relief from stress. A wide variety of techniques are used to clear the mind of stressful outside interferences.

Separation of meditation into four stages has helped many to better understand what is happening during meditation. Meditation may include all of these, or just some.

The first stage of meditation is physiological: the process of relaxing and achieving the relaxation response. Focusing (or being mindful) on the breath or a word will lead to a relaxed meditative state.

The second stage of meditation is insightful: gaining knowledge of the inner self. Observation of our thoughts after becoming relaxed will lead to great insights about our thinking and thought processes.

The third stage of meditation is an energy-healing one: by working with subtle energy flows through the body, symbolized by light, healing can be facilitated. This can be done for others using healing meditations.

The fourth stage of meditation is spiritual: becoming aware of a higher consciousness, the spiritual world and working in that world. When meditating many people have moving spiritual experiences, some even are able to make contact with the other side.

There are many ways to achieve relaxation and meditation; however, they all rely on being mindful and focusing the mind to distract the busy chatter, everyday, mind. The biggest challenge to the meditator is to become relaxed. Distracting thoughts (frequently alarming or fearful thoughts) keep entering our consciousness preventing the relaxation response. By the process of focusing or being mindful of an object or word we can chose what we think and then become relaxed. This takes practice, but fortunately with practice it is possible to meditate at will, even in a distracting setting.

Meditation is nonetheless best practised in a quiet place, in the upright position and with the back straight. There are some rules: it should not be done under the influence of mind-altering medication, for instance. It is easier to do in a group with a leader at the beginning.

One type of meditation that has become very popular is Mindfulness-based Stress Reduction, as taught by Jon Kabat-Zinn (the author of FULL CATASTROPHE LIVING, 1990) from Massachusetts University Medical Center, and the Center for Spirituality and Healing at the University of Minnesota.

This technique uses observation or mindfulness of the breath to begin the relaxation response. It can be done easily anywhere. It can rapidly lower the stress level and help in anxiety-producing situations. For some reason, the human autonomic nervous system will relax when we are mindful of the breath. The technique has no religious connotation so it is palatable to almost everyone, and is being taught in schools and businesses as a way to lower stress. Breathing relaxation has also been used in obstetrics to help mothers lower their pain, in which context it is called the 'Lamaze Method'. Students relax before tests by breathing deeply and slowly. Performers in the arts use the same technique. It is a great way to aid sleep. The ability to initiate the relaxation response should be available to everyone, and it would be great if it was taught in schools. The only time it shouldn't be used is when driving or doing dangerous work.

Another type of popular meditation uses repetition of a word. Dr Benson described what he called 'the relaxation response', which is the first part of meditation. This response can easily be obtained by being mindful of a repeated word (or a mantra) rather than being mindful of the breath. As the attention focuses on the word, the busy chatter mind settles down and the body begins to relax. I have covered this technique more completely in my book WHY MEDITATION WORKS (Polair), which will be republished as MEDITATION FOR THE REST OF US in the USA in July 2009.

Creative visualization, which uses the imagination, is another often-used meditation technique. Being mindful or focusing on something pretty a garden, lake, flowers, jewels, etc., may lead into meditation. In fact in my own experience this is one of the easiest ways to learn meditation. It is also possible to use visualization when having a medical or dental procedure, to 'take the mind to another place' and thus relax and reduce anxiety.

There are other techniques that are used to focus the mind such as focusing on a real flower, candle flame, or jewel. Music has been used by some; however, it is often difficult to use as once the mind starts to follow the music, it can then be distracting.

The last three stages of meditation use the relaxation technique to start meditation. After a quiet state has been achieved, more advanced meditation can be explored.

Meditation can be used positively in many ways, particularly in medicine. There have been many scientific articles establishing its benefits. Blood tests, MRI scans, PET, and EEG have all proven some of the effects of meditation—which are almost always beneficial. Here is a limited review of some of the ways that meditation is used in medicine.

First, meditation has been shown to facilitate the relaxation response—which is the opposite of the stress response. This makes it a powerful tool in combating the detrimental stress-related diseases. Stress causes or makes worse many conditions, including high blood-pressure, heart disease, auto-immune disease, infections, anxiety, GI diseases and cancer. As is well known, the stress response has been useful in our history, to help the threatened individual flee or fight. The sympathetic-adrenal axis goes into overdrive, and the body goes on high alert, with stimulation of the heart, blood vessels, muscles and respiration. At the same time, the GI system shuts down and the immune system rests (presumably waiting for the stressful event to be over). This was a good defensive procedure, and not harmful, as the stress response was often rapidly over. (The lion went away!) However in our modern society the stress often never leaves us, something which leads us into a state of chronic stress. We become 'stressed out'. In this continual overstressed state, the body begins over time to fail. Diseases develop.

Meditation can step in here and become a useful tool to reduce stress. If the technique is used daily, it is possible to lower the stress level to a baseline level and allow the body to heal. Meditation has been shown to promote relaxation and resilience with regular practice. This made mainstream TV news recently.*

New research has also determined that there is a direct connection from the brain to the immune system. Esther M Sternberg, MD., Dr R Glaser, and Candace Pert, PhD, along with many others, have pioneered work looking at the connection between the nervous system, the stress response, inflammation and the hormonal and immune systems. This is the subject now studied as Psychoneuroimmunology or PNI. It has been shown that negative thoughts can depress the immune system and delay healing. The mind can affect the body—'the mind-body connection'. For example, if small superficial punch biopsies are done on the forearm of volunteers, the rate of healing can be observed alongside the volunteers' mental state. It has been shown that being either happy or angry can change the rate of healing significantly. Meditation has been shown to help

*CNN, January 6th, 2009: 'For stress reduction, just say ommm' (CNN.com)

achieve a more relaxed, happy state, speeding healing. Surgery is stressful, but meditation has been shown to reduce the stress of surgery, allowing faster and improved healing.

Meditation will sometimes allow reduction in the amount of medication taken. For example, medicine to reduce blood-pressure can (under medical advice) be reduced or stopped altogether when meditation is practised regularly, for there are many studies that show a beneficial drop in blood-pressure with meditation. Many chronic diseases are definitely improved with meditation. Modern medicine has limited tools to treat many chronic diseases, but fortunately meditation is quite helpful with chronic diseases such as anxiety, asthma, Crohn's disease, psoriasis, and many others. It is even helpful with patients receiving organ transplantation.

A recent study published in the *Proceedings of the National Academy of Sciences* found that meditation, diet, yoga and exercise may even change gene expression in hundreds of genes in only a few months.* The changes are subtle but profound.

Because meditation is so helpful in reducing the stress of modern living and is safe, people are incorporating into their daily lives. It is being taught in health clubs, churches, and in the medical setting. Hopefully, in the future the majority of people will take the time to learn how to meditate—adding meditation to exercise, good nutrition, and stretching as ingredients of a healthy lifestyle.

* * *

The stage of insight meditation is more difficult and usually requires a teacher. It is not necessary to do insight meditation to be an accomplished meditator, although many accomplished meditators practise insight meditation, particularly those meditating in the eastern traditions such as Buddhism. In the East some meditators practise for hours daily, over many years. They become very deep meditators, and have written extensively on their experiences. This type of meditation may not be practical amid a busy modern life.

The simplified overview of insight meditation follows. After meditation is allowed to deepen, following the initial relaxation response, thoughts bubble up and are available for observation. By watching our thoughts,

*Wall Street Journal, Jan. 9th, 2009, 'Alternative Medicine Goes Mainstream'.

naming them and then letting them go, we can gain insight to our inner self. In a way it is like auto-analysis. For those interested, there are many books on insight meditation such as INSIGHT MEDITATION by Sharon Salzberg and Joseph Goldstein. Jack Kornfield has also written extensively on insight meditation.

Healing can be obtained using meditation in two ways. The first is to reduce the stress response and help the immune system. The second is to access healing energy directly. This method has only recently being examined by modern medicine, though many spiritual traditions have used prayer and meditation to improve the underlying energy of the patient. The eastern traditions talk about the Chi energy. Tai Chi, Chi Gong, yoga, karate, acupuncture, ayurvedic and Chinese medicine have all been able to cliam success by using the Chi energy to heal and revitalize patients. I have myself witnessed a Chinese physician revitalizing patients in an amazing way.

It is possible to use healing energy during meditation in many ways. People can use the energy to heal others or practise self-healing while meditating. This is seen by psychics, who can tell the condition of the person's energy field and their energetic body. When meditating it is possible to work with this energy and aid self-healing. There are also those who are able to send healing to others while meditating. Such energy work is also done in many alternative medicine therapies.

When doing a healing meditation, it is possible to be aware of spiritual energy, 'the energy of the body'. When the body energy becomes unbalanced with disease or the stress of daily living, it can be rebalanced in meditation. Light can be used to represent this energy. It may be helpful to consider when we are low on energy that our energy store or 'light tank' is empty and that it can be filled with light during meditation. While meditating, it is possible to imagine a beam of light shining down on the body. With every breath this light is visualized entering the body and circulating through the body, filling our 'light tank'. If this light breathing is visualized daily, it will balance and calm the system, aiding general health. Meditations on the light are used in many meditative traditions.

The fourth stage of meditation is the one I call spiritual meditation. Many meditators report significant spiritual experiences while meditating. Through the centuries there have been many mystics who have had a direct personal relationship with a higher being. Sometimes this has been during an ecstatic state, particularly after fasting and prayer. However, it is possible to have remarkable spiritual experiences during meditation without special preparation. Many who meditate report a spiritual experience, for example messages from higher levels. People report contact with a spiritual being who imparts love, knowledge and comfort. Others believe that they have contacted loved ones, during meditation, who have passed on bringing great comfort to the meditator.

There have been many mediums over the years who would act as an intermediary between the living and deceased. Some of these have been fakes but many were and are genuine. Grace Cooke (and many others like her) was one such who was able to give messages to people from deceased family members (as she did so successfully with Sir Arthur Conan Doyle). She also verbalized teachings of the teacher White Eagle. Those of both Conan Doyle and White Eagle were to help dispel 'the mad fear of death' as well help people understand the meaning of life on earth. Although few are as sensitive as Mrs Cooke, there are many people today who have significant spiritual experiences when meditating. In the meditative state, it is possible to receive intuition, or guidance that is very helpful and comforting.

As meditation becomes mainstream it will subtlety lead to more healthy and balanced lives. Meditation has value in helping us cope with stress, keep the body healthy, healing the body when necessary, teaching us about our internal mental life, and enriching our spiritual life. Until it is experienced, meditation almost seems too good to be true; however its worldwide popularity demonstrates its value.

References

Baltzell, James, MD, WHY MEDITATION WORKS. London. Polair Publishing, 2006

——, MEDITATION FOR THE REST OF US. Minneapolis, MA: Fairview University Press, 2009 (forthcoming)

Cooke, Grace, MEDITATION. Liss, Hants.: White Eagle Publishing Trust, third edition, 1999

Kornfield, Jack, SEEKING THE HEART OF WISDOM: THE PATH OF INSIGHT MEDITATION. Shambala (1987)

Benson, Dr Herbert, THE RELAXATION RESPONSE. Avon Books (1974)

Kabatt-Zinn, Jon, FULL CATASTROPHE LIVING (1990). Delacourt Press (1990)

Salzberg , Sharon, and Goldstein, Joseph, INSIGHT MEDITATION: A WORKBOOK (2001)

TO ALL OUR RELATIONS:
THE BROTHERHOOD OF ALL LIFE

Elyan N P Stephens

'UNIVERSAL Brotherhood', 'The Brotherhood of Man', 'All our Relations' are phrases that attempt to approximate the vast concept that all mystics and sages throughout the ages and from every culture have observed, to the effect that All Life throughout the Universe is connected in a continuum of interlinked web-like threads, whereby the experience of any single entity within this interconnected web instantly has an effect upon the whole, which in turn has an effect upon each of the other individual entities within this unified organism.

The concept of the universe being a unified organism entered the realm of Science in the modern era through the research and publications

Elyan NicDomnhaill P Stephens was born on the day that President Truman declared a Day of World Peace (2.9.1945), into a family that included English and Scottish Protestants, Irish Catholics, Clans Macdonald and Campbell, so she has had little option but to endeavour to learn the potentials of a recipe for peacemaking ever since. Somewhat of a Wild Child during the 1970s, having somehow achieved an Honours Degree in English Language and Literature on the way, she has worked in the London parks as a 'common or garden' gardener, filed away in offices, made excellent Shetland ganzies in a Shetland crofthouse, terrorized children in the Isles and in North London and Hackney Schools while quietly absorbing all she could about spiritual healing meanwhile. For livelihood since 1987 she has maintained private practices in Person-Centred Counselling (www.bacp.org) and in Radionics (Registered under Energy Medicine with the Institute for Complementary Medicine: www.icm.org). She has the privilege of being one of the healers trained by the White Eagle Lodge, for whom she is also a Co-ordinator of the Star Centre for Wales alongside Jane Trevelyan. Currently she is happily living and working in a wooden cabin high in the oak woods overlooking the Dovey Estuary.

of Charles Darwin. Although his theory has been infamously abused by some who had an agenda of social engineering (eugenicists and Nazis), his amazing revelation was that every individual of every kind and species is interconnected. This of course led to the true science of ecology, as well as to philosophical concepts about Gaia.*

With an understanding of Carl Jung's theory of synchronicity, along-side an understanding of the wider implications of an astrological horary, it must be significant that the year of Arthur Conan Doyle's birth was the year too in which Charles Darwin published his 'Origin of Species'. This heralded the birth of debate about scholastic religious values, and offered a vehicle that allowed freedom of thought to enter the public domain. Synchronously also, 1859 was also the one hundredth anniversary year of the birth of Rabbie Burns (Robert Burns), who was arguably the poet par excellence who defined the nature of egality as an aspect of liberty, in his universally known lines:

> 'A man's a man for a' that
> And a' that, and a' that...
> A man's a man for a' that.'

Burns is of course referring to the effects of class division upon the Scottish society of his era, but his poetry has an international following right through to today, and this means that people generally have expanded his original meaning to that of the universality of the human 'Brotherhood of Man', in a similar evolution of meaning as has occurred with Beethoven's 'Ode to Joy'.

We understand that the word 'Man' is said to encompass both genders in the English language, but, as with this limitation of the language, the liberation of Woman from her social invisibility is a process only barely begun—certainly if we take the use of language as a touchstone! However, for Eighteenth Century Europe, this was cutting-edge stuff; just as Arthur Conan Doyle's influence in the early Twentieth Century through the Spiritualist Movement expanded consciousness beyond anything he himself may have intended or expected.

---

*The Gaia Hypothesis was expounded by the scientist James Lovelock in 1966. In summary, he theorized that the Planet Earth should be viewed as a single living organism.

The Blossoming of Liberty

It may be helpful to view the period since Arthur Conan Doyle's passing from his physical body into the Light (via the astral plane, whence he gave such cogent message, with the help of Grace Cooke's mediumship), in the form of thirty-year cycles (a Saturnian cycle, approximately). The first of these, from the mid-1930s to the mid-1960s I shall better leave to other contributors to this book. Here, I'd like to consider the changes that I've lived through: the wider, sometimes extraordinary, social and cultural effects that might be supposed to have emerged synchronously with the release of these new vibrational energies, during the second thirty-year cycle, from the mid-1960s until the mid-1990s.

Liberty of thought and of lifestyle choices manifested vast changes during the thirty–year cycle from the mid-1960s. A growing demand for civil liberties, concurrent with an emergent mutual respect between individuals of every social category throughout this era, nowadays manifests in that generally people do not assume that they have the right to sneer at another person for being different in some way: such as by being female/gay/lesbian/transgendered/darker-skinned, Jewish/lower class/minority dialect speaking/disabled/under- or overage.

The Able-bodied Heterosexual Married Caucasian Male from a Public-School heritage whose social and cultural hegemony was undisputed for centuries has given way to a generally new pattern of social consensus since the civil rights disputes of the 1960s in the USA, the ANC Rebellion in South Africa as led by Nelson Mandela, 1969 Stonewall Demonstration in the USA, *inter alia*.

There was a consequential influence upon attitudes in Britain. The civil rights movement had huge support amongst gay and feminist individuals and activists, and in a major way even coalesced the groundswell that had been growing here throughout the UK into a resurgence of political and cultural activism.* Concurrently, what had been dubbed 'the Class War'—in which, as a residue of feudalism, there had been a consensus pretence that

*Feminist activism during the 1960s, drawing strength as it did from previous waves of feminist demands for suffrage and for equal access to higher education, very quickly raised political consciousness to the point that Parliament passed several new Laws within a decade: Criminalization of Marital Rape; Protection of the Working Rights of Pregnant Women; The Equal Pay Act; The Sexual Harassment at Work Act

classes and castes are a part of the 'Natural Order'—had by now given way to a general sense of shame about social divisions continuing to keep pockets of gross poverty hidden in every city of our Island nations, as well as quite widely dispersed throughout the rural areas. Since 1990, indeed, the social rift between those who are comfortably well-off and those living along the edge has led to widespread discussion about the damage to our social fabric— should we drift into becoming 'two nations' within the one franchise.

Spiritual philosophies that point the way into the new Age of Aquarius are more widely tolerated, if not fully accepted, as a result of the mental and spiritual ferment during this era, emerging in parallel, as it were, with the social and legal reforms that were being both demanded and indeed implemented.

The Blossoming of Wisdom

I was living in the Stone Age still, during the early 1970s, in a derelict croft-house by the shore on the West of the Shetland Mainland, when information began coming to me about the Wrekin Trust, Sir George Trevelyan's New Age College. Like so many of my generation at that time, a disillusion had set in about our capacity to influence the trend of our Society in its warmongering ways, after the great work of CND appeared to be having little effect upon political policy. This had led many of us to pursue a grassroots change in our lifestyles, to learn to live our dreams and beliefs in simplicity, harmlessness and truth.

Despite my living in such a remote outpost of the British Isles, I found myself able to synthesize various intersecting circles of ground-breaking philosophies that were taking practical form within the wider society.

I was visited in my remote crofthouse in 1975 by people who were active in the feminist and gay movements that were concurrent with civil rights activism in the USA. They also brought me pamphlets and books about the Bach Flower Remedies, the Wrekin Trust and Attingham House with its New Age workshops sprouting up there; the Centre for Alternative Technology, set in a quarry near Machynlleth in western mid-Wales, and invitations to both 'Mind–Body–Spirit' festivals' in Olympia and feminist conventions at the University of London, year after year for a decade or so. All of my visitors seemed to be following a vegetarian lifestyle, which hitherto had been lampooned and marginalized as 'cranky', as well as insisting upon organic wholefoods, herbal teas and alternatives to coffee—albeit none of these were easy to come by in Shetland (where the daily menu mainly consisted of 'Reestit Mutton & Taaties', or the ubiquitous Fish & Chips). Nevertheless, we did find that Marianne Tarrant had organised shipments of wholefoods by the St Clair ferry all the way from Edinburgh, which she was in those early days distributing from her crofthouse on the remote isle of Papa Stour! When I visited again in 1981, I found that she had progressed to opening a Scoop Wholefood Shop in Lerwick itself. Such was the speed of progress of New Age understanding at the practical level, during the second half of the last century.

I still rely on the Bach Flower Remedies, which I first tentatively tried out on my beloved little red hens in 1971! I use them daily, for myself and in my complementary therapy practice, as a Registered Counsellor and Radionics Practitioner. Recently, I have been further inspired in my understanding of them by reading the brilliant exposition of another contributor to this book, Gaye Mack, the author of IGNITING SOUL FIRE.

I never did manage to make a successful composting toilet in Shetland or a water-turbine from old oil-cans, let alone a wind turbine! Yet I did try, and some of my more mechanically-minded neighbours actually managed all of these forward-looking and ecologically necessary feats.

My biggest discovery during that era of burgeoning mental and spiritual adventure, discovery and lifestyle exploration was the White Eagle Lodge, which was literally put into my hands (in the form of a copy of its magazine, *Stella Polaris*) at New Year 1976 on Papa Stour, where I had gone to teach in the Bun School. I was a successor in this little school of Stella Shepherd, of 'Like a Mantle the Sea' fame, and very little had changed there since her spell as School Dame during the 1960s.

The moment my feet touched ground off the little mailboat that had carried me over the wild waters from Sandness to Papa's wee harbour, I was given this, my first copy of *Stella Polaris*, by the mother of a seven-year-old pupil whose horoscope had been drawn up by Ingrid Lind. I learnt she was one of the Brothers in the White Eagle Lodge, which had been established in 1936, and the only books on the school shelves apart from *Hymns of Praise*, I discovered, were HULLO SUN, OUR FATHER and ANGELS AND INDIANS, all written by Joan Hodgson, the elder daughter of the Lodge's founders, Grace and Ivan Cooke!

I had travelled a thousand miles from my birthplace in West London on my Sunbeam motorcycle, undertaken the thirteen-hour North Sea crossing on the old St Clair Ferry, and then finally braved a perilous lobster-boat-cum-mailboat journey to a place with no electricity, no cars, forty households and only half a mile of road among green trackways, in these two square miles of an Island ... before White Eagle had reached out to me! Thirty years old and through my first Saturn Return, I was ready.

My pupil's mother, Sabina Holt-Brooke, had been one of the team of gardeners in the early Findhorn Community of the late 1960s, where she discovered the teachings of White Eagle. She had brought these, along with her redoubtable gardening skills, to the exposed and windswept Atlantic isle of Papa Stour. Sabina was not of the first wave of helpers for the Findhorn project, though she was there in its early days.

It was Armyn Woodehouse, whom I met in 1975 and 1976 at her home, magically named 'The Manse o' the Braes o' Logie Coldstone' in the forested hills above Braemar, who told me the story of her involvement with Eileen Caddy at Findhorn in the 1950s, and in unforgettably graphic detail about how she and her friend Rhona had carted scores of wheelbarrow-loads of compost and 'pure muck' to lay on the first vegetable garden beds that were made according to Eileen's guidance from the Devas. 'It was not magic that caused those vegetables to thrive—those fairies had help from the sweat of my limbs!'

Always practical in her application of the tenets of the Ancient Wisdom, Armyn used White Eagle's teaching to inform every aspect of her work and life, from her intense love of gardening to her Radionics practice, which included research into horticultural Radionics. This she pursued in partnership with Enid Eden, Honourary Fellow of the Radionics Association and later Principal of Keys College of Radionics, from its inception in 1984. Enid was later to become my Tutor, mentor, healer and friend, shortly before Armyn's passing into the Light in the mid-1980s. It was Armyn who encouraged me to pursue my interest in Radionics, and she also inspired me with her example as a White Eagle Brother and healer. She led me to understand that quite a large number of those involved at the beginning of the Findhorn project were, like herself, Brothers of the Star in the White Eagle Lodge.

I had already devoured the wonderful 'Findhorn Garden', written by Eileen Caddy, which I had found in the Lerwick Public Library. It was Margaret Button, née Elphinstone (also, later, her nom de plume as a noted fantasy novelist) who, as a librarian in Shetland during the mid-1970s, had commissioned so many New Age, Ancient Wisdom and Complementary

Medicine texts for what I later came to realize was the best-stocked and most illustrious public library in Britain during the 1970s! (Certainly it beat any upon whose shelves I later searched for these titles throughout South, East and West London!). The books that introduced me to Radionics were found on its shelves—when they were not in my crofthouse!

Margaret and her then husband John had also been influenced by a residence at Findhorn, early in the 1970s. Among the very first desktop publishers in Britain, they were producing the first 'Green Catalogue' from their home in Sandwick, to the South of Shetland Mainland, when we were friends during 1975–76. The catalogue was an encyclopaedic tome that astonished me, as it listed endless New Age groups, businesses and spiritual centres in the UK, none of which had I known about before I left London in 1972. Certainly, some had been quietly thriving unbeknown to me, but many had sprung up, like Venus from the foam, fully-formed and new.

Who would have believed that my bid to retire from the world to Uttermost Thule would find me in the heart of a ferment of New Age ideas!

A few years later, in South London, at the beginning of my counselling training and early practice, I met Jane Trevelyan, who became a lifelong friend and colleague. When we helped out on the White Eagle Lodge stall in a 'Mind-Body-Spirit Festival' at Olympia in 1986, she introduced me to her father's cousin, Sir George Trevelyan. I found him to be 'a very parfit gentil knight', interested in and knowledgeable about all the spiritual and mental explorations going on around us.

He was my senior by about forty years, but so youthful in his manner that we launched immediately into easy conversation. I was at that time two years into my Radionics training with Keys College, and he enthused about it most encouragingly. He told us both that it was when he was in his forties (during the early 1950s) that he had been crippled with arthritis. It had been so bad that he was confined to a wheelchair; medics had assured him that there was no cure. Almost in despair, he began a search of alternative approaches to health and healing. He had been introduced to a Radionics practitioner, whose subsequent treatments were so effective that within a year he was out of his wheelchair, and within two years he was launching himself upon his new career as a spiritual teacher, lecturer and writer. He then founded the Wrekin Trust, when he inherited Attingham Hall by the Welsh Marches.

He explained that it was the challenge of understanding how Radionics, a subtle-energy form of treatment, actually worked so effectively that had encouraged him to study all he could find out about subtle anatomy, energy fields and spiritual science.

He too had found the White Eagle Lodge, of course, and was an 'Outer Brother' throughout the last two or more decades of his life. He told Jane and me that he based all of his teaching and work upon what he learnt from White Eagle. His unflinching stance for all that he had found to be truth in this New Age teaching had cost him much, as he found that his wife, along with many members of his family and erstwhile friends, most of whom were either staunch Church of England or held to Humanist convictions, considered that he had lost his mind! For most of the period for which we best know and admire him, he had to live separately from his wife and family. Most of them do not even regard him as one of the most celebrated members of the illustrious Trevelyan family, as we do; while for our modern era many of us consider that he was the great Gatekeeper, a way-shower who inspired thousands throughout Britain, Europe and America to look beyond the confines of spiritual materiality and politicised religion toward the dawn of a New Age! The Age of Aquarius had sent its streamers of Light ahead of its dawning, and Sir George had sent out a cry to everyone to awake to greet it.

Sir George also, very kindly, gave his Patronage to our small yet significant charitable venture in South London, 'Together Women', which set up 'The Rainbow Net Counselling Centre for Women' plus crèche, for the five years up to 1993, as a trial run for a 'Kindergarten of the School of Magic' (as we liked to think of it, in reference to Sir George's 'College of the New Age', and White Eagle's more recent 'School of Wisdom').

Since his death in the late 1990s (a true passing into the Light, one that he had heralded) Jane and I have both felt his generous influence from the spirit realms, still helping and encouraging us in our work for the White Eagle Lodge now, in Wales, where we lead the 'Bro Ddyfi White Eagle Group—*Grwp Fro Ddyfi Eryr Gwyn*' and facilitate the 'White Eagle Lodge Star Centre for Wales—*Canolfan Seren Nhgymru dros Llety Eryr Gwyn*'.

I subsequently learnt about (and marvelled at) the wideranging influence of Sir George's Wrekin Trust as a college of the New Age. At Attingham Park, numerous residential and day workshops with extraordinary titles that no-one before in any form of education had ever seen or heard, were offered by young leaders, teachers, lecturers and facilitators, who emerged to pioneer a totally new style of Adult Education. The Growth

Movement was henceforth established in Britain. It has continued in a state of constant metamorphosis until the present; now the websites of 'Places to Be' and 'Neal's Yard Agency for Inner Journeys', *inter alia*, offer myriad New Age workshops and retreats.

Concurrently with Sir George's way-showing, and later encouraged by him, Ruth White and her spirit guide Gildas had built up, throughout Britain and Europe, a similar following of circles of people open to learning as much as they could about the spiritual dimensions of the human psyche. Ruth was herself guided in her own psychological development by Mary Swainson, the pioneering counsellor at her teacher training collegeand the author of THE SPIRIT OF COUNSEL (another who was an early Brother in the White Eagle Lodge). With Mary, Ruth wrote and published her first three groundbreaking books, beginning with SEVEN INNER JOURNEYS. I was privileged to have Ruth as my teacher in her 'Inner Guide' series of workshops for a period of seven years, during which time she was more than a friend to me. It would be impossible to describe the depth of gratitude that I feel toward her for all I learnt with her.

Both of these influential spiritual teachers, Sir George Trevelyan and Ruth White, brought the exploration of inner space into practical reality for many thousands of otherwise ordinary people. Both were frequently invited to offer lectures and workshops at Findhorn and other places.

Meanwhile, during the 1990s, in the White Eagle Lodge the founding era of direct trance mediumship was deliberately handing on its torch to what Grace Cooke herself called 'the New Mediumship'. The Guided Journey style of meditation that White Eagle gave us to use within a highly-raised spiritual ambience has become the main vehicle used now to guide seekers into their own contact with the source of their being, and also with their loved ones in spirit. Grace Cooke thus gently handed over her mantle (and with it her trust for the maintenance of her work) to her daughters Joan Hodgson and Ylana Hayward, shortly before her passage into the World of Light in the night of September 2nd–3rd 1979. This spiritual mantle is still worn by Ylana, now in her early nineties, though she shares with her niece Jenny Dent, who has ably taken up the challenge of continuing to offer White Eagle's wisdom teachings—which are so needed for our modern era, as the new Mother of the White Eagle Lodge—based at New Lands, near Liss in Hampshire.

The remarkable story of the White Eagle Lodge is well documented in beautiful publications, including the recent THE WHITE EAGLE LODGE STORY (2008). The work of being a lighthouse continues daily, by thought–projection of the white Light to enlighten the thought-field of humanity and to bring healing to world conditions, as well as to individuals of every species, continuously, through the commitment of countless volunteers in every part of the world. As it is, thankfully, not a proselytizing organization, you must make your own first contact with them should you wish to take part in this most rewarding and desperately-needed endeavour.

As we know only too well, it only takes 'good people to stand by and do nothing, for those who wish ill to prevail'. As all that manifests in physical form upon the earth plane began as a thought-form (whether in the Mind of our Creator or in the minds of the human created beings) we must make a choice as to the trend taken by our own thinking. 'As Above, So Below...' to quote a modern translation of Hermes Trismegistus in the Emerald Tablet (which some believe to have derived from among the nine-thousand-year-old archives mentioned by Plato in his *Timacus* and *Critias*).

And so we come to the message of Arthur Conan Doyle, given by Spiritualist mediumship when he found himself 'trapped on the astral plane', one aspect of which is that we would do well to examine our own habitual thoughts, fantasies and feelings. He warned us to take care about what we habitually imagine, because all these products of our mental and emotional life take a manifested form on the inner planes. It is from here that we are affecting the thought-field and feeling life of all Humanity, through what Carl Jung named 'the Collective Unconscious'.

For myself, when I first studied THE RETURN OF ARTHUR CONAN DOYLE in the 1970s, and again the next edition in the 1980s, I was deeply affected by this admonition, which had the effect indeed of giving pause to my own ambitions as a writer of fiction. ACD painted such a dramatic picture of how he was assailed by astral forms of his own creating from his Sherlock Holmes stories and others, and how remorseful he felt about the effect they were having upon the collective unconscious of humanity, that it has kept me paused, as a writer, ever since! Many may, perhaps, consider this a mercy.

In the White Eagle Lodge I have found a way to begin to train and discipline my own use of thought, through the Absent Healing work. I have also, of course, learnt to harness the power of thought to a good and healing purpose in my practice of Radionics.

Many people whose parents would have considered themselves members of the Christian Church have been seeking forms of meditation, once mainly provided by Buddhist and Hindu Teachers but also in the White Eagle Lodge, which is the gateway to control of wayward human thought. The Age of Aquarius is one in which the faculty of thought and the vast powers of the mind will be studied and will become better understood.

Those who seek to abuse such knowledge have already manifested, since some of Hitler's medics fled to the USA in the late 1940s, and taught businessmen how to target their advertising upon the wider population using a knowledge of the human psyche based upon Freudian psychology. It is now the work of all of us who care about the future for the next seven generations (of all species!) to learn how to train and harness our own capacity for creative thought and envision a beautiful world, in which mutual respect is a paramount value throughout every aspect of our relationships with people of every nation, and with all other species of creature upon this planet. There is more, according to White Eagle, but if we can make a start in our own back yards, then the vibrations of our intentions will reach through the whole fabric of the subtle web of Light that links us together.

'Bake your own bread' is the exhortation of both Mahatma Gandhi and Satish Kumar. Make compost from all our food waste; grow whatever food plants we are able, regardless of the limitations of our personal territory; recycle our clothes, our books, our endlessly accumulating IT equipment. Learn, learn and go on learning all we can about ourselves, each other and our environment, both physical and subtle…. The Age of Aquarius is dawning now, and we are the pioneer generation whose thoughts, behaviour and choices are creating the world to be inhabited by the next seven generations—among whom, no doubt, our own souls will be reincarnated.

References
White Eagle Lodge, THE WHITE EAGLE LODGE STORY. Liss, Hants.: White Eagle Publishing Trust, 2008
• Keys College of Radionics may be found on: www.keyscollege.co.uk
• Radionics Practioners may be found on the website of the Institute for Complementary Medicine, where the British register of Complementary Practitioners (BRCP) is held. They are listed under the 'Energy Medicine' section: www.icnm.org.uk
• The Vegetarian society may be found at: www.vegsoc.org
• The White Eagle Lodge worldwide may be found at: www.whiteagle.org

RETURNING TO NATURAL MIND

Peter Russell

People are disturbed, not by things, but by the view they take of them. Epictetus

'IN THE final analysis', said the Dalai Lama, 'the hope of every person is simply peace of mind'. As with many great truths, these words resonate with something we know deep down. Beneath all our endeavours, we all want to be at peace, to feel content, fulfilled, at ease. None of us want to be in pain or suffer unnecessarily.

We may decide to change jobs, start a new relationship or take up a new hobby because we believe we will be happier. I may choose to go hiking because I expect to get some pleasure from it, a tangible endorphin rush from the exercise, or a feeling of warmth and closeness from spending time with a friend. I may spend time writing a book, foregoing other pleasures, because I gain satisfaction from my creative expression.

The gratification that we seek may not always be immediate. Most of us do not enjoy visiting the dentist, but we go in the hope that we will suffer less later. Or we may forego some personal gain and devote our time to helping elderly relatives or others in need; yet we do so because it brings some inner fulfilment. Even the masochist, who sets out to cause himself pain, does so because he takes some comfort from it.

Seeking a better state of mind is the fundamental criterion by which, consciously or unconsciously, we make all our decisions. This is our ultimate bottom line. It is not a bottom line that can be measured in numbers,

Peter Russell's principal interest is in the inner challenges of the times we are passing through, and his work integrates Eastern and Western understandings of the mind. He has degrees in theoretical physics, experimental psychology and computer science and is the author of ten books, including THE GLOBAL BRAIN, WAKING UP IN TIME, and, most recently, FROM SCIENCE TO GOD.

but it is nevertheless the true arbiter of all our decisions. We may think we are seeking an external goal, but we are seeking that goal in the hope that, in one way or another, we will feel better for it.

Why then do we seldom find peace of mind? After all, we are intelligent beings, we can look ahead and plan for the future. Moreover, we have many tools and technologies with which to create a better world for ourselves. One would think that we, of all creatures, would be content and at ease. Yet the very opposite seems to be the case.

As far as I can tell, a dog spends more time at ease than its owner who is busy seeking the various things he or she thinks will bring satisfaction and fulfilment. Leave a dog with nothing to do, and it will probably lie down, put its chin on the ground, and watch the world go by. Leave us human beings with nothing to do, and it is not long before we complain of being bored, get restless, and start looking for things to fill the time. We worry what we might be missing and how we might improve things, or we go check off one more thing on that neverending 'to do' list.

Samsara

Paradoxically, it is our remarkable ability to change our world that has led us into this sorry state. We have fallen into the belief that if we are not at peace, then we must do something about it. We think we need to obtain something we don't yet have, get others to respond as we would like, enjoy a new experience, or avoid some circumstance or person that is causing us distress. We assume that, if we could just get our world to be a particular way, we will finally be happy.

From the moment we are born our culture reinforces this assumption, encouraging us to believe that outer wellbeing is the source of inner fulfilment. As young children we learn from the example of our elders that it is important to be in control of things, that material possessions offer security. As we grow up, much of our education focuses on knowing the ways of the world in order that we might better manage our affairs and so find greater contentment and fulfilment. As adults, the daily deluge of television, radio, newspapers, magazines, and advertisements reinforces the belief that happiness comes from what we have or do. The net result is that we become addicted to things and circumstances.

Our material acquisitiveness may not look like a drug addiction, but the underlying pattern is the same. With drugs—whether they be alcohol, tobacco, coffee, tranquillizers, cocaine or heroin—people take them for one simple reason. They want to feel better. They want to feel happy, high, relaxed, in control, less anxious, temporarily free from some suffering. In this respect drug-takers are seeking nothing different from anyone else; it is just the way in which they are doing it that most societies find unacceptable.

Similarly with our addiction to having and doing, we are seeking a better state of mind. And, in the short term, it may appear to work. But any pleasure, happiness, or satisfaction we do find is only temporary. As soon as one 'high' wears off we go in search of another 'fix'. We become psychologically dependent upon our favorite sources of pleasure—food, music, driving, debating, football, television, shopping, whatever.

When this fails to bring any lasting satisfaction we do not question whether our approach may be mistaken. Instead we try even harder to get the world to give us what we want. We buy more clothes, go to more parties, eat more food, try to make more money. Or we give up on these and try different things. We take up squash, or look for new friends. Yet true peace of mind remains as elusive as ever.

We live in what Indian philosophies call the world of *samsara*, whose original meaning is 'to wander on'. We wander on, looking for fulfilment in a world which provides but temporary respites from discontent, a momentary pleasure followed by more wandering on in search of that ever-elusive goal.

The Clinging Mind

Throughout human history, there have been those who have woken up from the illusion that, if only we could get the world to be the way want, we would finally be content. They are the rishis, roshis, mystics, saints, lamas and other 'wise ones' who have each, in their own way, rediscovered the same timeless truth about human consciousness: The mind in its natural state is already at ease.

By 'natural' they do not mean the state of mind in which we spend most of our time—which clearly is not usually one of ease and contentment—they are speaking of the mind before it becomes tarnished with worry, wanting, analyzing and planning. Time and again they have reminded us that we do not need to do anything, or go anywhere to be at ease. On the contrary, all our doing, all our seeking to change things, takes us in the opposite direction. We imagine something is missing, and this self-created sense of lack creates feelings of discontent. These cloud our consciousness, overshadowing the intrinsic ease of the mind in its natural, unsullied, state.

This was one of the Buddha's key realizations. He saw that we all experience what he called *dukka*. The word is often translated as 'suffering', leading to the common misconception that Buddha taught that life is suffering. The word *dukka* is actually a negation of the word *sukha*, which has the meaning of ease (originally, a wheel that runs smoothly). So *dukka* means not-at-ease, and is probably best translated as discontent or unsatisfactoriness. Suffering, as we think of it, is an extreme form of discontent. Much more common—indeed, so common that it usually passes unnoticed—is the discontent that comes from wishing that things were different, worrying about what happened earlier, or hoping for a better future. Buddha realized that the root cause of this discontent was our clinging to our ideas of how things should or should not be. As soon as clinging enters the mind, we lose the natural state of ease.

Thus, to return to a state of ease, we have only to stop creating unnecessary discontent. That means letting go of our attachments as to how things should or should not be.

Letting Go

Letting go never seems easy. This is because we treat 'letting go' as another task to do. We've become so enmeshed in the habit of doing that we mistakenly approach letting go in the same way. But you can't 'do' letting go—however hard you try. It is our doing that is the problem. To let go we have to cease the 'doing' of holding on. We need to allow the mind to relax, accepting the present moment as it is, without resistance or judgment.

This is sometimes misinterpreted as accepting the world as it is, which can lead to a Pollyanna attitude of 'everything is OK'; the world is perfect as it is. But there is a subtle, and crucial, distinction between accepting our experience of a situation and accepting the situation itself. Sadly, the world around us is rife with injustice, self-centredness and unnecessary suffering. No-one, I hope, is proposing the kind of acceptance that says we can simply let such ills be. Accepting our experience of the situation, on the other hand, means not resisting what we are actually perceiving and feeling in the moment. There is nothing we can do to change our present experience. Wishing it were otherwise is a pointless waste of time and energy.

All it does is create additional discontent.

The most commonly recommended way to become more present is to bring our attention back to our physical experience, noticing how it feels to be a living being—the feelings in our bodies, the sensations of breathing, the air against the skin, the sounds around us. Our immediate sensory experience is always in the present moment. It is when we start thinking about our experience, what it means, and where it might lead, that our attention is drawn into the past or the future—and back into the world of *samsara*.

The more often we can come back to the present moment, the more the mind is able to relax. When it is fully relaxed, totally at ease, we rediscover the mind in its natural, undisturbed state.

In Indian philosophy the profound and delightful ease of natural mind is often called *nirvana*. To many, the word conjures images of some blissed out, euphoric state of consciousness. But its original meaning is very different—and much more instructive. The word 'nirvana' literally means 'to blow out', as in extinguishing a flame. When we accept our experience of the moment, as it is, without lament or resistance, the flames of greed, hatred, jealousy and the many other unwelcome ramifications of our discontent die down; extinguished by a lack of fuel.

Then, no longer blinded by self-concern, we are better able to see a situation for what it is. Free from imagined lacks and needs, we can act in accord with the needs of the situation at hand. Whether it be helping others, righting injustices, taking care of our health, raising children, whatever we choose to focus our energies upon, we can do so with greater commitment and deeper compassion.

We spend so much energy trying to find contentment in the world around us. If we spent a fraction of this energy allowing the mind to relax, letting go of some of our attachments, we would find more of the peace of mind that, in the final analysis, we are all seeking.

A HOLISTIC SCIENCE FOR THE SOUL-AGE

Ruth Hadikin

IT IS beyond doubt that we are at an evolutionary point in human consciousness, one which brings understanding of our true nature and our role here, on this planet, at this time, hence this book. In studying the evolution of humanity it becomes apparent that we are on the verge of what some might call a spiritual dawn. From the earliest apes that walked upright as humans, not knowing that they were 'aware' (conscious), we have evolved through stages of 'knowing', to the point where we are now 'aware that we are aware', or conscious. Awareness has become aware of itself. We are realizing that we are not helpless victims in a Universe that does things 'to' us, but rather are conscious co-creators of our own evolution. For the first time, the realization is dawning on us that we are co-creating the reality that we experience. Not only is our environment affecting us, but we are having a huge effect on it. We are facing the reality that we are part of one whole system, not separate from it. This knowing brings a need for us to study and understand our world from a very different perspective. A truly holistic one.

This new awareness raises many questions that traditional science

Ruth Hadikin is an author and ongoing student of Soul Astrology. She spent eighteen years in the UK Health Service and had many articles published including a coaching column. Author of EFFECTIVE COACHING IN HEALTHCARE, she co-wrote INTERPERSONAL SKILLS and THE BULLYING CULTURE with Muriel O'Driscoll. In 1999 she founded Ruth Hadikin Associates Training and Development, where she provides training, coaching and consultancy in communication, emotional intelligence, relating, stress and workplace bullying. She has been studying esoteric and spiritual teachings, astrology and psychology for over thirty years, in which time she has supported clients using many modalities: nursing, midwifery, teaching, coaching, counselling and Soul Astrology.

doesn't have answers for. As we step into our role as conscious co-creators, we might wonder: Where are we going? What are we co-creating? Who are we co-creating with? Who, or what, is God? This shift in consciousness is known by many names. It has been described as a global spiritual awakening. Certainly there is an increased awareness of, and interest in, spiritual matters. In times to come this period of human evolution may well be called the Soul-Age. It is written that during this period of our evolution we are to have a conscious experience of our soul. Not just one or two, like the saints and avatars in ages gone by, but this time we will all experience this. We are set for a mass quantum leap in human consciousness.

As we move forward into the Twenty-First Century, we will need a different approach to science. The science of the Nineteenth and Twentieth Centuries was based on separation: dissection, categorization, classification and labelling. It was a product of the consciousness of the age, which thought the key to understanding anything was to observe it and label it. From the newly-evolving consciousness that is emerging within the mind of humanity, we can see obvious flaws in this approach. We cannot observe wholeness from the outside because in wholeness there is no duality, and so there is no outside! (Nor inside for that matter). It is clear that in moving forward from here we will need a different approach to science. A holistic approach that brings us to deeper understandings of unity, wholeness, the interrelatedness of all things, and oneness. We will need sciences that are congruent with our spiritual being and experience. Maybe we already have in place some of the rudimentary elements for this. Maybe wisdom teachers through the ages have been guiding us, but we didn't have the consciousness to recognize what was before us, until now. Soul Astrology has the potential to become a comprehensive applied science of energy and relationships that gives us a framework for understanding the nature of the universe, quantum physics, the mind, and healing. We just need to recognize it and learn how to use it properly, in the way it was intended. Before this can happen, we need to understand what Soul Astrology is, what science is, and the purpose of each.

Soul Astrology is the name given to forms of astrology that draw upon psychological astrology, transpersonal psychology and esoteric astrology, to create a model of the Universe and how we fit into it. It is one thing to put forward a model, or framework, for understanding the Universe; it is quite another to suggest this can be applied as a science. So let's take a moment to understand what Soul Astrology actually is, where it originates from, and how it can be used as a practical applied science for this new age, to enable us to understand the nature of everything from the universe to the mind. Indeed the true nature of everything.

Many eminent people throughout history have also been astrologers. Carl Jung, one of the fathers of modern psychology, and the great mathematician Pythagoras, were also accomplished astrologers. Yet in the Twentieth Century, astrology fell from grace and, rather than being considered a science, it was relegated to the status of fortune telling. What happened? Were Pythagoras, Carl Jung, and many other wise teachers throughout history mistaken? Or, in our arrogance at the height of twentieth-century materialism, was there something about astrology that we couldn't understand because, in our ignorance, we didn't have the consciousness to comprehend it?

Most Westerners only know of Pythagoras as a mathematician. Few know that he was also a mystic and scientist who ran an ancient mystery school. His students began with the study of mathematics. Once accomplished in mathematics, his students were required to study music. It is said of Pythagoras that he heard the 'music of the spheres'. Certainly he held music in high regard. Each of his students was given a 'monochord': a one-stringed instrument, and told that once they understood the secrets of the monochord, they understood the secrets of the Universe. So what could his students learn from this instrument? Well, they could learn the relationship between notes on the musical scale. They could also learn that a musical note never dies. Once that string is struck, the vibration continues until infinity. It may pass beyond the current range of human perception, but it doesn't end there. Once we grasp this fundamental truth, we can begin to realize the possibility of omniscience. That it could be possible, just as many mystics and yogis have told us over the ages, to expand human perception to the place where 'all is known', and that this potential lies in each of us, because we are not separate from that place, but just 'blind' to it at this time, by virtue of our limited perceptions.

Astrology in its truest form is an invitation to us to expand our knowledge by expanding our perceptive abilities. We can only fully understand and comprehend this through personal experience. Twentieth-century science was limited by its own obsession with materialism: a limiting fixation with 'objective' research almost to the point of ignorance, whereby evidence had to be externally verified in order to be valid and, if it could not be, then it was rejected. Twentieth-century scientists continued along this vein, in spite of an awareness of 'the observer effect': a well-known phenomenon in scientific research whereby 'that which is observed is changed by the observation'. Much evidence of this is found in quantum physics, whereby results often depend upon what researchers expect to see. The researcher cannot remove themselves from the equation, and everything affects everything else, because all is inter-related. During the latter years of the Twentieth Century a field known as 'heuristic research' was developed as a tool in certain social sciences, such as psychology, especially those which are trying to understand the human mind. In heuristic research the researcher uses himself as the 'subject'. At last 'self' observation has found a place in conventional scientific circles. As yogis and mystics have told us, there is no other way to explore the realm of human consciousness, other than from within, because our mind is creating that which we observe.

'There are no levels of Reality; only levels of experience for the individual'
Ramana Maharshi

What is science? The meaning of the word 'science' changed over time, deviating from its origin in the Latin 'scientia' meaning knowledge or knowing. It was only from the Nineteenth Century onwards that the term 'science' came to be used only to denote 'knowledge obtained through a scientific method'. Neither was there ever a consensus of opinion at the time as to what these methods should be. In its striving for some externally verifiable objective 'truth', and distorting the original meaning of the word 'science', Western science became divisive in nature. The totality of 'all that is' was reduced to subject/object. The more we explore things from this standpoint the further it takes us from the truth of our being. Yet if we simply return to the original meaning of the word 'science' as 'knowing' then it is perfectly possible to have a science of wholeness, integration, unity.

How can astrology inform us, give us knowledge, and be considered a true science of inner knowing? To answer that question we now need to look at astrology in itself. True astrology has also been distorted by the dualistic mind. The planets were considered to be 'out there' and separate. Astronomy came to be the science of choice for the study of planets because we get to be 'over here', studying planets which are 'over there'. Subject/object. As we shift our consciousness to increasingly embrace wholeness, we can begin to understand astrology as a science of wholeness, energy and interrelatedness. More accurately, astrology is a body of wisdom gathered over thousands of years by wisdom teachers such as Pythagoras who, through their own inner knowing, developed a deep understanding of the true nature of reality, and left this science behind for us, as a map to follow in their footsteps.

The work known as 'Esoteric Astrology' was received by Alice Bailey (A.B.) from 'The Tibetan', later to become known as the Master DK. At the time he was alive and well and living in a monastery in Tibet. He transmitted wisdom teachings by telepathic means to A.B. In itself, this is an exciting testimony to the power of a highly-developed and crystal-clear human mind. One of the first questions I had upon reading this work was how the teachings related to Tibetan Buddhism. Although the teachings are very different, there are core truths which can be related not only to Buddhist teaching, but to the teachings from other wisdom schools. They are in agreement about the presence and capacities of the higher mind, telepathy, the subject of reincarnation, and the interrelatedness of all things. In the Pythagorean school, knowledge of reincarnation was also a fundamental principle. It seems that, irrespective of religious belief or tradition, there is core wisdom that we in the West have forgotten how to access. Soul Astrology is giving us the tools to access and understand this wisdom.

The Tibetan tells us that we exist within a living organism, with whom we co-create in every moment with our minds. Albert Einstein is reported to have said, 'I want to know the mind of God'. The Tibetan reminds us that we are not separate from God, so this is possible, but first we have to develop our perception enormously to be aware of this. Just as a cell in our big toe has no knowledge of our mind, this is the difference between the small capacity of our mind, and the mind of God! The cell in our toe cannot stand outside our body to understand it, it can only increase its awareness until it realizes there is a body, of which it is a part. The current state of Western science sends rockets to the moon and beyond to see what is 'out there', when indeed all of 'out there' is really 'in here'. This is tantamount to our toe sending a rocket to our head to see what is 'out there', when the best way to know and understand would be for the toe to expand its perception so that it could feel and thereby know its connectedness to the rest of the body.

The Tibetan does not ask us to accept the teachings in Esoteric Astrology on blind faith. He tells us to corroborate the teachings and, if we cannot, then of course we must reject them. How do we corroborate them? He tells us that it can only be done through developing the intuitive faculty and accessing 'the illumined mind'. The human body is the only instrument of perception that can corroborate these teachings, and while we seek for truth outside of ourselves we will remain in ignorance. The true science of the future will increasingly be based on heuristic research—looking within. Only then will we develop the skills of expanded awareness that allow us to discern the subtle energies that were known to Pythagoras, and are described in Esoteric Astrology.

The Pythagorean model of the Universe used music and colour to illustrate seven creative forces, which issued forth from the mouth of 'the One'. Judaism tells us that seven creative 'lords' (Elohim) issued forth from the mouth of God. There are seven colours in the spectrum and seven notes make up the musical scale. In Esoteric Astrology the Tibetan tells us that seven energy 'rays' issue from one. The one divides into two and from that issues forth a third, from which issue rays four to seven. We ourselves are energetic fields vibrating, resonating, within one larger energetic field. As we begin to stand in the truth of this and expand our awareness of these energies we will realize some of the deeper truths of which the ancient Masters spoke.

How do we recognize these energies? Through our perception. We perceive them as positive emotions and sensations. Buddhist teaching refers to 'subtle winds' to describe the various forms of energy that flow through, and from, our body. There are seven chakras, or energy centres, in the human body, which correspond to seven chakras, or energy centres, in the solar system.

In Esoteric Astrology the first ray is known as the will of God, the second ray as love/wisdom and the third ray as active intelligence. This is similar to a Tibetan Buddhist prayer that asks for 'enlightened power' (will), 'enlightened compassion' (love/wisdom), and 'enlightened wisdom' (active intelligence). The seven rays of which the Tibetan speaks are literally describing the fabric of the Universe in terms of loving, compassionate and powerful energies. The very energies that saints, mystics and yogis have told us are always there for us, if we know how to access them. Energy, Chi, Prana: although known by different names in different traditions, the nature of these fundamental energies remains the same and possesses the qualities of love and intelligence.

'Someday after we have mastered the winds, the waves, the tides and gravity, we
shall harness the energies of love. Then for the second time in the history of the
world man will have discovered fire.'
Pierre Teilhard de Chardin

Quantum physics is amassing a wealth of evidence that supports these
teachings. Nothing is solid, everything is energy, and there is no such thing
as 'empty space'. After many attempts scientists have finally accepted that
it is impossible to create a vacuum in a laboratory, because whenever they
try, there are always at least photons (particles of light) present. In other
words, there is no such thing as a vacuum, or space. Everything is connected and, more importantly, it is connected by light. As we move away
from the concrete literal-mindedness of early science, we are beginning
to realize that everything in astrology—the zodiac with its animal signs—
and the planets, is symbolic of an underlying energetic reality. The zodiac
signs were given as symbols to an ancient people who were much more
closely connected with nature than we are. Because they understood animals, they understood the energetic qualities of Aries the ram, for example, through symbolism. Soul-centred astrology has been trying to point
us toward a deeper understanding of the underlying energy, the differing
energetic qualities that we command and receive, and the relationships
between the various forms of energy. Soul Astrology teaches us about the
nature of energy through metaphor and simile. When we say 'the Moon'
is an accumulation of past learning, it is nothing to do with the physical,
actual Moon. This is where confusion arose between science and astrology in the Twentieth Century. We are talking energetically. We are talking
about a wave, an energy pattern, that is in us and is reflected above in the
constellations and planets. As above, so below.

We can only understand these energies by coming to know them in-
timately through personal experience. Many forms of healing have arisen
in recent years based on energy and vibration. We are slowly beginning to
recognize ourselves as energetic beings: living, intelligent, energy fields.
Esoteric Astrology gives us a blueprint of the entire energy field. A personal soul-based astrological reading gives us the blueprint not only of the
mind that created the physical form which we have now, but what we are
creating for our future lives, and what we have the potential to change.

The most important part of our natal chart is the rising sign, or ascendant. This is the constellation that was 'rising' on the horizon at the point of our birth, and as such marks the 'dawning' of our life, and the dominant energy that prevailed at that precise point in time. As above, so below. You are a product and co-creator of this energy. It indicates the nature of your soul and therefore was a natural medium for you to use as a gateway into this physical incarnation. In contrast, the positions of the Sun and Moon indicate the dualistic nature of our lower egoic mind. By 'ego' I mean the mind thinking of itself, or our general sense of 'there is a me in here'. The Moon represents what Carl Jung called our 'shadow', meaning those aspects of our psyche which are in the dark: our unconscious mind. The Sun represents that which is in the light, our conscious mind. Neither is our 'true' nature. The Moon is an accumulation of conditioning, learned behaviour and traits, from many past lives, while the Sun can be thought of as the present. Through self-observation we can not only come to know and recognize the subtle energy patterns in ourselves that lead us to re-peat behaviours, but understand those thought-forms that we ourselves are perpetuating that create our future experiences.

Along with others both the Tibetan and Arthur Conan Doyle have told us that physicians of the future will want to know a person's birth chart before treating them. Just like an electrician would need to see a wir-ing plan before detecting a fault in the system, doesn't it make sense that if blueprints of our whole system are available, then our physicians and therapists would need to be aware of them? An awareness of the habitual energies dominating a chart can tell us which dis-eases that individual will re-create in this and future lifetimes. It is the ultimate in preventive medi-cine. Imagine being able to correct 'mis-fires' in your energy field now, to prevent illness in your future lives!

Through deepening our understanding of energy, we begin to answer those really big questions about the very nature of our being such as 'Who am I?', 'Why am I here?' and 'What am I supposed to be doing with my Life?'. In Soul Astrology we have a frame of reference that assists us in un-derstanding the nature and causal relationships between karma, energy, and our experienced reality. It helps us to understand the bigger picture through a deeper understanding of ourselves, and our part in it. If our Sun, Moon and rising sign help us to distinguish between soul-based and ego-based behaviour, it can also help us to understand the complex nature of karma. As mentioned above, 'ego' in this sense refers to our self-concept:

who or what we have been 'conditioned' to believe ourselves to be, what we identify with, including all our beliefs, skills, talents, fears and limitations. Karma refers to that conditioning which has been carried over in our psyche from previous incarnations. There is a saying in Buddhist teaching that if you want to know your past actions, look at your present life, if you want to know your future life, look at your present actions. Zen teaches:

'Karma creates the body, and the body creates Karma'

This is known in Buddhism as the wheel of *samsara*: the cycle of death and re-birth. The energy of our past thoughts, actions and behaviour is mirrored in our Moon-sign. A storehouse of karmic 'seeds', which we are unaware of, ready to ripen in any moment. It is not 'past' in the sense that it is gone, but rather that we created it with our past thoughts, words and actions. It indicates energy which we still carry and are unconscious of. The Sun can be thought of as karma which is currently ripening. Although created in our past, it is coming into our conscious awareness in the present. Thought-forms which are currently expressed in our conscious awareness. The qualities of the signs in those positions tells us much about who we were and who we are currently becoming, as a living energy form. In this way, using our natal chart with a process of self-observation, we can distinguish our soul's evolving nature from our individual and collective karma, and realize we are so much more than we currently experience ourselves to be. Soul Astrology is the key to unlocking why we came in to this specific incarnation, what we are here to heal, and what we are here to grow. We may even have a conscious experience of our soul, and realize ourselves as a soul-based being.

In observing ourselves, we deepen our understanding of the nature of 'mind' and karma, and adopt a very different approach to Astrology. Soul Astrology in the future will include deep personal development. Students of soul-based astrology will develop knowledge based on experience of their own individual journey. As we touch and come to know our own soul, we naturally develop a deeper understanding of the nature of mind.

What do we mean by mind? Tibetan Buddhists have no distinction between heart and mind as we do in the West. Emotions are also considered part of the mind. The Tibetan speaks of the plane of emotions as an aspect of 'lower mind' as distinct from the clear, higher mind we can access where the wisdom of the Masters can be found. According to Buddha, we are a continuous stream of mental moments. Practices such as meditation help us to slow down to the point where we can see the gap between thoughts, and discern what lies underneath. With deeper awareness we can see the relationship between our thoughts and the reality we experience. Understanding this distinction between 'lower' and 'higher' mind leads to a fundamental understanding in Esoteric Astrology.

In Esoteric Astrology, each zodiac sign has a lower and an upper octave, a mundane and an esoteric ruler, indicative of our lower and higher mind. Buddhism again speaks of mundane and ultimate reality. Until relatively recently, Western psychology has approached understanding the mind from the perspective that we are our personality. We in the West tend to be attached to our personality as if it is a fixed thing, an intrinsic part of who we are. Soul Astrology invites us to consider that the roles and behaviours that we attach to as our 'personality' are not inherently 'who we are' but are learned behaviour, with which we have become identified. Although we may identify ourselves with our personality, we can also understand that we are part of something greater—that is, bigger than this small 'I'—and understand that the two realities are really one. We understand that we have a dualistic nature. Karma is trying to tell us something about why this is so, and how we experience at least two levels of being. Soul Astrology, in contrast to conventional Astrology, addresses both our dualistic nature, and our Oneness. More than ever before it is emerging as a complete psychology, and even more than that, it explains the physical universe.

There is a direct connection between thoughts, emotions, and physical health and illness. Sigmund Freud, the father of modern psychology, based his psychodynamic theory on 'thermodynamic theory', which was popular at the time. The Victorian steam technologies, steam-powered ships, trains, factories, were all based on thermodynamic theory, which states that when water boils it becomes steam and as steam cools it returns to water. Freud realized that energy doesn't go anywhere, it just changes shape and form, and that this applies to people. So he based his theory of psychodynamics on the same idea: that mental and emotional energy cannot go anywhere. It just changes its state, and can become physical illness. From this we can deduce that energy patterns, or past 'karma', can be locked into our patterning at birth. Future students of Soul Astrology will be able to recognize energetic patterning in a natal chart that could be potential for dis-ease, and understand what needs to change for healing to happen. At this point we can only imagine our deep understanding of the nature of disease. The Tibetan tells us that all dis-ease is caused by separation. The solution is a return to wholeness.

Daily self-examination was a requirement for students of the Pythagorean school, just as modern counsellors, psychologists and psychotherapists are required to undergo their own inner process work. Just as heuristic research is now valued, self-examination is valued in any study of psychology because of what can be revealed to us through understanding the inner workings and patterns of our own mind. Through exquisite self-observation we undergo a transformative process whereby we can access higher truth. We begin to widen our perceptive capacity and can recognize the inner gateways to the Universe. These inner doors, sometimes referred to by mystics as the 'Bhagavat in the ten directions', are our gateway to the Universe through inner space. We have access to ultimate truth because we are not separate from it. We can expand our capacity to reach the place where, as the Tibetan said, 'The will of God is known'.

As we expand our perception, through using this instrument of higher perception, we will recognize and know what the Tibetan means by our being 'living cells within one larger living organism'. We will come to an intimate knowing of our individual soul, its relationship to the group soul and, in turn, the greater Being, of whom we are part. Heuristic research, the modern science of self-examination, allows us to compare and validate our experiences and personal truths. With thorough, deep, self-examination, as advocated by Pythagoras, we will come to understand the deeper truths contained in the Tibetan's teachings and Soul Astrology can become a true science: a transpersonal psychology that supports our expanding consciousness through inner knowing.

Soul Astrology gives us a map of our journey so far. Everything is in our natal chart. It is a snapshot of our evolution and everything we have picked up along the way, good and bad! It is the sum total of our individual and collective karma, or psyche. This means that we are, as all the great wisdom teachings have told us, defined by our goodness. We really do have an innate inner light at our core, and all our 'negativity' is not inherent in our nature, but rather the result of past conditioning. A very negative side effect of our modern age is that it leaves us stuck with all our negative feelings and doesn't give us a way forward. Soul Astrology is telling us that yes, we do have a core essence, a vital spark, a light, and we are moving, growing into something, evolving. All our negative thoughts and emotions are learned and, as real as they feel to us right now, they are habitual patterns in our field of consciousness which we have the power to change if we know how. Our natal chart tells us how to tell which is which. It gives us a personality tool so we can see what kind of personality we have, what the positive and negative traits are and what we can change, whilst letting us know that we are so much more than that.

We have so much more understanding about various subtle forms of energy. We could almost dispense with the animal analogies for the signs of the zodiac, although it would be a shame because they are such great metaphors.

The true nature of mind is one of pristine clarity like a stream of crystal clear mountain water. From this place, our perception is exquisite: all is known. We are clairvoyant, clairaudient, and clairsentient because all is clear: nothing is in the way, we have clear sight, sound and knowing. We are omniscient, all really is known. For most of us the spiritual path is a way of returning to this utmost clarity. Soul Astrology is simply a tool, albeit a comprehensive one. It allows us to understand our true nature. It also allows us to understand why we don't experience expanded perception: what gets in the way in the form of habitual patterns of thinking, feeling, and expressing, that have clouded the clarity of our perceptions. It indicates those areas that we can heal or change so that we can experience our true nature.

> 'Light is undiminishable, eternal and omni-present. In every religion that existed these qualities have been recognized as divine. So that we are forced to the conclusion that light, actual sensible light, is indeed the direct vehicle of divinity: it is the consciousness of God.'
> Rodney Collin, The Theory of Celestial Influences

When each one of us has become an exquisite observer of Self, with integrated knowledge from our personal experience and an intimate relationship with our own soul, we will recognize our true nature as one of light, and Soul Astrology as a true science of inner knowing.

IN THE LIGHT OF A NEW DAY

Anya Sophia Mann

IN THE light of a new day, you are anew. You are fresh. You are rejuvenated. It is true.

Only you can know this for yourself. Bringing this idea into your conscious awareness can be the welcoming point of each new day. Upon reflection at the close of each day you can look for what you are grateful for, to include lessons learned from your life experiences. What a beautiful, conscious, way of melting into the unconscious slumber of a good night's sleep!

In the light of a new day you are refreshed. You can do anything different or better than the day before. There is so much hope. So much promise. Potential and possibility abound. When we awaken to the moment, the present–here–now moment, it is all there is. Living from there creates something new and different from what has gone before. You are growing, changing, evolving and, by presenting this in many ways, will wake up something in you that will recognize the truth on a body and cellular level. You will vibrate differently. Your resonance will be higher as you claim for your self what you have always known. Nothing stays the same. Everything is energy and movement. You are energy. You are evolving. You are life living through you, as you.

In the light of a new day you can feel the clear light that refreshes. If you watch the day by greeting the dawn light with your intentions for that day you can feel the support of knowing that you are not alone. Knowing

---

Anya Sophia Mann is an evolutionary Life Coach, Consultant and Mentor in transformational personal and professional development. She specializes in shifting global cultures through conscious leadership, from families to corporations, and beyond. Balancing any system holistically, including the human body, is part of her visionary healing work as a highly-developed Empathic, Medium and Intuitive.

that you are a part of the whole of it. Everything is you, and you are everything. Every breath you take you exchange with everyone. We breathe each other in every moment. To not know this is to deny truth.

In the light of a new day, in the crystal clear light, life emerges from within. If you are open to it, you can feel it. Let it move you in ways that your mind would keep you from. In every moment, of every day in every way, allow your compassionate heart to lead the way from within, with light and love. Drop the labels that shape your light and shine bright in new ways that you are discovering. Paying attention to these, as you journey through life, will make you more aware of what is not you. Self-reflection is the greatest teacher and guide for which path to go down. It does not mean live from the past, just reflect for coincidences and synchronistic events that are not coincidences but signposts showing you the ways to the higher purpose which we all have.

In the light of a new day we can ride the rays of crystal clear light that will lead us to right places, right people and right situations which are our next best step in living a life intentionally full of purpose and meaning. In this chapter, of which I have been invited to write and share, my intention is to bring a timeless message from all that is divine and true in life. A message from the future here now that only you can get in your readiness to hear it for your self. A potent message meant for you, like in the series 'Conversations with God' by Neale Donald Walsch that so powerfully opened up my view of life and living, of which I am deeply grateful. THE POWER OF NOW and A NEW EARTH by Eckhart Tolle also moved me on a soul level of recognizing the truth on the pages, like it was written just for me to awaken to that which was brought forth in those books.

In the light of a new day we are fresh. You can awaken rejuvenated by giving all your cares and concerns to a higher power just before falling asleep. Set that as your dominant intention each night: to let go and allow life to sort things out for you in the night hours. The answers, guidance, people, places and situations will show up the next day to show you, that you are not alone and are listened to. Your thoughts are heard. Your thoughts create your world.

In the light of who you are, pay particular attention to children as much as possible. They are your future evolved self. Make it a point to go places to watch the spontaneous behavior of children. They don't think. They just do. There is nothing in the way of being. Children just be with what is. It is natural. There is much to be reminded of in their presence. You too have an 'aliveness' in the form of a child within you. Return to that with awareness. See the world from the innocence and non-attachment of a child.

In the light of a new day is the free flowing space of new ideas. New imaginings that will lift you up vibrationally. You will resonate to higher purpose and naturally attract matches to that. We must take responsibility for unintended, unconscious creations that we are living up against, all because we were not made aware of our powerful ability to create and co-create worlds that we live in.

In the light of a new day you can evoke timeless energy for all healing. We, the people, can transmute, transcend, and transform energy flow. That is the simplest idea one could have of themselves and why you are here on this planet earth. As a human being, we are flow-ers of energy. Life-force energy. How you feel is an indicator of how you are flowing life-force energy that grows what it is focused on. Life-force energy leaves when we release the body. Our consciousness goes on. As often proven by evidential mediums who can connect with those who have passed on. We are eternal.

In the light of a new day our consciousness can shift and we can really view ourselves and feel ourselves as 'People of the World'. We, the people of the world, are individually united. Remember the words, 'United We Stand, Divided We Fall'. We are a human family. We are a system. We go nowhere without each other. I really resonate to the expression 'we don't go until we all go'.

In the light of who you are, contemplate in your day that every single situation you encounter has had, at some point, a human being involved. Where would we be without each other? If on every loaf of bread there were the names and pictures of the human beings it took to get that bread on your table, you would then have the true ingredients as opposed to just wheat and flour, etc.

In the light of a new day we can come to deeply realize that me, is we. I, am you. You are the one in every one. We need each other. We are capable of so much more together than apart. We can be, and are, healers for each other. Healing can take so many forms. Think of healing as being the balancing of a system. Any system, be it the human body or a corporation. When we are out of balance, re-balancing is what is needed. We can be that for each other and the world. Re-balancing by re-cognizing and re-member-ing that which we already know as truth that is in every cell of our body.

In the light of a new day we can hear the timeless message from then to now. One is all. All is one. You are the one in everyone. We are different expressions of energy. We vibrate at different rates. We are much better together than apart. I am that, I am.

In the light of a new day we step into the bright light of who we really are. Beings of the light. Here to shine. Our consciousness evolving every day with our life experiences.

In the light of a new day we are born again and then again. Each moment of each moment of each new day we are changing. Different than the moment before. Evolving. Not from anything to anything. Just movement. Not good, not bad. Movement.

In the light of a new day we are reminded by nature that we are divine. We come from the divine. We are nature. We are a part of all that is and the 'isness' of it all. I wonder what life would be like if we could all carry the awareness that we are here to be the light of lights that we are. Guiding, reflecting that light for and with each other.

In the light of a new day, look to nature to constantly and consistently remind you that you are ever-changing, ever-evolving and not to become fixed or attached to mental ideas. Your thoughts about things can be moving like the wind.

In the light of who you are you can share the love and the wisdom that is so readily there when you are connected, clear and compassionate. In the awareness that we are a global human family that is interconnected we can start right within our own homes to be different with each new day. With each new learning. How can we be better human beings? How can we be an expression of the highest of who we are with consciousness as to the fact that we are that? We have always been consciousness experiencing itself.

In the light of who we are we drop labels of societal and familial conditioning. We be with what presents in our lives, for our soul growth. We experience ourselves having new eyes to see with. New ears to hear with. When we come out from under what has been conditioned onto us we can clearly see that we are not those labels.

In the light of who we are we realize that we are not the names our parents gave us. We try so hard to live up to someone else's idea of who we are instead of embarking on the journey of self-discovery and defining for ourselves, who we are. Self-reflection will change your view of you. And from that view we will see a very different world. A world where people are often acting out that which they are not, eventually getting to recognize that which they are. The longest journey is from the head to the heart. One we travel in the fullness of our aloneness.

In the light of who we are we can come to know ourselves as reliable, trustworthy, intuitive, knowing individuals that are contributing to something greater that is happening. Whether we know this fact or not, we can feel it from the place of deep connection and palpable inner-knowing. When we are not connected to our core, evidence is, everything looks and feels foreign. We are often fear-driven in this state. When connected we know that there is no authority outside of ourselves. Nothing and no-one can control you. Your mind is free. You can see beyond illusions.

In the light of who you are you can come to know yourself as someone who is meant to be here on this earth. Playing out a vital role. Contributing in unimaginable ways. You can't know until you know your life-purpose; then you will 'get it' in a way that no one else can tell you. Paying attention to what gets your attention is very important. This is life calling you up. Calling you to stand in you. To be you. To be in touch with you.

In the light of a new day a new you can emerge. Be open to that. You are the centre of the Universe. Y.O.U. You are the centre of 'Your Own Universe' (Y.O.U.). You are the point of change within each individual that will change the world. One of my many roles is that of Life Coach, and when I look into the eyes and heart of one person I see the world breathing there. So my work often involves individuals who I can feel are ready, able, and willing to make some profound transformational shifts in their personal and professional lives. We partner together for a while on a journey that releases the old stuck places and creates new movement in all directions of their life. You are that change waiting to happen in your own life. You can change the world by changing you for the better. For the higher awareness that we all are.

In the light of who you are your uniqueness 'is' your success. Discover, determine, define what is unique about you. Touch your essence. In doing that you will flow your divinity into a world that will receive it like a missing link that it has been waiting for to reveal a beautiful, harmonious view of life here on earth as it relates to the Universe. We are all here to contribute to the whole what no one else, not one other person can contribute in its uniqueness and expression. You are a combination of energies that is like no other. You are an individual in the whole of it all.

In the light of a new day if you want to get to know who you really are, notice who you are expressing yourself to be with each person you meet. We are all designed to evoke something in each other to show each of us who we are and who we are not. When you see who you are not coming out, choose differently in the next breath. Expressing the higher light of you. We are meant to light up each other's path as we travel along.

In the light of who you are whisper in a child's ear or hold the thought in your third eye of, 'You are light. And light you shall remain. You lowered your vibration to be here. You are an uplifter of humanity with your every thought and breath. And I see you. And I know you'. We all need to be re-minded. Often. And in many ways. This is why we are here. To remember and to wake each other up.

In the light of who you are how have you made a difference today? A difference in your own life as well as in others. This very action is what will grow you on a soul level. You are an evolving being whose most natural expression is that of love. Be in love. In everything that you do. Be in love. Not like romantic love. Be love. Let it flow to you and through you. Allow your heart to open, fill, flow and overflow.

In the light of a new day, be mindful. Watch. Observe. Ponder. As the Buddha says, 'accept everything that comes to you'. Be curious. Have child-like wonder. Express through soft eyes. Graceful hand gestures. Purpose-ful body movement. Grounded feet with a spring in your step. Lighteart-ed sharing. Peaceful posturing. Vibrant voice. Simple, meaningful, words. Unwavering stillness. Creative expression. Compassionate concern. Core connection. Be awake. Always available. Surround yourself with beauty in your environment. Let sound soothe you. Be where light can bathe you.

In the light of who you are look for reflections that resonate as good feelings in you. This is your innate guidance system showing you the way for more of the same. When something doesn't feel good, the same ap-plies. Alter your course until you feel waves of good feelings again. This is a communication that was agreed upon before you arrived to be on this earth plane as spirit having a human experience. You as co-creator here are manifesting in every moment. Raising your consciousness and creating with awareness will bring forth a peaceful, harmonious world. The one we are all meant to share. Together, as one. One being.

In the light of who I am I feel moved to share with you parts of my life that will give credence to the above statements. We learn best by example. So I will be giving real life reflections that have existed in my life. Of which it often feels as though I am on my fourth re-incarnation in this life. Many roles and expressions have been played to many people in many situations. People who called me forth and called me out in ways I never knew existed within me. As a stream of consciousness I will begin to list words that describe those roles, not necessarily in order: daughter, sister, cousin, aunt, great-aunt, mother, grandmother, wife, lover, housewife, divorcee, single, friend, student, teacher, coach, consultant, mentor, employee, employer, traveller, meditator, follower, leader, reader, writer, intuitive, psychic, medium, citizen, manager, gardener, truth-seeker, truth-teller.

In the light of who I am, in the roles I have played, some of the qualities brought forth that I got to experience myself moving in and out of are: liar, truthful, cold, warm, soft, hard, quiet, expressive, sweet, silent, loud, aggressive, suppressed, timid, caring, loving, hating, connected, mad, angry, passionate, peaceful, sad, confused, wise, stupid, heartfelt, careless, irresponsible, unconscious, conscious, light, asleep, awake, happy, miserable, optimistic, enthusiastic, scared, frightened, broken, broke, full, empty, gracious, kind, mean, critical, knowing, ignorant, emotional, forgetful, stressed, relaxed, clear, connected, restricted, expanded, insightful, inspired, ignorant, selective, listener, appreciative, irreverent, reverent, present, mature, childish, agitated, calm, heartfelt, cold, clear, deceitful, calculated, bright, gentle, curious, vibrant.

In the light of who I am, I as you, too, can get to see how you are all of it. We are energy. Energy moving. Energy expressing. Moments of movement we call life. Playing roles and expressing different levels of consciousness depending on where we are in our evolution in life. All moving us to being at choice in a higher expression of our most evolved self in any moment.

In the light of a new day I know that you too have acted out these roles and expressions. This is what we do as human beings. However we are all moving us towards an awakening that is happening in spite of ourselves. All of the Universal energies are lined up to support this new way of being for all of us here now on the Earth. You can see it in the children. Something is more awake, alert, aware in them.

In the light of who I am I can now see you in me. I can see me in you. I know through becoming aware of all my expressions, I can now be more compassionate toward my fellow human beings because I am to myself.

You are my family. Often we hurt the ones we love. Often we love strangers more than our own family. Let's be more aware.

In the light of who I am I can see how everything and everyone has brought out the best and the worst in me. Right out into the open so that I can see me in the best of times and the worst of times. From this perspective I wouldn't change anything. I have no regrets. All of it honours who I am, have been, and am becoming.

In the light of a new day I found myself really respecting myself and the gifts that people brought out in me. Gratitude fills my heart for all the role-playing we do for each other. We are brilliant in who we are to each other. Catalysts on a soul level. All the roles. All the expressions. All the people, places, and situations evoking aspects for us all to experience. Often I use an expression while coaching: 'there is only one of us here'. This just makes more and more sense to me, because coaching another is coaching aspects of myself. We are all cells in the mind of God. How can you know who you are, until you know who you are not. When 'who we are not' is reflecting back to us so we can see, we are not that. Yet we are all of it. This is the beauty of the evolution of consciousness. We are evolving through lower thought forms and expressions into our higher self. This is our destiny. The destiny for all of us who have been, and are here now, living on Mother Earth.

In the light of who I am now I can see me, the real me, not the one that I thought I was, or was trying to be, to fit in or please others' ideas of me. I now see myself and experience myself to be creative, capable, intelligent, intuitive, loving, generous. All of the qualities I would admire in another person and now recognize for myself through all my interactions with others. I am coming to know myself as a soul being. Growing towards a brighter, lighter expression of source energy.

In the light of who I am, learning how to relate to another has been a journey. It went from an unconscious journey to a more conscious journey now, which is how I refer to my work with people in coaching, consulting and mentoring. I can see how each and every human interaction has been knocking on the door of my soul to call out my growth and expansion. I can see now how all my life experiences, including childhood, were destined to awaken me into all that I am, from an environment that was a direct contrast to that.

In the light of a new day what I would want for the world is to be peace. To live harmoniously in light and love. We can be that for each other. Being that for ourselves first is the wake-up call. We can recognize each other, in each other. Why would any one want to hurt another? Simple. They are disconnected from their core self. Not that you can ever really be but you can live from the illusion of that. When connected you realize you are dishonouring your self on many levels.

In the light of a new day it is such a wonderful realization to know that we the people are connected to all that is. And that every thought and action sends out a vibration like a ripple in a pond that has a direct effect on the whole. There isn't a planet or star in the sky that is not affected by us as individuals and collectively the same is true. When the energies shift above, so do they below. We are directly connected. We are source to all in our life. We are oceanic in our consciousness. And oneness in our being.

We are the point of attraction for all that is in our life. This is a powerful knowing. Look for evidence of this fact, everywhere.

In the light of who you are, be there for each other in small ways. It truly is the little things that count. A twinkle in your eye. A smile on your face. A warmth in your voice. Be that for each other. What can you do today that empowers another person? Who can you be today that says 'you matter' to someone who needs to feel that? Where can you be of the most benefit in your community? What situations can you put yourself in so that you feel good about you? How can you shine in your life, so others can see your brilliance? What can you consciously overlook, so another can move through their shadow aspects?

In the light of who I am in this moment of writing I can feel my future self in all of you. I can feel you being inspired and called up to stand in you. Be the best you that you can be. While writing this I am evoking in myself what I am wanting for you to live. When we share our heart, our life, our love, we expand and from there you can feel the future and how it is going to be, because it is being created now, in the present.

In the light of a new day wake up to you as co-creator in this universe. Choose wisely.

In the light of who you are shine bright, love long, live free. Be presence.

In the light of who I am, I will live the highest of you, which is me, knowing that you are on your way now.

VISIONARY MEDICINE MAN FOR THE AQUARIAN AGE: DR EDWARD BACH (1886-1936)

Gaye Mack

WHEN Edward Bach abandoned orthodox medicine in the late 1920s in favour of his work with flower remedies, his reputation plummeted from that of genius to charlatan. Sadly, this affront from his own colleagues deeply affected Bach's way of life both professionally and personally, as often happens to visionaries. Nevertheless, in spite of the limitations that had become a part of his life, there was a deep 'knowing' within Bach that fuelled a determined foresight far beyond that of his contemporaries. Thus, we should not be surprised that this vision has been in the background of the whole mind–body–spirit movement from the time of his first discoveries in 1928, on. As flower remedies have been, and are increasingly emerging as the modality of choice behind so many other therapies and world views, it seems that Bach's humble work with the healing vibrations of the natural world was no less than divinely inspired.

The story of Dr Bach's career as a highly-respected orthodox physician and the course of events which led to his groundbreaking discoveries of the famous Bach Flower Remedies between 1929 and 1935, are well known, through numerous books on alternative therapies and other 'New Age' subjects. Although these publications are very informative and useful, with few exceptions, Bach's esoteric interests and spiritual beliefs con

---

In the United States, Gaye Mack was among the early group of Registered Practitioners with the Dr Edward Bach Foundation. Through the her graduate work and practice, her work with flower remedies has progressively expanding. She is the author of several articles on the Bach work, plus two books: IGNITING SOUL FIRE: SPIRITUAL DIMENSIONS OF THE BACH FLOWER REMEDIES, and MAKING COMPLEMENTARY THERAPIES WORK FOR YOU. For additional information on Gaye and her events in the USA and UK, go to www.womencreatingchange.com.

tinue to remain unexplored to any great depth. However, in his two books, HEAL THYSELF (1931) and THE TWELVE HEALERS (1933) these interests are very evident. His highly-developed sensitivity and symbiotic relationship to Nature clearly come through his words, reflecting his own spiritual nature and practical mysticism. Most importantly, it is these facets of Bach that were at the core of the remedies' discovery over eighty years ago.

Today, science has far less issue with the proposal that all form is actually condensed energy and that energy is vibratory in nature. This is something Bach intuitively knew as early as 1930. In his article, 'Some Fundamental Considerations of Disease and Cure', written at that time, and referring to the highest class of plants and their healing qualities, Bach states that such plants have 'the power to elevate our vibrations, and thus draw down spiritual power, which cleanses mind and body, and heals'.* Furthermore, in an address delivered in 1931 he is quoted as saying that the remedies 'which have been Divinely enriched with healing powers, will be administered, to open up those channels to limit more of the light of the Soul, that the patient may be flooded with healing virtue. The action of these remedies is to raise our vibrations and open up our channels for the reception of our Spiritual Self'.†

Nowadays, flower remedies are considered one of the major alternative healing modalities in the world. There is no question that the current use of and clinical research into flower remedy therapy in the global arena is because of the quality of Edward Bach's pioneering work and vision. As with other foremost vibrational therapies, they are 'medicine for the Aquarian Age', and a medicine or therapy that is increasingly gaining notice and use by the allopathic community.

What specifically stimulated Bach's interest in esoteric matters we shall never know, as this information is not available to us. But what is quite clear is that although Bach had a considerable interest in various subjects which were fashionable within the 'Spiritualist movement' of his day, it appears that his interest was not simply stimulated by the tide of popularity. As reflected by his own writings and talks between 1931 and 1936, esoteric matters resonated with him at a far deeper level. In other words, these matters didn't just resonate with him because he was a Freemason, but rather, they were part of Bach's very soul fabric.

*Mack, IGNITING SOUL FIRE, p. 72
†Bach, COLLECTED WRITINGS, ed. Barnard, p. 117

Clearly, Bach worked, spoke, and wrote within a metaphysical frame-work that feels quite familiar to us today. Further evidence of his esoteric con-templations can be found in his unmistakable reference to the collective of evolved souls known in metaphysical spirituality as the 'White Brotherhood'. In a letter written to a 'Brother' (presumably a fellow Mason) in 1934, Bach describes his anxiety for the future and that while lying 'near the tow-path at Marlow-on-Thames' a 'message came through'. He goes on to explain that this message was not only for himself, but also for all of those 'who are striv-ing to help'. Bach concludes his letter by stating that this experience would mean nothing to many people, but to him it was a clear indication of how 'the White Brotherhood work, amongst us, not by miracles, not by appari-tions, but by just leading us, if we are willing to be led, by every-day affairs'.*

As part of his soul's core fabric, Bach's interest in esoteric subjects was something that seems to have gradually emerged long before his discovery of the flower remedies. In her book, MEDICAL DISCOVERIES OF EDWARD BACH, PHYSICIAN (1940), Nora Weeks, who worked alongside Bach and then car-ried on his work following his death, relates through her personal experi-ence Bach's remarkable history. Even as a very young man, she notes, Bach was a keen observer of human nature, and seemed to possess a highly-developed intuitive sense about the suppressed emotional states of those around him. In his later years as a physician, this 'sense' extended to an awareness of obscured physical imbalances in others.

While his success as an orthodox physician and man of science grew in traditional circles, a major shift occurred in his experience with medicine in the later 1920s, one that had a tremendous impact on the direction his life was to take. Weeks relates that at this point he had become increasingly dis-satisfied with the methods utilized by those that practised traditional medi-cine. Privately, as a student of the esoteric, for him healing had become something other than a matter of treating the symptomology of illness or disease. For Bach, it was a matter of treating soul and spirit as well.

Bach's observations of his patients and those around him led him to formulate a theory on the origins of illness and disease, namely that they were a result of disharmony between the soul and the personality. Further, he was adamant that the method of regaining wellness came through harmonizing this disharmony.

*Bach, ORIGINAL WRITINGS, ed. Howard and Ramsell, p. 92

For Bach, *integrating the soul and the personality was the key to avoiding illness altogether.* He was also convinced that Nature held the keys to attaining this harmony. It was as if, in addition to what knowledge he had of the esoteric, he *intuitively knew* that the soul's message is to teach us how to feel. Through this process of both painful and joyful emotions, we develop our intuitive sixth sense, the voice of our soul. It would appear that this conscious awareness of the relationship between the soul and the personality was an indication of his own expanding awareness and the soul path intended for him.

What is particularly extraordinary is the realization that Bach's greatest work evolved during the darkness of the Depression of the 1930s. In this climate, there was 'something' that gave him the ability to 'see' light through the oppressive darkness that was sweeping across the globe.

If we consider what we know of Bach's personal history within the context of spirituality and how this context relates to his discovery of the flower remedies, we are offered an intriguing glimpse of Bach not only as a natural healer and psychic, but also as a mystic whose vision not only saw far beyond the mundane world around him but most importantly, his vision reached out to the threshold of our entry into the Aquarian Age. But, as with many visionaries through the ages, these gifts came to him at a heavy price.

Within the realm of esoterics, it is generally accepted that fragile nervous systems are not unusual in individuals who are gifted with the heightened intuitive nature we find in psychics, but also those who have the gift of clairvoyance or ability to see images or visions. In her writings, Weeks reports that he suffered intense episodes of physical debilitation during the discovery of the final nineteen remedies (1934–35). This discovery notwithstanding, Bach's health had always been chronically very fragile, and only soothed by the natural environment.

She reports him as saying to her, 'Are you ever unconscious of your body?' When she replied, 'Yes', he continued by saying, 'You do not know how fortunate you are. All my life my body has suffered in some way from pain and discomfort and distress.... I must know what pain is like and experience every kind to have a true understanding of what others suffer.'* Additionally, although Bach had a recollection of past incarnations in which he had always been a healer, Weeks notes that these memories meant little to him, and that his particular gifts of healing and 'sight', which he also acknowledged, were,

---

*Bach, ORIGINAL WRITINGS, ed. Howard and Ramsell, p. 181

as he put it, 'in higher hands' and could not be passed on to others.* Thus, seemingly, he was more concerned with the work he had come back to accomplish, because his work with the remedies could be passed onto others.

As noted, Bach, however, did find relief for mind, body and soul in the freedom he found in the countryside and it is in this context that we discover Edward Bach, Mystic.

In his beautifully written book, THE MYSTIC HEART (1999) lay Brother, Wayne Teasdale discusses the subject of mystics and mysticism at length. Unfortunately, this subject is too vast for extended exploration in this space, but we can, however, place Edward Bach in Teasdale's category of a Nature Mystic for this discussion and the impact that it has for us both presently and as we move forward into the age of expanded consciousness.†

Teasdale tells us that many people believe they have had at least one mystical experience in their lives. Furthermore, according to the nineteenth-century American psychologist and philosopher, William James, such singular experiences are identified by four general characteristics, namely,

1. They are more to do with feeling than intellect and cannot be conveyed using ordinary language
2. They have a noetic quality that manifests as a state of awareness beyond linear thinking.§
3. They transcend linear time, but rarely last more than a few moments.
4. They involve a state of passivity in the subject, as if the subject was 'swept up' and held safely by a supreme presence, not unlike an out-of–the-body experience.¶

However, there is a huge difference between the singular experience and identifying oneself as being a mystic. While the mystic path includes some of the general characteristics stated above which pertain to a single mystical experience, the reality is that it includes a great deal more. The mystic pilgrim is engaged in an ongoing process of travelling a very long and arduous path. Along this, there are certain markers or characteristics of identification.

*Bach, ORIGINAL WRITINGS, ed. Howard and Ramsell, pp. 181–2

†Readers interested in a more extensive exploration of Edward Bach as a mystic, please refer to my book IGNITING SOUL FIRE

§As used in this context, the term 'noetic' refers to states of knowledge that are beyond the ordinary intellect.

¶ *Harper's Encyclopedia of Mystical and Paranormal Experience*, p 384

According to Teasdale, the mystic pilgrim experiences distinctive states of consciousness and ways of being. Moreover, the path of the mystic is one that is practical and active. The mystic participates in his/her process, one that is beneficial to the ongoing soul-growth, and an experiential one. In other words, those on this path are in contact with what is ultimately real, according to Teasdale.* A mystic lives his/her path; he or she does not just talk about it. In addition, like the singular mystical experience, there are moments of awareness that lack sufficient descriptive language, but are implicit through a different way of knowing.

For the mystic, there is illumination of a universal connection between the temporal and cosmic world that does not require proof or explanation; it is integrative, absolute…. It simply *is*. Finally, Teasdale tells us that mystic spirituality is a practical, spiritual wisdom. In addition, within this wisdom there is particular knowledge of cosmic law and its process. The intuitive knowledge of this wisdom connects to the Divine at deep levels, and for some there is the added gift of sensing the emotions and motives of others when they are on their own journey.

While the path which the mystic treads manifests in many forms, expressions and traditions, there are specific characteristics that identify the mystic and the mystical path. It is in these characteristics that we can come to understand why Bach was a mystic.

Spiritual teachings, teachers, and scholars identify characteristics that are broadly-applied across many traditions and philosophies. However, because there are countless portrayals of mystics through the ages, we find that there is a collage that cuts across boundaries both sacred and secular alike. Mystical characteristics are to some extent subjective. Therefore not all 'mystics' will adhere to a precise list of identifiers, nor do all mystics exhibit mystical characteristics in the same fashion.

In exploring Bach from this perspective, we can discover the essence of this man beyond his gifts as a brilliant physician. Leaping into the new territory, we have the opportunity to witness an expression of absolute and contemporary mysticism, and in the process perhaps discover mystical characteristics within ourselves as we enter into the age of Aquarian consciousness.

A pattern that seems to appear with most mystics is that they disconnect, in a sense, from a life that has been familiar. How and when this dis-

*Teasdale, THE MYSTIC HEART, p. 23

connection takes place varies individually. For many the driving force is an inner struggle between the incessant chatter of the rational mind and listening to the voice of the Soul. As Bach began his work with the remedies, he identified this conflict as the cause of illness and disease.

According to Teasdale, who has quite a lot to say about the characteristics identifying Nature mystics, it is Bach's unique rapport with Nature that places him in this category. As a group, Nature mystics have an intrinsic connection to all of life through the natural world. For them there is an innate understanding of the symbology and messages nature freely offers to humankind.

For the Nature mystic this connection to the natural world is a 'reality [that] is revelational ... that trigger[s] higher states of awareness.'* In other words, there is an intimate relationship and, most importantly, a level of consciousness with the Divine through the natural world that simply does not resonate to such depths with others. Edward Bach expressed his symbiotic relationship with Nature and his service to humanity through the discovery of the remedies and his passionate desire that others freely learn how to use them for their wellbeing and discovery of soul purpose.

Some pilgrims on the mystic path also possess the extraordinary gift of high sensitivity to the motives and emotional depths of others. Edward Bach is included in this group. As Bach's intuitive abilities became increasingly stronger, he had the ability to heal by touch and, on occasion, had the ability to foretell events. Weeks notes:

Through his finely developed sense of touch he was able to feel the vibrations and power emitted by any plant he wished to test; and so greatly was his body receptive to these vibrations that it reacted instantaneously. If he held the petal or bloom of some plant in the palm of his hand or placed it on his tongue, he would feel in his body the effects of the properties within that flower. Bach's great compassion and links with all things and people formed a link between them and him, and by reason of this sympathy, he would hear the call for help from any in distress.*

In reality, Edward Bach's work with the remedies evolved into a therapy which functions on several vibrational layers within us. For most people familiar with them, the remedies are a therapy that addresses the imbalance or disharmonies we experience when are emotions are distressed. This

*Teasdale, THE MYSTIC HEART, p. 192
*Weeks, DISCOVERIES, pp. 50, 107

imbalance occurs within temporary situations and situations with which we have a history. However, Bach *knew* that they worked deeply on our spiritual body as well and was not reticent in speaking to this facet of their power.

Bach was intrigued with the patterns of numbers, which is not surprising as Freemasonry has its roots in mathematics. Referring to our 'emotional hindrances', he maintained that the keys to their transformation (so that we may access our spiritual self) rested in the spiritual heart of twelve distinct soul-types or soul personalities. Alongside these soul-types, he placed the first twelve of his remedies, those he identified as the 'Twelve Great Remedies', later calling them 'the Twelve Healers'.*

Clearly, the universe may hold an infinite number of soul-types, but Bach chose not to tackle the prospect of such a massive field and instead opted to keep his work simple within the twelve. He also maintained that these twelve soul-types comprised individual collectives, or groups, and that each of us belong to one of these 'soul-groups'. His message in all of this was that our own spiritual responsibility, along with that of our companions in the group, is about transformation. By working through the hindrance or soul-lesson of our particular soul-collective we have the opportunity to realize its 'virtue'. Thus, by engaging in the process of our soul's lesson, we each carry out our responsibility of imparting its particular virtue to the rest of humanity.† For each of us, this is *our service for all humankind, which is brotherhood in the widest sense and the universal message that drives the Aquarian consciousness.*

It is from this perspective that Bach believed that if we can identify our soul-lesson (by way of the soul-profiles of his Twelve Healers) we have the opportunity for transformation.

While there are slight variances in his philosophical language depending on the audience he was addressing and his own level of awareness, the essential spirit of his message remains constant. That message is that, at their foundation, the Twelve Healers are soul-medicine, capable of providing light into the hidden corners of a person's soul. They provide a bridge of light between the soul and our conscious awareness, bringing the wisdom held safely within the intuitive heart upwards into our reality.

Bach had a great deal to say on this subject, but overall, it is important

---

*Barnard, BACH FLOWER REMEDIES: FORM AND FUNCTION, pp. 140–41
†Barnard, BACH FLOWER REMEDIES: FORM AND FUNCTION, p. 139

for us to keep in mind, and have appreciation for, the fact that he himself was on a path of continual soul-growth and awareness. As a true mystic and healer, Edward Bach had the ability to facilitate the connection between his mind and intuitive heart, but this does not mean that his path was clear or easy. As his understanding and intuitive abilities deepened, he made modifications in some details and impressions concerning the remedies as a system of healing.

According to Bach's friend and colleague, Dr F. J. Wheeler, 'the last seven years of his [Bach's] life were lonely ones for him; his work, during that period, was based entirely on the knowledge that he gained intuitively and for such, the world has little understanding or encouragement, needing causes, scientific provings, before it is ready to believe.'* From statements made in one of his last public appearances before his death, it is evident that Bach had found solace in and connection to the Divine through his work with the remedies. He said:

> We carry a Spark of the Divine, that within us resides a Vital and Immortal Principle. And the more that Spark of Divinity shines within us, the more our lives radiate Its sympathy, Its compassion and Its love, the more we are beloved by our fellow-men.… From time immemorial, man has looked at two great sources for Healing. To his Maker, and to the Herbs of the field, which his Maker has placed for the relief of those who suffer. Yet one Truth has mostly been forgotten. That those Herbs of the field placed for Healing, by comforting, by soothing, by relieving our cares, our anxieties, bring us nearer to the Divinity within. And it is that increase of the Divinity within which heals us.†

Edward Bach was a man who did not view life through a tunnel but envisioned the entire universe. Whatever he learned, it seems that it was never enough. He concluded in 1935 that for this lifetime his work was finished. Bach *knew* that his time in this incarnation was coming to a close in the fall of 1936. He wrote of this to a friend that he was expecting 'a call to a work more congenial than of this very difficult world'.§ In all of his humility, his burning desire was to leave all human beings with a way to heal themselves. Were this not so, his discovery of the Remedies would

*Weeks, DISCOVERIES, p. 139
†Masonic Lecture, 1936, in Bach, COLLECTED WRITINGS., ed. Barnard
§Bach, ORIGINAL WRITINGS, ed. Howard and Ramsell, p. 173

long ago been relegated to the fate suffered by suspect cures of the times.

Fortunately this has not happened, in fact quite the opposite. Other healing therapies which are also based on energy or vibration, such as acupuncture, homeopathy (which Bach also practised), therapeutic touch, and laying-on of hands, just to name of a few, are slowly being embraced by the western bio-medical model. If Edward Bach were physically with us today, I think he would be astonished at the global breadth his work has reached in the last eighty or so years. Presently there are numerous major flower-remedy repertoires around the globe. This does not count the thousands of individuals who prepare their own flower remedies from their gardens and the fields of Nature, as Bach himself encouraged people to do. The fact that the discovery of flower-remedy therapy is universally acknowledged as exclusively his, speaks for the brilliance of Bach's work.

The magnitude of his work and its present significance can be further evidenced by the response to the international conference to celebrate his 120th birthday, held in Cromer, Norfolk, in October 2006. Spearheaded by Julian Barnard of Healing Herbs, Ltd. and like-minded colleagues, this two-day conference was attended by over four hundred medical clinicians, alternative therapists, flower remedy producers, and individuals from related disciplines representing thirty-two countries.

I have mentioned that there are numerous flower remedies being produced all over the world from indigenous plants. However, a specific example of this expansion can be found in the work presented at the conference by Patricia Kaminsky and Richard Katz, founders of the Flower Essence Society and the FES North American Flower Essences. Building their work and ongoing research upon Dr Bach's discoveries, Patricia and Richard have produced a collection of more than one hundred flower remedies from North American plants which are used all over the world. Moreover, using templates from her own work and as a mentor to flower remedy practitioners, Patricia opens our awareness to the depth of healing possible through the use of flower remedies.

Her 'Stages of Flower Essence Response' (Four R's) is a straightforward guide useful to both practitioner and individual as it clarifies both the action of the remedies and what can be expected in the healing process. She identifies 'Stage One' as the Release, Relaxation or Rejuvenation stage. In this initial stage the experience of the remedies is 'characterized by many sensations, which are often registered in the body. These changes may be experienced as a release of excess or dysfunctional energy, a general feeling of calm, or a sense of renewed stamina. Many diverse, but short-lived symptoms may accompany Stage One; these shifting symptoms occur as the energetic relationship between body/soul comes into a new alignment.' Stage Two brings 'Recognition and Realization' in which the

> 'benefits of the flower essences can now be more distinctly felt in the mental field, producing a variety of cognitive responses. Thoughts and feelings that operated just below the radar of consciousness can now be identified; there is increased objectivity and clarity. The flower essences help us to compare and contrast old behaviours or feelings with new alternative choices and solutions.'

In Stage Three, the individual is likely to experience Reaction, Resistance and Reconciliation. At this stage, 'it may appear that the condition has worsened or has regressed to an earlier stage of dysfunction. True change involves conscious choice and this often means that the soul must revisit its original wounding or trauma in order to bring renewed understanding that may not have previously been possible. Stage Three addresses underlying or unhealed aspects stored within the memory of the soul.'

Finally, Stage Four brings 'Renewal' and what Kaminsky refers to as 'Reconstellation'.

> 'In this stage we often see the emergence of entirely new aspects of the self. The active transformation of character defects results in new strengths and creative choices which would not have been possible without such inner work.*

Even though in his writings Dr Bach was not as specific in describing these processes as Patricia has been, nevertheless similar processes are implied if one reads Bach's words carefully. In describing and teaching the action of the remedies and the healing processes involved, Kaminsky has also created a more sophisticated model that places the multi-layered healing dimensions of flower remedies within an alchemical template that connects mind, body and soul. Although this model of Patricia's is more complex, particularly regarding its relationship to the current fields of consciousness studies and modern psychological theory, nevertheless, it is also precisely *in sync* with Edward Bach's intuitive vision long before.

*Kaminsky, Patricia, FLOWERS THAT HEAL

The work of Kaminsky and Katz are but two examples wherein this conference provided a forum for presentations that also included legitimate clinical studies of flower remedy therapy. Internationally, there is a great deal of ongoing clinical research into the value of flower remedies as an integrative element within healing models. These research studies are particularly active in Asia and South America, where ancient traditions of healing have not been disregarded in favour of the 'modern' bio-medical model for healing.

An example of the clinical research currently taking place is a published study into Dr Bach's well-known 'Rescue Remedy' as a pre-anaesthetic medicine.* The summary of this study was presented by Dr Shigeyoshi Toyota, Department of Anaesthesiology, Tsudanuma Chuoh General Hospital, Japan at the fifty-second conference of the Japanese Society of Anaesthesiologists, held in Kobe in 2005. The study followed the standard guidelines for a randomized comparative test and double-blind study using patients who were undergoing surgery and either having general or spinal anaesthesia. The ethical committee of the Tsudanuma Chuoh General Hospital approved the research. The outcome of the study indicated that Dr Bach's combination of flower remedies in 'Rescue Remedy' was successful in alleviating anxiety and tension prior to operations, and that it should be considered to have potential as a pre-anaesthetic medication.

Thus, through such efforts as provided by these examples, we can begin to see possibilities before us in the realm of healing if the concept of collaboration rather than exclusivity is embraced. Working with our differences rather than against them is the key if we are to evolve. In recent years there have been several visionary pioneers in the field of medicine who have recognized that this attitude is imperative.

As one of these pioneers in mind/body medicine in the United States over thirty years ago, Dr Herbert Benson of Harvard University recognized the value of meditation in reducing stress. Other physicians who were educated within the bio-medical model have followed Benson by exploring frontiers of healing that can not be explained or rationalized through the mechanistic model so championed by René Descartes three

---

*Rescue Remedy is a combination of five of Dr Bach's thirty-eight flower remedies, produced by the Edward Bach Centre in Oxfordshire. This combination is also known as 'Five Flower Formula', when produced by Healing Herbs, Ltd.

hundred years ago. James Gordon, Rudolf Ballentine, Andrew Weil, Deepak Chopra, Christine Northrup and Memhet Oz are among this group of physicians who have had the courage to wake us up to possibilities similarly envisioned all those years ago by Edward Bach.

In his book, HEAL THYSELF, Bach wrote of the future of medicine and healing:

> Healing will pass from the domain of physical methods of treating the physical body to that of spiritual and mental healing, which by bringing about harmony between the Soul and mind will eradicate the very basic cause of disease, and then allow such physical means to be used as may be necessary to complete the cure of the body.... It seems quite possible that unless the medical profession realizes these facts and advances with the spiritual growth of the people, the art of healing may pass into the hands of religious orders or into those of the trueborn healers of men who exist in every generation.*

He further envisioned that hospitals 'of the future' should be places of healing and how that would be accomplished:

> 'Let us now glance, for a moment, at the hospital of the future. It will be a sanctuary of peace, hope and joy. No hurry: no noise: entirely devoid of all the terrifying apparatus and appliances of today: free from the smell of antiseptics and anaesthetics: devoid of everything that suggests illness and suffering.... The object of all institutions will be to have an atmosphere of peace, and of hope, of joy, and of faith. Everything will be done to encourage the patient to forget his illness; to strive for health; and at the same time to correct any fault in his nature; and to come to an understanding of the lesson which he has to learn. Everything about the hospital of the future will be uplifting and beautiful so that the patient will seek that refuge, not only to be relieved of his malady, but also to develop the desire to live a life more in harmony with the dictates of his Soul than had been previously done. The hospital will be the mother of the sick; will take them up into her arms; sooth and comfort them; and bring them hope, faith and courage to overcome their difficulties.†

*Bach, COLLECTED WRITINGS, ed. Barnard, p.145
†Bach, COLLECTED WRITINGS, ed. Barnard, p. 115

Thus, the portrait of Edward Bach as a mystic and visionary well ahead of his time is one that we can learn from if we are awake and paying attention. It is a portrait that brings into focus some compelling realities about the man. In our contemplation, we come to realize that were he alive today, his compassion would undeniably reach out to us. Whether physician or friend, acquaintance or not, he would sit beside us, hold our hand and encourage us through our distress. He would stand at our back as we face difficult challenges and he would be healing us with his insights, energy, and medicine of the future through his remedies and the remedies of those dedicated to following in his footsteps.

'We each have a Divine mission in this world, and our souls use our minds and bodies as instruments to do this work, so that when all three are working in unison the result is perfect health and perfect happiness.'†

Edward Bach, MB, BS, MRCS, LRCP, DPH

†Bach, COLLECTED WRITINGS, ed. Barnard, p. 91

References
Bach, Edward, COLLECTED WRITINGS OF EDWARD BACH, ed. Julian Barnard. London: Ashgrove (1987)
—, THE ORIGINAL WRITINGS OF EDWARD BACH, ed. Judy Howard and John Ramsell. Saffron Walden, Essex: C W Daniel (1990)
Barnard, Julian, BACH FLOWER REMEDIES: FORM AND FUNCTION. Hereford: Flower Remedy Programme (2002)
Kaminsky, Patricia, FLOWERS THAT HEAL: HOW TO USE FLOWER ESSENCES. Dublin: Newleaf (1998)
Mack, Gaye, IGNITING SOUL FIRE: SPIRITUAL DIMENSIONS OF THE BACH FLOWER REMEDIES. London: Polair (2004)
—, MAKING COMPLEMENTARY THERAPIES WORK FOR YOU. London : Polair (2006)
Teasdale, Wayne, THE MYSTIC HEART. Novato, CA: New World Library (2001)
Weeks, Nora, THE MEDICAL DISCOVERIES OF EDWARD BACH, PHYSICIAN. Saffron Walden, Essex: C W Daniel (1973)

This chapter contains substantial excerpts from the author's book IGNITING SOUL FIRE: SPIRITUAL DIMENSIONS OF THE BACH FLOWER REMEDIES *(Polair).*

COMING OF AGE

Helen Petrow

THE DATE 2012 is more and more on our lips and in our minds with all of us aware that it represents the end of the Mayan calendar, but not quite sure what to anticipate further. In my view, just by an awareness of a common goal, just by a consciousness of time leading us somewhere, we tend to interpret the intervening time as a preparation, and inevitably to lend it a heightened importance, as if we were preparing for our 'coming of age'.

What might 'coming of age' mean, other than reaching our full potential, stepping into our power as individuals, expressing our creativity? And indeed, there is, in my experience, the increasing desire to take ourselves in hand, especially as far as health is concerned, and to explore possibilities which now abound to make ourselves well. Medicine, which was the prerogative of the medical doctor, has now left the hospitals and is in the hands of the individual. Patients, from being in the receiving role and accepting unquestioningly the advice of the physician, now read up on their condition to the point of being as knowledgeable as, or even more knowledgeable than, the 'expert', so they can challenge what happens to their body. They do not accept a governmental guideline for health just because it has been efficiently marketed and cleverly advertised, based on arguments which tap into their guilt and fear: they are able to glean information from many sources, discuss experiences of friends, decide what might be correct for their body or their children's bodies. We have all understood two fundamental principles: that there is more to being well than slavishly taking medication, and that each of our bodies is unique, and as such requires its own road to health.

These apparently simple and quite commonsense points have enormous implications. They hold the possibility that our illness, however complex it

Helen Petrow is a medical doctor specializing in rheumatology, and a clinical psychologist. She was trained in vibrational medicine by Jack Temple and now practises full time in Nairn, Scotland, where she lives with her husband and daughter.

may be, can be not only 'held at bay', but reversed, that in fact true healing can occur. In the past healing was seen as being in the hands of a few individuals with esoteric powers, who could bestow miracles on those who suffered. However this excluded the contribution of the 'will' of the individual. In participating in our own health, our free will is paramount, and penetrates right down to our sense of self: do we believe we can be well, do we believe we deserve to be well, are we prepared to make the necessary changes in our lives to achieve this? Again, in the past 'change' seemed a heavy and unappealing prospect, all intricately wrapped up in 'giving up' all that we liked best, and embracing a lifestyle of frugality and self-deprivation. However, if we accept that change is the very fabric of life, that each new moment is itself coloured by all the circumstances, quite new and different, prevailing at the time and with no necessary resemblance to what has gone before, then we can view it with curiosity and interest, and decide how we would personally like to influence this change. And if change is seen as a 'coming of age' and a stepping into one's power, then it contains the promise of creativity.

Thus free choice or free will is the element that is now the intermediate step between the symptom and the healer, and in understanding how it contributes to healing we must also ask why, in the past, the 'miracle worker' managed to create miracles for some, but not for all. We have always understood that a lack of healing implied that the individual, for reasons to do with his destiny, was not 'meant' to heal. We cannot exclude the possibility that at some level, factors prevail on healing that are beyond the powers of the healer and the free will of the patient. However let us try to understand more about the role of free will in 'allowing' healing.

There is no doubt that free will can be exercised negatively (impurity of thought) as well as positively (purity of thought). It is also clear that purity of thought may be present when the rest of the body is very ill, or full of dis-ease, which is why patients can know clearly what they need for their bodies to be healed, and sometimes travel a long way to reach the source of healing. This may not be easily explained rationally to others, and may not even be clear to the patient, so that 'free will' is not necessarily conscious thought. It is also not synonymous with unconscious thought, since our unconscious is influenced by our past life-experiences, but these may not affect our freewill. It is true that in the past miracles have been achieved with the complete submission of the patient to the healer: not, indeed, to the thought of the healer, but to what goes beyond thought, the intuition of the healer, or the extra-sensory perception of the healer, which dwells in the realms of the pure and the sacred, just as a place may capture and hold elements of healing which go beyond its physical attributes. Our intuition is reached through our 'third eye', or brow chakra, which Carolyn Myss in ANATOMY OF THE SPIRIT describes as 'the meeting place between our will and our spirituality'. As a patient seeking healing, we can temporarily link through our 'third eye' to the sacred in the healer or even a place, and 'drink in' what we need in order to heal. Love and devotion can help us establish this link more easily, since it focuses us on attaining the sacred.

We are trusting that the healer temporarily has more power than we do, and that through our access to the sacred we may be lifted up beyond illness and disease, in order eventually to tap into more of ourselves.

If we think of this in terms of energy it all becomes so much clearer. Energy has the power to create, be it love-energy, will-to-survive-energy, thought-energy, artistic-energy—and it equally has the power to destroy. Then it is fear-energy, anger-, guilt-, grief- or shame-energy. Interestingly, greed-energy, or thirst-for-power-energy, which we all imagine drives the frenzied materialism we perceive all about us, can always be understood in terms of something deeper, in particular one of the five emotions above.

If thought can change structure, it can do so at the level of the most infinitesimal particles, the tachyon, the atom, the molecule and also the cell. It can achieve this by transmuting the negative emotions into positive ones—compassion, happiness, peace and hope. These emotions carry their own power to create symmetry in the cell. Much of the body's immune function is based on recognition, in particular of proteins. Perfect structure represents a language universally understood, perfect recognition.

Why should compassion be such an important emotion for us? It derives from the Latin *patire*, which means 'to suffer', and means literally to suffer alongside, to feel with the other. It is interesting that the word passion comprises the opposite end of the emotional scale, the extreme of joy. It is as though inability to enter into the other's perspective excludes us from our own salvation. A system debilitated with dis-ease may need an infusion of healing to help to restore communication. Dis-ease in energy terms means disjointedness, disconnectedness, isolation from the whole. It implies inability to give or receive information correctly; for the cell it results in imperfect metabolism and division. Structure, in other words, directly influences cycle. It affects, therefore, future generations, whether it be of the cell or the individual. We still feel surprised to think that a negative experience in early life may affect us many years later. How much more surprising is it to think that experiences one hundred generations back may still be affecting our cells today? Is it thus not exciting to think how much wisdom, how much joy may be waiting for us in our own cells once we have managed to remove the dross? Then, indeed, we shall be able to allow positive, higher vibrations to prevail over the lower. What are these 'vibrations' other than the energy field surrounding the atoms, molecules, cells and outer body? They are easily picked up by those around us as harmonious or discordant, peaceful or resentful.

At an ordinary, everyday level we have a choice as to which it shall be— not, admittedly, to erase instantly the effects of the unwitting misdemeanours of all previous generations, but to set in motion a process allowing greater harmony at all levels. In the course of our day we function at several levels all the time, so that even when we are carrying out the most mundane of tasks, our emotionality is not far from the surface, and nor indeed is our spirituality—we have a kind of free-floating attention which registers a bird, a leaf, a flower, and which, in so doing, connects us to the universe. Despite us bringing all this to a simple task, these aspects are in fact disparate, and can aid or hinder us in our task. If our emotional energy is distracting us from our practical efforts, we accidentally cut ourselves or bang our head. If the impact of the woes of our existence is too great, it equally diverts us from our task.

At a cellular level the same is true. To fulfil its practical role of metabolism and division, a cell must be able to harness all its available energy—we do not want a distracted cell! The choices we make either generate peaceful, harmonious energy directed to a common goal—our desire to create a painting, for example, or to be well—or disparate currents of energy which detract from attainment of our desire. It follows, a little disconcertingly, that there are no arbitrary actions, no throw-away comments, every thought or action carries its own weight, and may be enhancing or damaging in its turn. If desire fills our thought, its attainment is in aligning our choices at every level, practical, emotional and spiritual. Then it does not matter how much of what we do is consciously understood, it only matters that we keep our goal before us and act only in accordance with it. Not only will this help us to heal ourselves, but it will take us to the highest pinnacle of our potential, while having the effect of making us respect ourselves and every other aspect of our world. Perhaps that is the meaning of our coming of age.

CREATING OUR EXPERIENCES

Dale Pond

WE LOOK around ourselves and see our life as we live our experiences. Sometimes we celebrate the wonder of it all, and at times we wonder how we got into the current mess. All the time not knowing where and how it all comes into being, who to thank or who to blame.

The good news is we are it. We create the good and celebrate and we create the challenging and whine about the misfortune. This is of course good news, because it puts responsibility back into our hands, hearts and minds. It means we can get a grip and make our experiences anything we want.

We've all heard these ideas before—that we can change things, be happier, be thinner, be wealthy and yet we remain as before—wanting better. Wrapped up in this idea we can change at will is a promise. This promise has been made to humanity for centuries. Even so notable as Jesus the Awakened One told us it was so. But where do you ask are the instructions? Where is there a path laid out simply and clearly that anyone could follow it to achieve their heart's content? Believe me when I tell you there is a simple and clear path. This path has been discovered, bit by bit, over the centuries and it has been proven to lead straight to a better you with new and improved life-experiences.

For this path to make sense to you we will look at some science of the mind and the force it uses to create what you are now experiencing and have experienced. For with an understanding of the working principles,

---

Dale Pond is a 'Renaissance man' with a broad background in many fields as author and lecturer and in acoustics and engineering. He has written over twenty books and many papers. Mr Pond is resurrecting the sacred science, philosophy and art discovered by John W. Keely and Walter Russell through the reconstruction and investigation of Keely's original Musical Dynaspheres. For a fuller biography, see http://www.svpvril.com/dalebio.html

which are all quite simple, you will see what you have been doing to create your life and how changing that activity you change your future experiences. It does not take a rocket scientist to change your life. It only takes some paying attention, will or desire to change, some insight sufficient to create a simple plan for yourself and the discipline to work your plan. So let's look at how it works.

After nearly forty years of investigating consciousness and higher level science supporting same, I can say with some degree of certainty that there are two fundamental states of energy in the universe, these being a dispersing state and a concentrating state. These two states can be expressed as discord and harmony, fear and love, or split and whole. These two states are the give-and-take building blocks upon which all else is built, whether a spinning galaxy composed of countless stars or the atom in your big toe. Everything everywhere and every time works on the same basic universal principles. These two seemingly opposite states are the root and substance of your thinking, being and life. They constitute the warp and woof of consciousness, materiality and Space and Time. These two states are the dynamic duo making up the duality of material and spiritual existence. Master these two states and you master life and all it contains or all you desire to create for yourself.

The First Principle is you are not a victim. You are a Creator. You are not an accident. You are a vital, meaningful and important part of what goes on around you. After all, you created it! And your continuing presence in your life is essential for it to unfold its purpose, which is to serve you. How is that for a cool insight—your life exists to serve you! The you referred to here is your consciousness awareness of 'I' and all its dragged-along appurtenances such as its dreams, spirit, body, wants and desires— the whole you. The real you is your mind, your consciousness, your awareness of being you. You cause your life by what and how you think on all the various levels of consciousness. Therefore you are Cause.

The Second Principle is your ongoing life. Your life is an expression or an Effect of your Cause. 'Your life exists to prove to you that you are right.'* Which may be expressed in diverse manners as a coming together or a falling apart. Your Life includes the various ways Effect manifests such as the car you manifested and drive and its condition and colour, the

*A COURSE IN MIRACLES

friends you attracted to yourself and associate with and everything else composing the elements of your life experience. Other synonyms for these two states as manifestations in and through your created life are peace and war, love and fear, quiet and noisy, warm or cold, health and disease, rich or poor, light and heavy and many other expressions* of this seemingly opposite duality.

Using these two principles it is plain to see that we can be in one of two mental states: calm, at peace and creative, or anxious, unsettled and destructive. The very interesting part is that we get to choose which state of mind we are in from minute to minute throughout the day. Sometimes we feel like we are blown around by circumstances, but when we know we are creative we can assume control. For some, our assuming control of our thoughts may take practice, but such control is attainable for everyone unless they have physical or neurological damage. We all know what being anxious, unsettled and destructive looks and feels like. As a mind persists in this chaotic state, it modulates the environment to be like itself. Chaos in the mind creates chaos in the life. Or chaos inside manifests as chaos outside. The calm mind is a mind at peace with its self, your life and all that is around you. As this consciousness persists it has an effect upon the environment and fashions that environment to be like its self—calm, peaceful and constructive.

It is clear to see then that if we change our mindset to one of perpetual peace and contentment (but never satisfied) our environment and all that it contains will likewise be peaceful and productive.

The unintended consequences come from aberrant thinking patterns. These embedded thought-patterns function much as a knot on a violin string. They inhibit coincident action by introducing discordance into the ordinarily harmonious chords of your creative thought. Almost always, these negative thought-patterns are on a level of consciousness we are usually not willing to access. It is possible to have good, clear and constructive thoughts on our more conscious levels of mind while at the same time having negative knots of thought on deeper unconscious levels. In these cases, conflicts are set up in our Creative Mind Forces, and our life-experiences consequently reflect those conflicts.

The ideal creative mind, then, is one that is purified of the negative

*http://www.svpvril.com/Cosmology/cosunity2.html

thought-patterns. Such a mind is whole and harmonious without disturb-
ing or destructive thoughts on any level of that mind. This state of mind
is usually referred to as the One Whole Mind, whereas the disturbed mind
is a Split Mind and discordant or egoic mind. The Whole Mind is in a pure
state of what some call universal and unconditional love. It is at peace. The
Split Mind is in a state of inhibition, fear and war.

There are many ways to achieve Whole-Mindedness. First and foremost is to take control of your thinking processes and stop creating new
negative thoughts and reinforcing those already present. Secondly, we
must undo or neutralize the negative embedded thought patterns, knots
or blockages.

Returning to a pure state of Whole Mind or Love has been addressed
by religions, philosophies and various disciplines since the dawn of time.
The details of this process have been sought after by the Pharaohs of
ancient Egypt, the mystics of the East, the various religious belief systems of yesterday and today. It is being pursued today all over the planet
by countless individuals making efforts on their own in their own ways.
Some refer to this purifying of the Whole Mind as Awakening or Self-
Realizing.

No matter what it has been or is being called, it boils down to clearing out the negative thought-patterns such that the mind is seen as whole
again. The interesting thing about this is the Whole Mind is ever-present.
It was never disturbed by our thinking mind, which is disturbed. So we
believe we have two minds when in fact there is actually only One Mind
misbelieving it is at war with itself. This brings us to the idea we are attempting to heal something that is in truth not broken or diseased. If this
were not true, then instant healings of the mind would not be possible.
One would be left with an arduous and lengthy process to rid the mind
of negative thought-forms much like the Dianetics process which does indeed work albeit slowly.

Instant healing or clearing comes from undoing the core belief we are
something other than what we are—Whole Minded awareness of I am.
Everything that is held in egoic consciousness is a mental creation—a belief or thought created by ourselves. And any thought can be rearranged
to be another thought. Therefore to change your life is to change your
thoughts. As they were created by you, you have total control over them.
Undo those original thoughts by whatever method works best for you and

all aspects of your life change to reflect your new concept of yourself.

You are free to transform your thinking and hence your life incrementally, to have better experiences, or you can let it all go and transform your entire existence by undoing the core misbelief that you are something other than Whole. These thoughts were beautifully expressed in my all-time favourite book A DIALOGUE ON AWAKENING:

Where does the healing of the world take place? When your mind again is seen as whole. The instant you look into a brother's eyes and see your Self reflected there. When your whole mind is known by you to mean every mind, all minds merged as One, the world will instantly change. It will be healed because you will see it to be so. You will have changed the cause by healing the thought of being separate from the Mind of God. The effect of then seeing only the world of God's Perfection is instantaneous. With the misperceived thought now gone, cause and effect have become the same.

In your place of knowing, you resonate with the truth of what I am saying. Yet even now your ego will stand in dispute, asking how it could be possible for you to heal your mind and thereby heal all the world. On this detail have you laid the foundation for your belief in separation. It is from this belief all other misperceptions of truth seem verified. For it is from here you have become convinced that you are a product of the world's creation, subject to all its laws and influence. You believe you are the effect and not the cause.

What is it like to be enlightened or awake? It is when you see only God as cause and effect being you expressing Him wholly. You will no longer feel the need to see your mind as separately identified within the whole Mind, but you will feel its presence there and you will recognize your Self in it. Fear of any nature becomes unknown. Joy abounds with every thought as Love is once again remembered. The bonding that takes place, that gels the mind as a whole, is this Love. It is not an exclusive expression of love you experience within your state of limitation. Here is God expressed. And His Love makes no distinctions.

I have referred to a concept I describe as the power of One, the power that results from individual expressions of the Infinite Mind as they come into recognition of their absolute unity—the infinite expression of wholeness, or One. It is this truth when fully grasped that will allow you to recognize yourself individually in the whole, as the whole, expressing the whole and coincidentally being wholly, uniquely you.*

*DIALOGUE ON AWAKENING

References

1   http://www.svpvril.com/Cosmology/cosunity2.html

2   A COURSE IN MIRACLES

3   Tom and Linda Carpenter, A DIALOGUE ON AWAKENING. Atlantic Books (1996), pp 3–4

4   Dale Pond biography http://www.svpvril.com/dalebio.html

WAKE UP!
OUT OF 'THE MATRIX' …
INTO 'THE DIVINE MATRIX'!

Morag Paterson

THE FILM 'The Matrix' had an electrifying emotional effect on me. It was one of life's 'Aha' moments, to which I resonated strongly both consciously and (I now realize) subconsciously. Suddenly I saw that what appears to be reality is but an illusion: nothing but a set of spoken words, thoughts and behaviours that are perceived by each and every one of us according to our own, literal, point of view, world view or paradigm.

What a fabulous gift to be broadcast to the world for all to see! A wake-up call indeed, I thought … yet I wonder how many of us 'see' something more behind the razzmatazz of fabulous film effects and compelling acting? How much had I missed and do I miss?

And even when we do grasp the deeper meanings at an intuitive level and 'get it', how many of us grapple with holding onto 'it' (the understanding, the feeling) for long enough to do more than simply notice? Even those who are 'consciously waking up' know it can be a fleeting and transient experience, this notion of consciousness. More urgently, how can we integrate 'it' (even transiently) into our being, into our day-to-day lives? This is, for me, vital: by consciously waking up to this awareness, we are not only true to our 'authenticity' (our true selves), we become a powerful (and ideally harmless) transmitter (and receiver) of evolutionary, positive energy in the world.

An 'evolution coach', writer, speaker, consultant and energy therapist, Morag Paterson encourages people (including herself) through transition and to live more consciously, wherever they are, whatever they do, however she can! She loves the magical simplicity (and complexity) of energy and natural systems, and lives mostly in France and Scotland.

Given the tide of twenty-first-century challenges we are facing, in our society, environment and economy, to learn to live consciously, to co-create together, is both an invaluable gift and a vital action: vital for the healthy continuity of all life on our planet Earth. We urgently need to wake up.

An example is the story of the boiled frog: if you put a pan of cold water onto the stove, add a frog, and turn on the heat very gently, the frog will sit pretty happily, until it gradually but effectively is cooked, without being conscious of what is happening. Take another frog and put it directly into a pan of already boiling water, and the frog will jump out. It feels, reacts and stays alive.

If we don't learn how to feel the subtleties, read the signs and take action, the same happens to us. Consider the recent economic crisis: it's been coming for a while, like the gradual warming up of the water....

You, dear readers, are already on the journey of evolving your consciousness, or are in one way or another consciously endeavouring to evolve. You are thereby also contributing to our 'collective consciousness', which, according to many evolved beings and writers across the ages, is gradually emerging now, and with significant shifts occurring up to, around and beyond the year 2012. So it is time to wake up.

The purpose of my small contribution to this eclectic cluster of 'vital messages' is to be a kind of midwife. Just as in any birth there's the right time, there's a process to go through, with symptoms and feelings, there are some things that can assist and nurture, others that can become barriers, and there's a result: a new-born. I want to help those of you who (like me) can get stuck in the birthing process, between worlds of unconsciousness and consciousness. I hope that in so doing, through the sheer practice of sharing, that we will feel encouraged, that the pain will be eased into joy.

It's about how to move out of 'The Matrix' (and all that represents unconsciously living) into the magical, light-filled and universal (one-verse) matrix of consciousness itself—'The Divine Matrix' (as Gregg Braden so beautifully calls it). To wake up to the Divine.

[Bear with me while I struggle with my own transient moments of consciousness and self-expression ... This is my first written piece on the subject, although I have been rehearsing for years. Procrastination is another symptom of being in the clutches of 'The Matrix'...].

Anyway, most books tell us that it's easy. It is simple. Anyone can do it. It's natural. And just like giving birth, it can be, and often is. But it's always different, and unique for each of us. So here goes....

An overview of the fundamentals is a good place to start, and in my view include:

Awareness of 'mind, body, spirit and soul with self, culture and nature' (thanks to Ken Wilber) which integrates anything you'd like it to, some included here but the list is, as they say, not exhaustive: social, economic, environmental, ethical considerations; learning styles: touch, see, hear, smell, experience, observe, think, react; core values, personalities, world-views, politics and Politics, behaviours; cultural differences and similarities; religions, beliefs; animal, vegetable, mineral kingdoms ... and any other category or sub-category of life as we know, sense, see, feel or perceive it.

To become alive, awake and whole, it seems we explore these multiple aspects as best we can, and as we become more aware, notice areas that we can balance out, explore further, or even touch on for the first time, so that we can become more 'holistic' and evolve in the true sense of the word, which takes us beyond our current thinking.

We might describe our consciousness through a spiral of evolution, of the thinking, beliefs and values that underpin our behaviours, and how we are affected by our life-circumstances.* A tiny proportion of the world population is currently 'able' to think and be in truly emergent ways: holistic, collaborative, big picture, interconnected, dynamic, managing complexity for the good of all, with good grace. And yet, a tiny proportion of the population thinking differently can initiate a change in consciousness....

As Einstein said, 'The solution to a problem is never found from the same thinking that created it'.

So everything is connected.

We have trodden our path, to date, and you (like me) have undoubtedly found that books, people, poems, music, words have struck you as important, useful, sometimes paradigm-shifting. Many of us believe that we 'attract' what we need to hear, see, know, 'get', and sometimes it can be quite obvious: 'if at first we don't get the message from the universe, it'll come harder and harder until we do' is a fairly common understanding and one that I have believed and trusted in for the last twenty years, as consciously as I could. Some messages have hit me from the outside (re-

*see Don Beck and Chris Cowan, SPIRAL DYNAMICS

lationship breakdown, car crashes, books, circumstances) others from the inside (inspirational Ahas, brought about usually after times of crisis, pain or chaos and resulting pressure, or through times of feeling more detached and open).

Many authors and seers over so, so long have enthused about positive thinking, affirmations, that matter follows thought, that we create every thought that we have, have been so clear that this is the secret of success-ful living, of overcoming barriers to love, money, health. And so we read the books, listen to the tapes, get excited, start the new discipline, begin the journal-writing, write wish-lists, recite affirmations, write down and burn our old beliefs on bonfires or by candle light, learn to meditate, to ask through prayer, talk to friends and say our life is now changing, and we want to believe that it is. And sometimes it does. And undoubtedly it is, to one degree or another—because everything IS connected. And it lasts for a while—a few days, some months, whatever. Or so it feels.

And yet somehow we still don't 'get it'. The sense of hope, the feeling of change, the desire to continue wears off ... and before we know it, we [... OK, I...] feel back at square one. Pulled back into 'The Matrix', having had a sense of the 'Divine'. It's as though the force of the environment—of the newspapers, TV, mainstream media in general and reported news in particular; the general craziness of the world; the mundane chatter of some relationships and the lack of honesty in others; the dull expectations that we have of each other; the 'plastic' feel of policies and procedures that make no sense, the lack of authenticity—pulls us back into a world of sleeping, a flatland, monosyllabic, monotone, robotic rut where we are powerless once again. As depicted in 'The Matrix', the movie.

Until the next urge takes us to start over (the next person, their sparkle, the words in a book, the film, the conversation, the therapeutic session) and moves us out of our lethargy...

This seems to be a cycle that goes on and on for many. I know: it has for me. And yet it is natural process, almost like a natural blue-print of life, and it will pass, as all things do.

So energy flows naturally.

Strangely—much like giving birth to a baby—there is much explora-tion of the preparation to the birth, explanation of the process itself, what to do (and sometimes we give up the natural process so that we can be 'properly taken care of' to ensure a safe birth, and sometimes of course it is helpful to know that help is at hand as required). However, the simple fact that our own experiences will be unique to us, and probably unexpected, is never explicit. It's as though we want to override the unspoken, to make it safe, to show the way, to control a natural process.

So my bit of midwifery is to remind us this is so. That there is often a 'pause' between the in-breath and out-breath, a mixture of chaos and order: a cha-ordic cycle. The books I resonate with and that inspire me are written by people who, in a sense, are already out of 'The Matrix', and are in 'The Divine Matrix'—they are 'unplugged', more awake, are developing their sense of consciousness, are speaking the language of 'the universe'. By the time they are 'there', it is simple, just as any mother will find it hard to express what she went through to give birth to her baby. 'There' has become her 'here'. Nature works in miraculous and mysterious ways so that we 'forget' the details (otherwise we would find it hard to get motivated to give birth again!).

Sometimes, it feels as though I—and maybe you too—have started the birthing process, but it is not continued, or I don't continue. Is it my choice, or is it the environment that affects me? Anyway, it feels I am out of control and I am drawn back into sleep, into waiting. Ironically, that's when it can be comfortable and life goes on, day after day, reading, being, doing as best I can.... At other times it is about feeling abruptly shocked, shattered and deeply concerned by the reality of the world around me— the flatland, one dimensional reality I can be surrounded by, with others asleep, even though they are pretending to be awake ... in the media, in politics, in industry, along the street....

Like the caterpillar that transforms into a chrysalis and then emerges as a butterfly, it is part of a process. It does not 'think' about when it will be the best time to begin, how long it will 'incubate' for and how it will emerge ... with what colours on its wings. The caterpillar unconsciously is, and, guided by a universal consciousness, becomes all that it can be: a beautiful butterfly.

If a caterpillar could describe what it went through, it would talk of feeling tired, going to sleep, a feeling of being in glue, and being a bit stuck, with strange things happening which it had never expected or experienced before. And if it could see out of its chrysalis, it would look as though things weren't really 'happening'. Some chrysalises don't 'hatch' at all, some 'hatch' earlier than others, some take longer, some are eaten: all sorts of things happen, and yet it is part of a natural system.

So take heart: it's normal! Human-being symptoms in this chrysalis stage, or birthing process, can include:

Knowing that there is something more but being unable to grasp it.
Feeling not particularly present; in fact not feeling much at all, if anything.
Knowing something is happening but not sure what.
Trying hard a lot.
Feeling like life is a pretence, an act, a performance, 'plastic'. (An image came to be that I was a 'cardboard cut-out'—but that's another story!)
Not engaged, not really caring.
Not feeling 'alive' or energized.
Things are an effort—most things, everything.
Keeping trying new things: the next book, another course, being guided by others' ideas.
Comparing ourselves with others.
Lacking a sense of self, a boundary.
Feeling alone.
Feeling worthless, negative thoughts.
Feeling disconnected.
Depression and fatigue.
Feeling afraid.
Finding it hard to communicate with others, not making connections.
Forgetting all that we know, particularly those things that helped us so much very recently (the new discipline, the affirmations ...).
Things just don't feel right.
Dis-interested.
Stressed.
Body shape changes.
Constant ill-health issues (colds, aches, pains, small niggles).
More major health issues (disease).

It can take some time. Some things help, and it is a good idea while you are waiting to keep doing the helpful things. This is not rocket science. I know you know, but I'm repeating here for good measure (because we forget):

Laughing—having fun.
Relaxing your muscles, relaxing in general.
Exercizing.
Eating well—fresh, fruit, vegetables, balance.
Being with people who make you feel good.
Fresh air, being in nature.
Making your environment comfortable.
Checking that your needs are being met—even small ones.
Keeping things simple and easy.
Giving compliments, doing a good turn.
Thinking nice thoughts.
Breathing in and breathing out consciously.
Affirmations.
Meditation and Prayer.

(The opposites of all of the above do not help, and symptoms are likely to worsen, or take longer to pass.)

So everything is energy.

Metaphysics, cell biology, quantum theory, string theory, chaos theory … all that is explicit in the New Science shows that not only is everything connected, but that everything is energy. And this energy is Universal; that is, it just is. There is a field of energy within which we all and all of life exists: 'The Divine Matrix', that of which we are all part if only we can remember how to be it!

> 'We are spiritual beings having a human experience, not human beings having a spiritual experience' Wayne Dwyer

The difference between us as a human-being and a caterpillar is that we can and do 'think' and thereby shape our reality. Groundbreaking research by Bruce Lipton has shown that 'genes and DNA do not control our biology; instead, DNA is controlled by signals from outside the cell, including energetic messages emanating from our positive and negative thoughts'.

Many of the symptoms of being low, 'in The Matrix', asleep, or lacking consciousness relate to our thoughts. Part of the magic of the transformation is to realize that we ARE these thoughts! Quite simply, we are what we think. Matter does follow thought. And it is what many poets, writers and sages (among others) have known and shared with us for a very long time.

If we think something a lot, it becomes a belief. It follows that if we change the thought, we change the belief. This is where affirmations are important: they really do work (mostly). So part of the process is to first know what we don't want, then to discover, define and really know what we really do want, then think about it a lot (and write it down, say it and talk about it), and by so doing we create our reality (sometimes, if we can stay on track for long enough...).

And this is the extra bit of the process...

A vital part of 'waking up' is getting 'feeling' activated in our systems. Feeling expresses our emotion, and is the current that electrifies our thought, that translates the thought into a language that is understood by the 'Universe', where everything is energetically connected. If the dialogue is in our head rather than in our heart, and we do not 'feel' or resonate with our thought, it won't translate into reality. It's as simple as that.

Our body's energy system simply works like the software on a computer. Sometimes negative thoughts get 'stuck' in our body, in our energy system, much like a malfunction in the software of a computer. On the surface things appear fine, but internally there is a malfunction, a blip on the circuitry, which loops round and round, gets wound up, slows the system down, uses loads of energy and eventually crashes (like we crash with stress or disease).

Without clearing these blips, we can stay stuck 'in labour', literally, not feeling as though we are passing through the natural, creative process of transition and transformation. Energy remains low, we feel plastic, out of body, straining and striving, rather than energized, aligned, connected and in tune. And even affirmations don't work!

Since we are energy, we must clear any limiting beliefs so that what we think can truly manifest, and then believe it! Because it works! The important thing is not the technique itself, but that we find a way that speaks our own language, that taps into our energy fields and systems, thereby tuning into the vibration of the energy surrounding and supporting us. By getting our own internal language and communication cleared, we can communicate more openly—and play!—with the magical Universal energy, learning to let go and trust, rather than control through fear.

So, in a few words, everything is energy (including us), everything is connected and has a natural flow. We have the power to create our thoughts, and our reality, positive or negative. The midwifery of the process is simply that the language of the universal energy is feeling, so feel it and you are already creating your reality. The creation of our positive reality can take a while (as part of a natural process of incubation, and because of some limiting beliefs we may hold), so be patient and keep being. Clear the limiting beliefs, by clearing our own energy system, and then trust that our thoughts create our reality.

We can just as easily continue creating 'The Matrix' environment for ourselves and each other by continuing to do and be what we have always done or been, or we can just as easily wake up (through experiencing an 'Aha' moment!) to the power of clear, good, high-quality thoughts, and become part of the energetic impulse that triggers the magic of 'The Divine Matrix'. It is simple, after all.

Wake up!

References

Beck, Don Edward, and Cowan, Christopher, SPIRAL DYNAMICS. Oxford: WileyBlackwell (2005)

Braden, Gregg, THE DIVINE MATRIX. Hay House (2007)

Lipton, Bruce, THE BIOLOGY OF BELIEF. Hay House (2008)

Vitale, Joe, SPIRITUAL MARKETING. AuthorHouse (2001)

Wheatley Margaret, LEADERSHIP AND THE NEW SCIENCE.Berrett-Koehler (2006)

Wilber, Ken, THE THEORY OF EVERYTHING. Gateway (2001)

SYNTONY AND FLOW: THE ARTSCIENCE OF EVOLUTIONARY AESTHETICS

Alexander Laszlo and Kathia Castro Laszlo

Introduction

Have you ever wondered what it would be like to flow the universe—to live in harmony with Planet Earth and to consciously and ethically explore our human potential? To ruminate on such things is not the idle flight of fancy—it is an indicator of the evolution of consciousness and the mark of conscious evolution. For it is precisely such ruminations that stand the chance to midwife the emergence of life ways for the sustainable co-existence of humankind with planet Earth.

Sir Arthur Conan Doyle, to whose memory this book has been dedicated, engaged in such considerations together with his friend and colleague Edward Gardner, and ninety years ago penned his vision in THE VITAL MESSAGE. In the preface to that work he indicated that preparing for the future is less a matter of being 'rapture ready' and awaiting the 'descent of the spiritual to us, but [of] the ascent of our material plane to the spiritual, and the blending of the two phases of existence. It is, at least, a fascinating speculation'. For a man whose knighthood was bestowed for the writing of

Alexander Laszlo, Ph.D., is co-founder and President of Syntony Quest and Professor of Systems Science and Evolutionary Development at various graduate schools internationally. He is on the Editorial Boards of four internationally arbited research journals, active member of several systems science societies, and author of over fifty journal, book, and encyclopedia publications.

Kathia C. Laszlo, Ph.D., is co-founder and Executive Director of Syntony Quest and Professor at MA and Ph.D. levels at various universities internationally. Her work bridges scholarly understanding with practical application in areas of organizational change, leadership, and development of human and social capital for sustainability. She is author of numerous peer-reviewed publications.

a military analysis in defence of the United Kingdom and who is most well remembered for the mystery-solving sleuthing of the brilliantly reasoning Sherlock Holmes—to whom he referred as 'the centre of deduction and inference and observation' of his tales*—such fascinating speculation is well worth remembering ... and taking forward.

Toward an Evolutionary Aesthetic

Many have written about the need for a new world ethic, even an emergent or evolutionary ethic†, and there is no doubt that this is not only important but essential to the future wellbeing of our species. However, before even the ethics of evolution—which speaks to our transcendent moral response ability—comes the need to nurture and cultivate the aesthetics of evolution. This addresses our transcendent perceptual sense-ability—that which provides both seat and compass for all our ethical considerations.

Ethics is based upon reason, and such higher cognitive function is entirely dependent on the underlying capacity of individuals and groups to grasp something they deem worthy of reasoning about. We do not waste time with thoughts, things and dynamics that appear irrelevant, uninteresting or unworthy of our attention. It is our aesthetic sense-ability that helps us determine where to direct our attention and what to consider worthy of reason.

To a large extent, the quest to midwife the emergence of lifeways for sustainable co-existence of humankind with planet Earth has to do with an emerging domain of inquiry that can be called evolutionary aesthetics. All beings have a sense of discernment and discretion, that which biologists define as tropism. This allows for inclination toward certain stimuli and away from others, and in human beings fosters the ability 'to live in harmony with deep enjoyment.'§ Have we forgotten how to do this? Those who take inspiration from the likes of Conan Doyle clearly haven't. But many of our mega-industrial, hyper-technological, and super-rational societies have dampened down our everyday aesthetic sense to the point where it is this atrophied little thing dangling off the edge of our consciousness that blooms only in the safe havens of museums and concert halls. In despera-

*Chalmers, *The Independent*, August 7th, 2006, p. 1
†Loye, MEASURING EVOLUTION
§Barber, HUMAN NATURE OF BIRDS, p. 159

tion we turn to mysticism, magic or transcendentalism, but in doing so often 'tune in' to things not at all part of the organic evolutionary narrative. If some things diminish our aesthetic sense-ability while others amplify it, how are we supposed to know what to tune into? To come to grips with this question of the 'appropriateness' of our much civilized tropisms, it is well worth remembering how those of traditional or 'wisdom' cultures tune themselves.

'The idea of 'appropriateness' is central to the Indian experience of the natural world', says N. Scott Momaday†. He explains that in the native American Indian worldview writ large, appropriateness is 'a basic understanding of right within the framework of relationships, and, within the framework of that relationship ... between man (sic) and the physical world. That which is appropriate within this context is that which is natural' (p. 504). He tells a story about appropriateness that nicely expresses its lived essence.

> There was a man living in a remote place on the Navajo reservation (in Southern Utah) who had lost his job and was having a difficult time making ends meet. He had a wife and several children. As a matter of fact, his wife was expecting another child. One day a friend came to visit him and perceived that his situation was bad. The friend said to him 'Look, I see that you're in tight straits. I see you have many mouths to feed, that you have no wood and that there is very little food in your larder. But one thing puzzles me. I know you're a hunter, and I know, too, there are deer in the mountains very close at hand. Tell me, why don't you kill a deer so that you and your family might have fresh meat to eat?' And after a time the man replied, 'No, it is inappropriate that I should take life just now when I am expecting the gift of life' (p. 504).

This man was 'in tune' with his world, and in this sense had a well-developed aesthetic sense-ability. The ability to descry what is right 'within the framework of relationships' between humans and the physical world is perceptual. This ability lays the foundation for an associative reasoning that is more cognitive and valuative. As Momaday points out, this sense of appropriateness, of goodness of fit, implies a moral sense as well: 'There

†Momaday, 'Native American Attitudes Toward the Environment', p. 503

is this moral aspect, and it refers to perfect alignment. The appropriation of both images into one reality is what the Indian is concerned to do: to see what is really there, but also to see what is really there' (p. 505). This expression gets at the heart of the type of vision that can grow out of a well-developed aesthetic sense-ability used to cultivate a sense of ethical response-ability. To the Western mind, it may appear cryptic if not all together abstruse, but Western philosophy offers a complementary, though not identical, perspective. We might assert that epistemological reality (the world of thinking and knowing) is socially constructed, while ontological reality (the world of being and doing) is interactively emergent, and that aligning the former with the latter requires using the former to inform and guide the latter. Though less cryptic, this may not be any less abstruse. It bears mulling over, though. To understand it better, we can try to understand the 'perfect alignment' Momaday talks about by considering the two visions of the relationship between humans and the natural world that the Indians (particularly among the cultures of the Plains Indians) hold simultaneously. One is physical and the other is transcendent. According to Momaday,

> it's rather like looking through the viewfinder of a camera, the viewfinder which is based upon the principle of the split image. And it is a matter of trying to align the two planes of that particular view. This can be used as an example of how we look at the world around us. We see it with the physical eye. We see it as it appears to us, in one dimension of reality. But we also see it with the eye of the mind. It seems to me that the Indian has achieved a particularly effective alignment of those two planes of vision. He perceives the landscape in both ways. He realizes a whole image from the possibilities within his reach. The moral implications of this are very far-reaching...' (p. 503).

This effort at alignment finds its parallel in a variety of traditions. They may take many shapes and forms but in some way they all have to do with seeking to align or strike a balance between the spiritual and the material, the transcendent and the mundane, the perennial and the temporal, the archetypal and the idiosyncratic, the ideal and the real... This is very much what is entailed by a lived expression of conscious evolutionary aesthetics. The incorporation and subsequent embodiment and enaction of such a sense-ability involve creating (imagining/dreaming/visioning) images of reality that are both ideal and have this 'goodness of fit', or appropriateness, with the world around us. It involves listening with evolutionary ears, seeing with evolutionary eyes and feeling with evolutionary heart.

A Leap of Vision

Imagine what it would be like to live in the world with the sense-ability of an evolutionary aesthic and the response ability of an evolutionary ethic—fully functioning and fully engaged. Inspiration for what this might entail comes not only from the wisdom practices of traditional cultures but also from the imaginings of creative minds that reach out to portray future possibilities through fictional thoughtscapes. Isaac Asimov was just as much a master of the literary form as was Sir Arthur Conan Doyle, though his realm was science fiction rather than mystery. In the fourth of the five books of his Foundation Trilogy, he writes of a planet called Gaia. The planet is not our Earth and the story he recounts is set far in the future. However, as he tells it we are let in on a vision of what things could be like for us were the evolution of consciousness to develop to its full potential on a planetary scale. Let's follow Dom, a being from Gaia, as he shows his artscience hobby to Trevize and Pelorat, the intrepid space explorer and his donnish old friend who has accompanied him there....

> He led them way into another room where, on a small circular table, there was a group of smoky lenses connected in pairs.
>
> 'These,' said Dom, 'are Participations I have designed. I am not one of the masters, but I specialize in inanimates, which few of the masters bother with'....
>
> 'How are they used, Dom?'
>
> 'You put them over your eyes. They'll cling. They do not transmit light. Quite the contrary. They obscure light that might otherwise distract you—though the sensations do reach your brain by way of the optic nerve. Essentially your consciousness is sharpened and is allowed to participate in other facets of Gaia. In other words, if you look at that wall, you will experience that wall as it appears to itself'....
>
> Pelorat placed one pair over his eyes and they clung there at once. He started at the touch and then remained motionless for a long time....
>
> Dom said, 'What did you experience?'.

Pelorat said, 'It's hard to describe. The wall seemed to twinkle and glisten and, at times, it seemed to turn fluid. It seemed to have ribs and changing symmetries'....

Dom sighed. '… these Participations are enjoyed primarily for their aesthetic value, [although] they have their practical uses, too. A happy wall is a long-lived wall, a practical wall, a useful wall.'

'A happy wall?' said Trevize, smiling slightly.

Dom said, 'There is a dim sensation that a wall experiences that is analogous to what 'happy' means to us. A wall is happy when it is well designed, when it rests firmly on its foundation, when its symmetry balances its parts and produces no unpleasant stresses. Good design can be worked out on the mathematical principles of mechanics, but the use of a proper Participation can fine tune it down to virtually atomic dimensions. No sculptor can possibly produce a first-rate work of art here on Gaia without a well-crafted Participation and the ones I produce of this particular type are considered excellent—if I do say so myself'*

The idea that aesthetics underlie harmonious design comes across clearly in this piece. In fact, Dom implies that art is necessary to 'fine tune' applied science for the dynamics of physical existence to be not only harmonious but actually felicitous. Of course, his Participations are an advanced form of technology that can be used to heighten aesthetic sense-ability. However, it may be possible to evolve our consciousness so that such crutches are not necessary. The challenge is to interpret the flow of events through which we consciously participate in the shaping of our futures and those of all things with which we interact, and then to learn to intentionally align our actions with evolutionary purpose. In this sense, evolutionary aesthetics are the Participations of our consciousness, and it is up to us to craft, polish, continually refine—and above all—employ them.

It is a craft, you know. It is inherent in the human mind, but it must be developed in a very subtle and difficult manner. It takes many generations to reach its full potential, but once well begun, it feeds on itself. We have been at it for over twenty thousand years and the sense-of-Gaia is that full potential has even now not been reached. (p. 363)

* Asimov, FOUNDATION'S EDGE, p. 356

So it seems Gaia may have a bit of a head start on us, but it is not too late for us here on Earth! In fact, the timing couldn't be better. Who knows where this process of conscious evolution could lead given twenty thousand years, and the important thing to realize is that we are given twenty thousand years—and more!! What will Earth be like in twenty thousand years—like Gaia, or like a barren radioactive wasteland, or just another planet—maybe with life and maybe even with intelligent life, but without human descendants? Which narrative we participate in creating will depend on the vision we have and the volition we evince as conscious participants in the play of evolutionary emergence.

In the long run we may look back and, like one of Asimov's characters, think how 'we do not understand a human being who cannot sense his (*sic*) place in the scheme of things, who does not feel like part of a greater whole' (p. 389). At this point in the adventure of our species on this planet of Earth, it is the combination of evolutionary aesthetics and evolutionary ethics that stands the best chance of providing a future-creating, life-affirming and opportunity-increasing pathway. The first step on this journey begins with the heartfelt realization that what we do—both as individuals and as a species—counts, for this is the essence of evolutionary response ability. But even before we take this step, we must first let ourselves know that what we feel counts. This is the essence of evolutionary sense-ability, and without it we may never develop the necessary Participations of consciousness.

Toward an Evolutionary Normativism

What is needed to launch our global civilization with conscious and intentional participation is some sort of 'evolutionary compass'. The fact of the need for such launching has been provided in vital messages since Conan Doyle's day and before and is being continually repeated in this day and age: 'The ideas and visions we now produce could be the butterflies of the [near future]. It is up to each of us to flap our wings—and to make use of the chaos of our times to launch our bifurcating societies along the humanistic path'.* The compass by which we might do so ought to provide some way of guiding our efforts so that they are harmoniously aligned with the general evolutionary processes of which we are a part. Our accustomed world

*Laszlo, Ervin, THE CHOICE, p. 61

of particulars is not up to the task since it is, by nature, chrono-centric and homo-centric. This is to say that the visions of any given society are products of their time, and the values are based in civic, educational and religious institutions that inculcate dominant moral-behavioural norms.

The norm upon which to peg our compass is nature, not idiosyncratic human proclivity. Nature over time is evolution, and it is important to realize that we are not merely the products of evolution, in a very fundamental sense we are evolution.* Once we learn not only how to follow the snail trail of nature but how to dance it into existence through the applied aesthetics and emergent ethics of evolutionary action, then we will have come to a new stage in the evolution of consciousness marked by conscious evolution. Today, we stand on the threshold of this stage. We have the choice consciously to participate in the co-creation of the future. It is all a matter of tuning our sense-ability to perceive it, accepting our response-ability to engage in it, and demonstrating the volition to embody and enact it. With integrity of heart, mind and spirit, we can learn to create the conditions for the emergence of sustainable evolutionary futures.

> In systems such as contemporary society, evolution is always a promise and devolution always a threat. No system comes with a guarantee of ongoing evolution. The challenge is real. To ignore it is to play dice with all we have. To accept it is not to play God—it is to become an instrument of whatever divine purpose infuses the universe.†

The attainment of evolutionary consciousness involves a willingness to lead into the unknown. There are no maps to get us from here to the future, no blueprints for planning our way out, and yet the pragmatics of evolutionary leadership count with an internalizable evolutionary compass to guide the global societal macroshift from the end of one world age to the inception of another. As a western civilization, we currently live in a world of certainty, of undoubted, rock-solid, measurable and standardizable perceptions. This is changing here and there with forays into the relationship between quantum physics, the arts, psychology and spirituality finding their way even into fairly mainstream cinema. And yet, we continue to act and

*Laszlo, Alexander, THE NATURE OF EVOLUTION
†Laszlo, Ervin, EVOLUTION: THE GENERAL THEORY, p. 139

interact as though our convictions were sufficient proof that things really are how we see them—and furthermore, that there is no alternative to what we come to hold as true. This is *'la condition humaine,'* so celebrated in our materialistic, individualistic, hypercompetitive societies. On the gross societal scale, it is our common way of being human, and it limits us to what we think we can perceive. Evolutionary development, as a deeper and more systemic variety of sustainability, is about perceiving beyond.

Daniel Pinchbeck and others suggest that consciousness does not arise in the slow course of evolutionary development out of the seemingly life-less and inanimate play of matter and energy.* In fact, it seems almost unreasonable to think that at a certain point in the process of diversification, integration and coordination of ever-increasing complexity, animate matter becomes self-aware and, presto, consciousness emerges as a novel feature in the universe. What if, instead, consciousness were primary and served as the substrate upon which the interplay of matter and energy were catalyzed? If our universe is composed of an underlying field of consciousness this would mean that dynamic structures of matter and energy arise out of this field rather than the other way around.† What is fascinating is how, at the threshold of evolutionary consciousness, we gain a glimpse of the possibility of being at the very beginning of a journey through many layers of consciousness that surround and embed us in a broad and deep cosmos and which, in fact, provide the impulse through which we evolve. The self-reflective embodiment of consciousness in human beings is now reaching the point where we may begin to grasp the necessary interplay of volition, evolution and dynamic harmony that comprise the creative essence of this cosmos.

Once we get a sense of the warp and weft of general evolutionary dynamics, we can understand how the deeper currents of societal change are neither directionless nor directed. As a system that incorporates purposeful change agents with conscious intent, society manifests the potential for self-directed conscious evolution. So while society cannot be manufactured or engineered by planning or architecture, the conditions that favour the emergence of healthy, sustainable, and evolutionarily robust environments for its development can be consciously created.

*Cf. Pinchbeck, THE RETURN OF QUETZALCOATL, p. 287
†Laszlo, Ervin, SCIENCE AND THE AKASHIC FIELD

A Sense of Syntony

The integration of evolutionary aesthetics, ethics, consciousness and voli-tion is what we call syntony. The premise of this chapter serves as the basis for an actionable understanding of this term. To recapitulate, with the em-bodiment of an evolutionary aesthetic, a basic sense-ability emerges. This then serves to seat an evolutionary ethic and nurtures a response ability among those whose intensity of consciousness is dedicated to bringing forth a world in which life thrives. As an organizing force in societal evo-lution, syntony involves an embodiment and manifestation of conscious evolution: when conscious intention is aligned with evolutionary purpose, we can foster and design evolutionarily consonant pathways of human development in partnership with Earth. It is the effort to cultivate these dynamics that constitutes what we call a syntony quest.*

Erich Jantsch considers syntony as 'inquiry at the evolutionary level *par excellence*'.† He describes this inquiry as the process of cultural orga-nization which 'may be helped in an evolutionary sense by furthering cul-tural differentiation, a pluralism of as many ideas, life styles, and world views as possible. The invention and introduction of new forms of cultural organization ought to become increasingly a matter of conscious design' (p. 260).

According to Webster's Unabridged Dictionary, syntony can be defined as 'in radio, resonance', while 'to syntonize' is 'to tune or harmonize with each other'. So syntony is essentially a sense rooted in instinct and related to intuition but no longer operating subconsciously. Teilhard de Chardin postulated that syntony will unite humankind over time through direct resonance at the level of consciousness in a process not unlike that envi-sioned by Conan Doyle in his Vital Message. It is our challenge to learn to consciously tune into the general evolutionary forces that shape us as we shape them. As Jantsch puts it, 'we shall have to learn now to design systems of syntony' (p. 270).

As exemplified earlier on by the American Indian worldview described by Momaday and the Participations of Gaia described by Asimov, syntony is a creative aligning and tuning with the evolutionary processes of which we are a part. It involves listening to the rhythms of change and learning

*Laszlo, Alexander, 'Syntony as an Organizing Force in Societal Evolution'
†Jantsch, DESIGN FOR EVOLUTION, p. 103

how to play our own melody in harmony with the larger improvizational jazz ensemble of nature and cosmos. It is finding and creating meaning and evolutionary opportunity, both individually and collectively. As a first step along this path, it will be important to begin designing learning environments where people can learn together about the interconnected nature of our world, the ecological impact of our individual and collective choices, and the joy of finding a meaningful way to contribute to the emergence of sustainable and evolutionary futures. This can lead to more strategic initiatives involving the design of new ways of working, learning and living that embody social and environmental integrity.

The Vital View

Evolutionary Systems Design involves a form of sustainability that transcends the homo-centric and chrono-centric paradigms of Business As Usual.* It goes beyond the search for 'green tech' solutions in specific areas of market opportunity—an orientation that only shifts the paradigm marginally to become Sustainability As Usual. Sustainability requires sense-abilities and response abilities that are anything but usual in our contemporary world. True sustainability means evolutionary development and is, in essence, an inside job. The search for solutions to the challenges faced in common by all people will not be successful if limited to an outward quest for answers in the domains of science and technology—that is to say, without including the human factor as the essential ingredient in every consideration. The moral and ethical responsibility of the leader of integral development for long-range systemic sustainability is, in the first place, a commitment to the wellbeing of all living things in our planet as well as to their descendants. No longer can we afford the luxury of ignoring the secondary impacts of our technologies and the undesirable consequences of our paradigms. To be sustainable, we need leaders from all walks of life who draw upon an evolutionary framework of aesthetics and ethics to incorporate perspectives that are systemic, humanistic and relational at the heart of all that they do to advance their quest for syntony.

Such evolutionary leadership involves both intuitive sensing and informed understanding of the flow patterns of being and becoming that constitute evolutionary dynamics. Presence and practice of the following

*Laszlo, Alexander, 'Evolutionary Systems Design'

principles fosters the emergent processes of syntony:

- Passion—vibrant, intense, and compelling enthusiasm
- Integrity—dignity and congruency with your values; worthiness, honour and respect
- Balance—spin control and flow control in (not of) all situations
- Grace—simple elegance, presence, kindness and a composed way of being
- Flow—tuning actions and attitudes to harmonize with surroundings

As these characteristics become more deeply embodied, it becomes a matter of course to enact the evolutionary aesthetics and evolutionary ethics of syntony. Almost as a byproduct of this quality of being, the conditions that nurture sustainable communities are fostered. Once we begin to remember how to tune into our continually emerging world, we start to move from merely being peripherally aware of it to becoming fully conscious participants in its self-actualization.

The syntony of evolutionary development means to be so attuned to the warp and weft of the dynamics of change that every thought, action and inaction contributes to the emergence of life-affirming, future-creating, opportunity-increasing relationships—consciously, purposefully, and yet effortlessly, naturally. This is the promise of the next stage of our species—that of conscious evolution. To attain it, and to experience such complete consonance with the flow of life in what Teilhard de Chardin would have recognized as an authentic experience of syntony, requires the cultivation of new sense-abilities and the taking on of new response-abilities.

Like all forms of truly creative and life-affirming societal evolution, the fostering of an emergent evolutionary ethic based on evolutionary aesthetics can only be accomplished in relationship—with oneself, with others, with nature, and with the potential inherent in the bridge we represent between what has been and what is yet to be. And it involves training—and practice. Lots of practice, even though learning to develop one's syntony sense is more like learning how to love than it is like following a manual of instructions for how to do anything in particular.

⊙   At the first level—syntony with oneself; personal or internal syntony—the practices involve centring, quieting the monkey-mind, listening with every cell of our being. These practices cultivate intuition,
compassion, insight that matches outsight, and a willingness to explore
and follow our deepest calling.

⊙   At the second level—syntony with others; community or interpersonal syntony—the practice involves deep dialogue and collaboration.
Coming together to learn with and from each other and to engage in
collective action with empathy, considerateness, openness, and joy.

⊙   At the third level—syntony with nature; ecosystemic or transpersonal syntony—the practices involve communing; listening to the messages of all beings (whether they be waterfalls, animals, mountains or
galaxies) and acknowledging our interdependence and ultimate unity.

⊙   At the fourth level—syntony with the flows of being and becoming; evolutionary or integral syntony—the practices involve learning
to read the patterns of change of which we are a part; learning to hear
the rhythms of life and becoming familiar with the improvizational
jam session that nature has been playing since time immemorial. These
practices cultivate our ability to play our own piece; to sing and dance
our own path into existence in harmony with the grand patterns of
cosmic creation.

Integral responses to the complexity of contemporary global and local challenges—personal, organizational, planetary—require an expanded
perspective: a way of recognizing interconnections, of perceiving wholes
and parts, of acknowledging processes and structures, of blending apparent opposites. But most importantly, they require collaboration. Individual
solutions and breakthrough ideas are necessary but not sufficient. Real opportunity to affect change arises from the systemic synergies that we create together. The Club of Rome coined the term 'global problematique' to
describe the complex entanglement of the collective challenges we face at
any given point in time. It is our task to create 'solutionatiques'—systems
of shared solutions that arise from the genius of each person. To do so,
we need to create an ecology of new ways of working, learning and living
that embodies social and environmental integrity. Jantsch was right: we
must learn now to design systems of syntony.

Our evolutionary trajectory has prepared us for this moment in history.

We have the cognitive and emotional capacity to embark on this quest for syntony. The real question is whether or not we have the will, the vision, and the conviction to do so.

References

Asimov, Isaac, FOUNDATION'S EDGE. New York: Ballentine Books (1982)

Barber, Theodore Xenophon, THE HUMAN NATURE OF BIRDS. New York: Penguin Books (1993)

Chalmers, John, in *The Independent*, August 7th, 2006

Jantsch, Erich, DESIGN FOR EVOLUTION: SELF-ORGANIZATION AND PLANNING IN THE LIFE OF HUMAN SYSTEMS. New York: George Braziller (1975)

Laszlo, Alexander, 'Evolutionary Systems Design: A praxis for sustainable development.' *Organizational Transformation & Social Change*, 2003, vol. 1, no. 1. pp. 29–46

Laszlo, Alexander, 'Syntony as an Organizing Force in Societal Evolution,' *Proceedings of the 43rd Meeting of the ISSS, Asilomar (USA), June 27th–July 2nd, 1999*

Laszlo, Alexander, THE NATURE OF EVOLUTION. World Futures [forthcoming, 2009]

Laszlo, Ervin, EVOLUTION: THE GENERAL THEORY. New Jersey: Hampton Press (1996)

Laszlo, Ervin, SCIENCE AND THE AKASHIC FIELD: AN INTEGRAL THEORY OF EVERYTHING. Rochester, VT: Inner Traditions (2004)

Laszlo, Ervin, THE CHOICE: EVOLUTION OR EXTINCTION? New York : Tarcher/Putnam (1994)

Loye, David, MEASURING EVOLUTION: A LEADERSHIP GUIDE TO THE HEALTH AND WEALTH OF NATIONS. Carmel, CA: Benjamin Franklin Press (2007)

Momaday, N. Scott. 'Native American Attitudes toward the Environment' in CONTEMPORARY MORAL ISSUES: DIVERSITY AND CONSENSUS by Lawrence M. Hinman. New Jersey: Prentice Hall (1996). (Originally published in SEEING WITH A NATIVE EYE: ESSAYS ON NATIVE AMERICAN RELIGION, Walter Holdon Capps (ed.). New York: Harper and Row (1976))

Pinchbeck, Daniel, 2012: THE RETURN OF QUETZALCOATL. New York: Jeremy Tarcher/Penguin (2006)

Webster's New Universal Unabridged Dictionary. Second edition. New York: Simon and Schuster (1976)

WHY COMMUNITY NOW?

C Bryan Harrison

BRAZIERS is a community, a residential college and a listed country house set in a fifty-acre Chilterns estate twenty miles south of Oxford. A fascinating place, attracting interesting and diverse communards who stay and work for some two or three years and usually move on. A better balance between short-term and long-term residents would be good to achieve.

Braziers is a community with an idea behind it, a response to the Cold War and the nuclearization of the world; an attempt to explore creative exchange between individuals and create something greater than their sum. I've visited Braziers since 1976. It's been my 'brain gym'. Since 2006 I've been the non-resident chair of its management committee.

Also, my family and I share *another* rural estate—forty acres in North-East Hampshire—with seven families including ourselves who bought into this leaderless project thirty-four years ago, in 1975. Each family has a private, freehold section of the mansion, and we all share, manage and work the estate. Following our three decades plus, we're all still here—no one has moved! Very unusual....

Why do we humans gather together in groups to live our lives, pursue work ambitions, enjoy pastimes, or define nations? Are all these groups communities? What is a community? I suggest that a community is ANY group of more than two. So a hermit—by definition—isn't living in community; nor is a married couple, nor two people in partnership. But as soon as that partnership has one or more children, they are living in a

---

C Bryan Harrison qualified at the Royal College of Art as a furniture designer, the stress of epilepsy having put paid to his intended medical career. His commercial life started with kitchen design for the disabled and developed into remodelling large interiors, such as Bonhams in Knightsbridge and Sundridge Park Management Centre in Bromley. He married Winkie Northcott in 1967 and their two children, Clive and Ruth, are now settling down to their own married lives. For Braziers Park and college, see www.braziers.org.uk.

community, however small. And any group of three or more, right up to international companies such as Shell or mega-countries or groups of countries—the USA, the EU—is a community of sorts. The EU used to be called the European Economic *Community*.

We live or work in communities as on the whole we enjoy the company of others and because, a bit like ants, we find that (multiply this by 10, 100, 1000 or more to suit) two heads are better than one. Also a bit like ants, we tend to specialize and then as individuals we can offer to a larger group our particular gifts, training and experience.

When our seven families moved in to our dry-rot-infested Victorian mansion and shared Hampshire estate, we felt like iconoclasts, explorers, breakers-of-the-mould. We had *separate* freehold 'terrace' sections of the mansion; indoor lives fairly private, the estate shared. But we were so excited! This place has been my learning ground. Learning not to speak all the time, learning that none of us is 'boss', that a dozen-plus adults had thrown themselves together to try to live a richer, more fulfilling life thereby. Did the enthusiasm match the work to come? We had immense walled kitchen gardens, twenty-eight acres of pastureland to cut or animal-manage, and unending shared outbuildings that needed keeping—or putting—into good order....

Imagine the fun as our sixteen children, within a comparatively safe environment, always with friends around, lived the lives of explorers in our woods and fields, experienced childhood relationships typical in a Kibbutz; yet with the quiet comfort of a special friend or two next door, and the ultimate refuge of a family home.

I've always loved living here. I'm encouraged that most of us still fall into animated conversation one with another as if we'd just met. Maybe we're extraordinarily lucky with each other as neighbours. The jury's out on this: we don't like to assume that the kindly mantle of good relations will necessarily last. We go about our separate lives, serving business or charity, whim or duty, art or architecture....

Braziers Park School of Integrative Social Research, Ipsden, Oxon.
Situated between academic Oxford and commercial Reading, Braziers Park is ideally suited to host brain gym gatherings to discuss world challenges. The contrast between Braziers and our Hampshire estate share is of abiding interest to me. Our two estates are similar in size, both set in

remarkably lovely countryside. But Braziers is a 'Grade II* Listed' building, last refashioned in the Nineteenth Century after the Strawberry Hill
(gothic revival) style. So in our generation, as with those before us, we find
ourselves committed to act as guardians of this unique property.

In 1976, when I first visited, the two people I was most conscious of—
and instantly admired—were Glynn and Margaret Faithfull. This couple had
their three children at Braziers and all five of them lived within the mansion
for some thirty-five years. They were the principal family here from 1960 to
1998: Glynn, a polymath, was at once scholar and farmer, plumber, electrician and builder. He had by an earlier marriage fathered Marianne Faithfull.

Margaret, his second wife, was truly Braziers' chatelaine, the kindest
woman I'd ever met, and a friend to us all. I grew to know the residents
and the faith they all had in each other that all would work out for the best.
Nearly no money, almost no maintenance, insufficient people on their
courses—the life-blood of Braziers; yet they lived from hand to mouth
from day to day and disaster did *not* intervene....

BPSISR was founded in 1950 by Norman Glaister, a psychiatrist and
philosopher, in a courageous bid to observe how people of unlike minds
might fare if asked to accommodate their differences; and to be the host
body for a school holding courses to study what he called integrative social
research. Nowadays I guess we would have used a word as yet unborn in
1950, *holistic*, instead of integrative. Against the threat of a third world
war, and convinced that communication was of the utmost importance in
avoiding future conflict, he set up BPSISR. To this day Braziers has continued to strive to be a place of conciliation.

Its principal tool has been the Sensory–Executive process. We all have
a more sensory (considering, reflecting) part of our personalities and we
are also all capable of executive decision-making. At Braziers, two com-
mittees bearing these names have continued down the years to inform one
another so a reasonable consensus can be arrived at. We aim today, just as
was stated in the 1950 brochure, 'to make conscious in ourselves the process of which we are a part'.

Braziers operates as an ongoing community and residential college,
complete with hotel and restaurant functions, producing organic vegetables, fruit, eggs, lamb, and pork from the estate. All cooking, housekeeping,
administration and sales are carried out by ten to twelve full- or part-time
committed members of the community, and volunteers from overseas on

three-month stays, all living within the main house or in cottages nearby.

For a decade or so now, Braziers' major income has come from letting the house as a venue to visiting groups with their own organisers. The current brochure reminds me that we host courses on yoga, tai chi, pilates, reiki, meditation, dance, clowning, theatre and communication. We have an on-site sweat lodge used by a regular group. Our summer camps celebrate music, nature, dance, singing and life. Remnant artefacts in our woods still recall memories of John Woodcock's Time Walk whereby he dramatically recalled how all human life has occupied merely the last moments of a cosmic day. For fifteen years, BIAW—Braziers International Artists' Workshop—has offered to artists from every peopled continent the chance to spend seventeen days at Braziers. This mix has proved intoxicating and provocative. Their final weekend exhibitions, spread as they have been throughout the mansion, outhouses and estate, have by turns been poignant, political and pragmatic; but always with the sense that the shared experience is worth so much more than the sum of the parts. Braziers' way of recognizing BIAW's contribution the BPSISR is to offer them its most illustrious platform—the coveted annual Glaister Lecture in May 2009.

The Braziers Community at present offers Creativity Sundays and Estate Work visits for no charge! Typical seasonal festivals may be held at Easter (creativity), Mayday (open day for all), Midsummer, Autumn Apple Day, Guy Fawkes Night and the New Year. Not, you will notice, too much there about solving the crises of the world…. Braziers has relied too long upon its ability to sell its remarkable space to courses arranged by others. These are excellent in themselves and we're proud to promote them. But, even collectively, they do not make a theme or solve a world situation. They will, of course, continue, as they are our life blood, but we hope shortly to bring our seventeenth-century and as yet un-refurbished Barn into operation as a second venue, potentially doubling our day-sales.

This will allow us to get back to delivering Braziers Courses—i.e., those planned and carried out by Braziers. We will be appointing a new part-time Director of Studies, and a publicity and PR volunteer, to spearhead these revitalized Braziers Courses. Whether these will mainly centre on sustainability or on personal development or on ways of working together or on philosophy we can't yet see clearly. Our mission is so very wide.

Over three years as Braziers' Chair I've frequently thought of our forebears—the Glaisters, the Faithfulls, the Woodcocks, Hilda Salter,

Jean Robertson and others. I thank them for carrying the burden of this privileged and beautiful place through to recent times. Inheriting the mantle of probably the longest-surviving non-religious community in the UK is daunting. I'm under no illusion that this inheritance is some kind of success to show to the world. Yet every week new visitors arrive from around the country and the world to talk and engage with us.

It's hard, without a union with shop stewards, to discern the movement which underpins communities these days. There are so many communities, most utterly different from the rest. Perhaps diggersanddreamers.co.uk is the best 'Yellow Pages' for the community movement. Most UK communities are based in the countryside, most claim a raised awareness of life and the predicament of our planet earth. Most try some degree of sustainability. Some are vegetarian, a few are vegan. There are a few in the towns and cities. In each one there is an attempt by a group of individuals to live a full and rewarding life whilst celebrating the rewards of working, living and deciding life together. At Braziers we call this advantage of the group mind 'multimentalism'. It's but a stone's throw from Jung's 'collective subconscious'.

At its heart, Braziers is committed to reflecting upon and endeavouring to address the real crises that face humanity today. The world is indeed on a perilous and precarious time-chart. Everywhere everyday signs of a difficult, perhaps disastrous, future for humankind and our world announce themselves. For Glaister in 1950 the main fear was a third world war. Now, still surrounded by wars started in our own backyards—if waged at a 'comfortable' distance— we face terrorism at home; and—globally and personally—we need to take action against threats to our species, the animal world and indeed the very survival of our beloved planet earth. Climate change alone may see much of the world's populations decimated before the end of this century.

In February 2009, as I began this article, the Australian bush fires raging just North of Melbourne have been of quite a different order—temperature of the air, speed of spread, rapidity of wind change—and consequent much higher fatalities. This is merely another sign that our abuse of our home planet is catching up with us. We have such a short time in which to apply good principles of limiting CO_2 emissions, learning how to live sustainably, and aspects of personal survival. I have grandchildren and I fear for their lives as adults. Perhaps, if some of the best but not necessarily the most competitive of brains, could get together at Braziers and offer their inner reflective way forward, we just might have a substantial contribution to make to world survival.

Community in the near future

If we share heating, and heat—as Braziers will shortly do—by renewable carbon from biomass, if we try to work near (if not at) where we live, if we insist on manufacturers producing long-lasting electric cars, if electricity can, quite soon now, be more ecologically sourced, if we can learn to be satisfied with purchasing less, travelling less, heating less, perhaps we have a chance. In this special period up to 2012, I certainly hope so. But how?

I suggest we look again at community. In 2007 no one would have listened. For 2010, with the world looking again for its daily bread and shelter, a new look at this old idea is very timely. There are a lot of different ways community might manifest—if people are 'conscious of the process of which they are a part'. That very consciousness works better in community, for there are endless reminders!

Even as I write in the spring of 2009, the long-rumoured world credit collapse *has* happened. We are probably now forced into many years of lower confidence, manufacture, travel. Flatlining it might be called. Can I say '*good*'? If we seize this moment as our last chance to make sense of the globe and our personal lives, then, just perhaps, we can have a good life— enjoy our lives and live them abundantly, feel fulfilled; but not feel the need to be racing about the country or world on (usually) unnecessary travel. In the age of television entertainment, mobile phones, conference calls, e-mail and the internet, we should have less and less need to travel.

Just imagine—knowing our actual neighbours again, noticing if the milk bottle (which can still be delivered) *isn't* taken in off the elderly person's doorstep—a new life will dawn! Neighbours as friends? Remember the Australian lunchtime soap? Its rather corny singing intro ended: 'neighbours become good friends'. OK, but if you hadn't got alternatives? It might be a better life. How our grandparents lived, but with mod cons.

One more step: brave creating or moving into community! Now you have the very real benefits of sharing heating, childcare, granny-watch, entertainment, bulk purchasing of basics, and—good company. No, I can't resolve the problem that my (dear friend) solicitor who in 1975 told me we shouldn't move to the Hampshire Estate-share as we'd be swapping wives within months. We didn't. Thirty-three years on, now…. It's up to us all to have a bit of discipline. Creating a community is the best thing to do *now*; It's usually worth it and may help to save the world.

2010 and Braziers' Sixtieth Anniversary

Colleague writers' aspirations and focus in this book are upon the year 2012. It so happens that, two years earlier, Braziers celebrates its sixtieth birthday. So our eyes are now upon 2010. But I can see that our Sixtieth Anniversary efforts and renewed confidence may well mature in 2012. So I am with you all entirely. However, first we have our own special anniversary to consider. I hope it won't, like for many women and men, be a rite of passage to retirement.

I wonder how we will use 2010.... No common feat, a real live community lasting this long.... I know I want to help make it a benchmark year for Braziers to become better known and respected, so we can offer more of a solution to world crisis. I hope we increase our database to maybe 10,000 people, all interested and in some way able to contribute to what we do. Above all I hope we use 2010 to invite very many communities to gather with us and to work together in a sort of multi-partnership; reminiscent of our founder, Norman Glaister's notion of the multi-mental organism writ large!

Oh! But look at my syntax! As I get more excited about our potential, I get a firm grip on what we can do and I slip into *I* rather than *we*. Oh dear! Excruciating though it is (I was overheard when I was 20 saying: 'Community? Oh yes, I'd love to run one of those!') But we run by consensus! Those of us on the Braziers Management Committee lend an ear to those of us on the Sensory Committee and then we act.....

Postscript

Once I wrote a play for radio about a community set up by single parents. Oh, the adventures they had! There is no end to the idea once it excites you. And clearly, as *you* may be hooked on cricket or international diplomacy or writing the genome for the earthworm, so **I** am infected with enthusiasm for community: a richer life....

I find it especially poignant that I should be writing this account at the very moment when Charles Darwin is being celebrated for the 200th anniversary of his birth and a hundred and fifty years since the first publication of 'The Origin of Species'. When we consider how humankind has interfered to well-nigh end our civilization, it's not much of a way to say thank you to our ancestor of the Galapagos experience!

THE JOURNEY OF THE SOUL

Shirley Kilday
written in collaboration with Jane Patience

WHEN WE look at life through the eyes of the child everything is possible. We have a sense of freedom and adventure. We are willing to explore. But as the child that we are grows older, we become more aware of other people, parents, siblings, family, peers and the culture we were born into. We lose the sense of 'Self', our unique individuality, and create the illusion of a Self that will fit in and be accepted by others. We conform to what is expected of us, what pleases others.

Do you remember hearing the comment 'what will people say?'?

As a child, on my grandparents' croft, I had a sense of freedom and space and I felt I was on the top of the world. There was a scarecrow in the field and I would sit on the fence and communicate with this scarecrow. I spoke to it and it communicated back to me, in my mind. I could feel the energy coming from it to me, and this all made me aware of other forms of communication, links into other realms. I found that I was 'switched on' at a very young age. I 'knew' things but did not share this as I was aware that others would see me as being different.

I know that people ask and plea for guidance and help through prayers and mantras and sometimes think that no-one is listening or answering them. Always, always something comes back and connects with us. This life force/ God communicates with us if we can hear and see through a different set of ears and eyes. We are so busy 'doing' and not 'being'. As

Shirley Kilday channels healing and guidance from spirit, working with the Inner Self and the vibration of Self, as the frequency of the vibration is the key to all life. Shirley accompanies you on a vision journey with ascended Masters where you discover the unlimited opportunities that exist for us all. She is a Reiki Master teaching Usui and Karuna Reiki ® and also offers angel attunements and workshops.

you learn to listen and to trust in this guidance coming through, this inner knowing, you realize that this life-force / God is greater than you ever could have imagined.

We all have the same opportunities to experience this inner voice, this communication and, through this, to know more of who we really are. We have to look at the hidden aspects of Self that were created to fit in with the illusion of what others expected.

Our families are a wonderful source of growth. Personally, I have had a wealth of experience from being the eldest of seven and from a large extended family. I have been tried and tested in many ways to see how I would cope and this is still an ongoing process. These life experiences help us to understand the power we hold within and with this inner strength we learn to live from the heart. To think before we speak, to think how our heart would react to this situation. Instead of attack, the first form of defence, we understand that we don't need to defend all the time, just to stand back and allow others to be as they are. Everyone has a different perspective on the same situation; their way may not be our way, but we must be respectful of their choice.

I have had to learn to accept and love myself for who I really am, to free myself from the illusion that began the day I was born. As we peel away the layers of the onion, letting go of all these aspects, we begin to refine the vibration of Self, more and more. We each have our own, individual energy vibration, like the snowflake, unique but part of the whole. All parts are equal, all parts are important, each have their own special contribution to make.

Most people see this world as a physical reality and live a life based on the five senses: sight, sound, touch, smell and taste. Yet people from all walks of life are becoming aware that there is more to life than this, that they are more than a physical body. We have energy bodies, an energy field, and we have a spiritual Self.

It was in the early 1990s that I first became involved with healing. At first it was hands-on healing, then I did the Reiki training to become a Reiki Master, Usui and Karuna Reiki ® but it was when I began to listen to my Inner Self, listen to Spirit, that I really found my path.

Earlier I had denied the vision, as I thought that to have 'the sight' meant that I had to predict the future. One day I said 'If I have to use the vision, then I want to use it for healing'. How my words came true!

My vision grew stronger and stronger and the knowledge began to come through. In 2004 messages from an enlightened being, coincidences and visions came in, guiding me to work with the angels. I believe St Peter came forward and told me that he was the overseer of the angel work and that the angels are coming en masse to the earth at this time. He said that the angels want people to be more aware of their presence, to work with them and to ask for their help. They now want people to be personally and consciously aware of them and to invite them in to their everyday lives.

I received a guided attunement from the archangels and I started by using the attunement on a few friends. The results were truly rewarding so the work spread out to others through small groups and workshops.

At a workshop in Nairn, Isis came forward and gave us great encouragement with the following message:

> Gathering of friends, welcome. We come forward to join with you in appreciation of the work you are doing, to give you confidence, to show you the path before you. Joy is in our heart, the momentum will build from a small band of people. The word is to be spread, the work to be done is a responsibility on the shoulders of people on Earth and Great Beings send messages of Love and Compassion.
>
> Fear not, your steps will be guided on the path appropriate for you. There will be twists and turns on the road.
>
> None so great as the gift of Love we give to humanity but we give this gift to you also as a personal thank you from us to you.
>
> Know the sorrows that you hold deep in your heart, transmute them to the Light. Let the Light and the Love of the Creator enter in. Be a beacon for His Light and for His Work. Move forward in grace and humility. You are blessed to be given this chance, do not waste it, the importance of what you do, to reach out and to touch. The sorrows and sins of humanity are great. No matter the size of the pebble, all efforts make a difference. You cannot understand all at this time but in due time you will begin to see the bigger picture.

One of the ways to open the doorway from the physical to the spiritual is to work with the heart. Through working with the heart, we are working with the Christ Light that we all hold within our hearts. The Christ Light has been waiting for this and joyfully responds to your awakening.

The steps you follow for the angel attunement may seem simple, but the effect, though subtle, is very powerful. The attunement opens up your connection to the angelic realm, activating the energy centre at your heart in a different way. This allows you to receive and work with the beautiful healing energies of the angels, working with your heart for your own healing. This healing works with all aspects of Self: physical, mental, emotional and spiritual. As the energy changes within Self, so it reflects on the outer personality, healing the person, to bring them to their full potential.

You listen to how the heart feels and move in to the flow of being. The more you connect to the flow, the more change is created in the vibration of Self. It changes the light within Self, raising the physical vibration to the spiritual vibration of Self. The energy field is moving to a spiritual vibration. It is an illusion that the physical form is solid. We are a flowing, moving energy field.

In November 1999 I had been told to use the Fluid Movement, taking everything back to water. Water, because this represents the flowing, moving energy field. I didn't just accept what I was told and shown, but questioned it all, even 'ripped it apart' until I understood it all better. I worked with the atom for healing. I 'played' with this and questioned again. I would see the person on the bench as fluid and then the atom around the person, seeing the person as the nucleus within the atom. Again, St Peter came forward to work with this. The geometric shapes kept coming in to my mind and would not go away.

After doing my own angel channelling I saw myself as the nucleus of the atom, said the soul mantra, and then asked that all the relevant geometric shapes be placed in my heart centre. After a few minutes I saw geometric shapes flowing in to my heart centre. I left them to flow and I also saw colours. When you ask for the geometric shapes to be applied to your energy field, this sacred geometry changes the light within Self and when the light changes it affects the tone, the vibration.

In the summer of 2005 I was guided to work with Metatron's Cube, placing it in my heart centre. When you look at Metatron's Cube you are looking at all the platonic solids at once, they are all contained within Metatron's Cube. The platonic solids are the building blocks of the universe and, as the human body is a microcosm of the universe, so Metatron's Cube is connected to the structure of man. I was then given Metatron's Mantra, which I channelled in March 2006. *Metatron's Cube is the totality of man within the spectra of life.*

Using Metatron's Cube and Mantra again changed the light, the tone and the level of the vibration, further raising the physical vibration to the spiritual vibration of Self. I was told that the Sacred Geometry and Metatron's Cube are part of the Mathematical Equation of Self. We are made up of maths, geometry, light (colour) and vibration (sound).

The more you focus and work with the heart, with the angels, the stronger your connection with your spiritual Self and so with the higher consciousness. You begin to listen and respond from your heart, from your inner senses not just from your head and from your five physical senses. Through working with your heart and listening to your Inner Senses you begin to create unity and stability in Self.

When you work with your heart you think with your heart. You learn to love yourself through acknowledging the truth about how you really feel and the changes that you would truly like in your life.

Experiences in our lives (present, parallel and past) can have a profound effect on our life today, on how we function as a person, mentally, emotionally and physically. We think we can shut away these experiences, these parts of ourselves, but this can leave us in a fragmented state. As long as we remain fragmented we continue to perpetuate these experiences, repeating the same patterns.

Ask your angels to be shown one part of yourself to bring it home in to your heart centre with unconditional, compassionate love. Some people will work with few experiences, others with more. I, myself, have worked with many experiences and I still continue to do this work when I am aware of the need to do so. The Soul has come to grow and learn, to be free, to know itself in its purest form. We can never be whole and well until we recognize and accept all these fragments of ourselves, loving and accepting ourselves unconditionally. You are not just helping yourself but also your family because as this healing changes the memory of the experience at the cellular level for Self so this also changes what is familiar to the family.

All the above has been included into and shared in the angel attunements and the workshops. Many people have now had the attunements and work with this on a daily basis. Those who wished to take this further also share the angel attunements with others.

In March 2007, more Masters came forward and I was asked to refine the vision work, to work with people individually on a one-to-one basis.

Angels and Masters come forward and work with the person on the couch, and my role has become that of a channeller, a helper and a companion. Sometimes the work is specific to the energy body and sometimes we all go on a journey. A journey to the universe, to other realms and to other dimensions. The people who come wish to re-programme their lives, creating a new vision for their life. A vision brought forth from the heart and also from the 'heart' mind.

Master Kuthumi said to me: 'The greatest gift that you can give to yourself is to harness the power of your own mind. To aid the physical form to make the transition to the spiritual, you must harness the power of your own mind.' In April 2007, this Master came forward again and gave us this beautiful message: 'Beloved ones, you have made it home to the Light. Now the work begins within the heart of Self'.

A Master said to me, one day, when I had asked a question: 'It would suit you better to be working on your own heart than to be sitting in judgment on those who are not yet awakened. And what you must understand is that there are some people for whom it is not yet the time for them to be awakened. Their journey is just as important and as relevant to the bigger picture.' The more work we do with the heart of Self, the more this reaches out and touches all others. No effort is ever wasted.

People must understand how simple all of this actually is. By setting your intention, saying prayers, mantras and affirmations that resonate with your heart in a loving, peaceful way, your heart will begin to sing. A very simple but powerful affirmation is:

> I am a Beautiful, Beautiful Being
> I am Pure Love
> I am Pure Light
> I am Pure Joy
> I am whole and well in Mind, Body and Soul.

You are creating beautiful energy-patterns within your own Being. These energy-patterns are like a kaleidoscope of light, colour and movement, continually evolving within and of themselves. You know by the pattern and the colour, e.g the beautiful, silver, four-pointed star / diamond that you are moving in to another level of consciousness. The kaleidoscope is working with the totality of Self, all existences that are stored in the cells, the totality of your Being. Working in this way leads to the integration of the personality and the soul. Humanity becomes soul-infused, centred in the heart, and with a 'heart' mind, not a negative, egotistical mind. As we change within ourselves so our outer reality must change to accompany the inner changes. Always the outer will reflect what is happening on the inner.

A person can reach a certain level by working on themselves, but to reach the higher levels this work can only be done with help from the Masters and the angels existing in other dimensions. As we come in to even more contact with the Masters and angels we will be further awakened. These awakenings are then done with each individual on a personal level but in accordance with the love and the wisdom of the Masters and the angels for our highest good.

This refining raises the vibration of Self so we grow more aware of other influences and other realms; for example, the realms where the angels, the fairies and the devic kingdom exist. At this time in man's evolution, those of the devic kingdom have been gathering together (especially during the last two years) to help humanity raise its vibration and to be more aware of the earth, its resources, animals, nature and of each other as human beings.

Fairies are helping us in ways we just could not conceive. Recently I was shown that the fairies are bringing crystals from the earth to help align the vibration of humanity to a more evolved state, a crystalline vibration. Our vibration is becoming more crystalline and the sound waves within Self are attuning to a higher frequency. As we are moving to a higher vibration so the planet vibration is being raised, this is through all life, all existence. The angelic realm and the devic kingdom see us as being one with them, no separation. All humans are one, everything is one, this shift is affecting the collective of all Life.

Arthur Conan Doyle was able, unconsciously, to tap in to some of what existed parallel and simultaneously to his life at that time, these other realms, and brought this out in his books.

Sometimes his thinking was 'out of the box' to create and to solve the crimes in his Sherlock Holmes mysteries. There was an awareness in ACD's family. His father Charles was aware of other existences, as shown by his fantastical drawings. His uncle Richard was drawn to painting fairies, elves, gnomes, the devic kingdom. This would all have acted as a trigger and a key for ACD's own awareness and interest in the existence of those beings.

It is hard for humanity to believe that there are other worlds within worlds, other levels of existence, unless they have personal experience and insight. Although the vast majority of humanity are, as yet, unable to touch upon this vastness, this mystery of life, through the raising of the vibration, we will vibrate at a more etheric level and more people will experience the reality of other realms, other worlds. When we rediscover the playfulness and the adventure of the child we begin to be more willing to explore these other worlds.

No one person, no scientist, has all the answers. This vastness cannot be put in to a category, that is the way it is. We will never fully understand or appreciate how vast these worlds within worlds are and how we are part of all this. We are all on the same path, the pathway home to God, and we all have a great power within us, the potential to work for the highest good of all. It is impossible to separate ourselves from humanity, nature, Mother Earth, the planets, the constellations, the devas, the angels, the Masters and from God Himself. We are all one. Everything that exists, exists within us. We are all energy.

LESSONS FROM THE FINDHORN GARDEN

Dorothy Maclean
*written in collaboration with Judy McAllister**

I AM NOT an ecologist or an environmentalist. I am neither philosopher nor politician. Nor am I trained or experienced in helping to shape structures for housing, or finances or decision-making. In looking for ways to describe what I am, I realize there are several descriptions that rest reasonably comfortably on my being. One is that of planetary citizen. I even have a passport to prove it, although no country has ever recognized it. Another is as mystic. Although I refer to myself as a modern mystic, my story differs only in the details from stories that have been lived out and told through the ages. Ever since we humans began to try and name or codify that which is all around us, there have been men and women who found themselves caught up by the magnificence that is in our environment— from the stars to the tiniest creature. Nature is a doorway to an understanding of, and a relationship with, the Divine that defies description. Yet nonetheless we try to describe it, through storytelling.

For the past forty years, my efforts to describe and to share my experience have required that I become a storyteller of sorts, though the story I tell is primarily my own. The bottom line of my story is an unshakable knowing that each and every one of us can have a personal and direct relationship with the Divine, and that through that relationship we can also

*An edited version of a keynote address given at a Positive Energy Conference at Findhorn, Scotland, on March 23rd, 2008

Seeking the answer to the purpose of life, Dorothy Maclean made a conscious contact with her inner Divinity. Along with Peter and Eileen Caddy, she spent years developing this attunement. She then made contact with the conscious intelligence of nature, leading to co-creative cooperation between it and humanity, and from it the Findhorn Community grew.

have a co-creative relationship with the intelligence of nature.

The longer story of my journey is not for the telling now. Suffice to say that in trying to answer the great questions of life, questions like who am I, why am I here, I came to the conclusion that it is all about love. Everything I read, all the teachers I listened to, led me to the belief in spiritual principles, of which my key understanding was to be loving. I got tested of that belief. Was I willing to act lovingly enough for another, to give up my greatest personal desire? To cut a long story short: to gain the inner strength to go through with this action of love, over many months I chose to commit myself to doing it. Then, for the very first time in my life, I experienced God within me as a living cosmic presence. And my definition of God is as the life-force in everything. I was no longer a lonely misfit, I was part of a joyous universe.

As you can quite well imagine, this experience changed me completely, even changing my voice. With such an expanded experience of myself, I now had the courage to take action on my commitment. Fifty-five years later, that inner contact continues to give me courage to take actions.

After that initial contact, whenever I was alone a thought kept continually intruding into my mind, to 'stop, listen and write'. After being besieged by this idea many times, eventually I did just that, and turned within. To my wonderment, I opened up to inner perceptions which I wrote down in my own words. I should say here that I do not hear or see anything. I have an inner experience, like an idea that arrives whole, and I then translate it into words. At first I was amazed, because those knowings revealed a God very different from the Old Testament Jehovah God of my childhood. Here was a delightful Presence, full of love, joy, play and merriment: a God of celebration, connection and empowerment.

I want to share with you the love of God I experienced in my attunements, the helpful messages I received, and how empowering and necessary these were in leading up to and in the founding of Findhorn, and of course in my personal spiritual growth. Here is an example:

Come closer, come closer, so softly, on tiptoe. As quietly as a mouse creep up to Me. Let Me draw you nearer, in slow motion lest we disturb anyone, lest we raise any dust. Move closer to Me invisibly, hearing no evil, seeing no evil, speaking no evil. Only purity can come close to Me, and we do not want any ripple of impurity to trip you.

Draw nearer, draw nearer, with the movement of your heart. Let it expand into Me. Let it bridge any space that might be between us, until there is just one, big, glowing heart, so big that it holds up this universe.

For nearly ten years before the nature contact began, I attuned to that Presence daily. Initially I did this three times a day, and received thousands of wonderful teachings, some of which have now been published. The main theme of these messages was to empower me to bring the love that I was experiencing into my everyday living. A love, which for me embraces both the personal and impersonal dimensions. How could I not fall in love with that God? How could I do anything other than allow this energy to be the guiding force of my life?

In looking back, I realize I was in training in how to explore the deeper parts of myself. I was not alone in this training. Peter and Eileen Caddy and our colleague Lena were all in training, each of us learning to follow that inner wisdom in our own different ways. Again, those are threads of the story not for the telling now.

Here is an example of how I was helped from within:

A tiptoe awareness is needed to express My thoughts, the awareness being of Me and not of what you yourself are doing. When you are aware of Me, you will be doing the right thing. This can be achieved in all situations, and is not impossible. It is difficult, it is unusual, but it is the only way to live.

This state is reached by continual practice. Think of Me all the time and gradually you will not have to try so hard to turn your thoughts in My direction.

And another example, with helpful suggestions:

Stretch every particle of yourself towards Me, and I will fill every particle with Myself out of My abundance. Soak yourself in the stream of love inside and out, giving yourself up completely. Relax in it, drown in it, every atom of you, until there is nothing in you not made new and pure.

Then breathe again, like a newly emerged chick, breathing love in instead of air. It is My love that keeps you alive, that sustains you. Know this. Breathe it in softly, breathe it out gently.

Let all your thoughts come to Love for their life, that they breathe forth My dimensions of love. Let all your acts come to love for their life, that they abound only with love. Let all you see be seen in love, that you see only boundless loveliness.

At first I did not trust what I received, and had to learn to discriminate between my normal thoughts and those coming from my God-self. Throughout it all the patience of God never wavered. A fact I often wondered at! Over time these wonderful periods of inner attunement slowly changed me.

During those years we each learned to trust and act upon what we were receiving from our inner wholeness. What came applied to all dimensions of life. For example, God conveyed: Brush your teeth with Me. Everything was to be done with love. Whenever there was a problem, God was available as a source of help if we so chose. A great example of this occurred at Cluny Hill Hotel, when our alcoholic Head Chef arrived in the kitchen too drunk to stand up, and with two hundred dinners to cook. In this instance, Peter's intuition failed him and he was forced to ask Eileen to get guidance on this looming crisis. She went within and received, that if we wanted the Chef to cook the dinners, Peter needed to give him another drink. Believe it or not, it worked! Normal sensible minds would never have thought of such a crazy solution. Only God could have!

Another inspirational message that I like very much is:

You are close to Me but you can come still closer, further into My love. That is the marvellous journey ahead of you all, this glad venturing into My love, this delicate response in you to a new outpouring of Myself. This is the ever different, ever lifting, ever softening process which is the joy of My heart to behold in you and in all.

For each one My approach is different, for My one love is sensitive to all creatures. The warmth of My love, the surge of it into an open heart, is universal and unique; I am all things to all people. I pour it out on all creation, and it comes back to you as you open yourself to Me from all sides, within and without. The more you open your heart, the wider the opening through which I can come.

Eventually the storywriter brought the Caddys and me to the Findhorn Caravan Park. Unemployed and living with minimal financial resources, Peter set about creating a garden to augment our diet. Sand, which is all that was here, along with lots of rounded pebbles, is not conducive to great gardening.

One morning in my meditation I was told that I had a job to connect with

Nature. This was later expanded upon and I was told that everything in nature has an ensouling intelligence. I was to harmonize with that essence. I was also told that the forces of nature are something to be felt into, to be stretched out to. I was told that this would not be as difficult as I expected, that all forces are to be felt into, even the sun, the moon, the sea, the trees, the very grass, for all are part of God's life. I was to play my part in making life One again, with God's help. I was told to begin by thinking about the higher nature spirits, the overlighting angels, and to attune to them. This would be so unusual as to draw their interest to the garden, and they would be overjoyed to cooperate with humans who were eager to cooperate with them.

Eventually I chose a vegetable that I enjoy eating, the garden pea. I made contact with my inner divinity and then focused on the pea. To my surprise I made an immediate link and received a creative, helpful response, which I translated into words, as I did with my God-contact. I realized I was communicating not with an individual pea plant but with the soul of the species, with a formless energy-field. The nearest word I could find to describe it was 'angel', which to me had too much form. Somewhere I had come across the Sanskrit word *deva,* which means 'shining one'. That seemed more accurate, as to me it was formless.

As usual, I was sceptical about these messages, as well as doubtful about my ability to feel into nature.

Thus began our experiment of cooperating with the intelligence of nature in the garden. Luckily God helped me to understand the process, by telling me:

> You are pioneering in the true attitude to nature, to the one life. For this attitude, it behoves you to think of everything in terms of life-force, not merely an impersonal force like electricity, but a manifestation of a being. They can teach and help you, though what you see of them outwardly may be a lowly bee, a leaf, a stone. Behind all is a great chain of life leading to Me. Humans have been given dominion over all these on Earth, but only as you, too, fit into the great chain of life.

We got many answers from the devas to our gardening questions, though they never ordered us to do anything. The devas/angels/god, whatever word we are comfortable using, do not want us to be just obedient servants, but a humanity who is attuned to its own wholeness and who can cooperate with them as equals.

Just after my first contact with the garden pea, I became aware of a pre-siding angelic presence which seemed to be in charge of all levels of life here, including the human. I called it the Landscape Angel. In hindsight, this was a misnomer, for now I realize that this angel is the local representative of the Angel of our planet, of Gaia itself. It came to help us specifically in our experiments in attuning to God and the intelligence of nature. Suffice to say that it became my teacher, introducing me to all manner of other beings and stretching my understanding into new realms. All the while the garden flourished, and the community you see here today began to take shape.

The Landscape Angel gave us continuous help. For example, in order to grow healthy vegetables, it communicated that we needed nourishing soil, not sand, and the best way to achieve this in our situation, was by add-ing compost to the sand. I have hundreds of such essential and invaluable messages from the Landscape Angel, who is ever ready to help and be a source of inspiration and connection.

I continued to receive help from God in understanding this coopera-tion with the devic kingdom, and what I needed to do in order to listen to and be sensitive to their contact: God said:

> Remember that most of the beings you contact are highly evolved and can understand human feelings, so they will try to meet you to a certain extent. The various plant devas live in a sphere of immediacy of knowledge about anything which concerns them; all knowledge is open to them. This knowledge is yours when you tune into them. Their mission is to manifest My plant world.
>
> Mingle with these beings. It is an exchange and a beginning of a unique and far-reaching cooperation. They are amazed and delighted that their cooperation is sought and then followed so faithfully, and at this time in the world's evolution when humans are increasingly harm-ing their work. It is not only important, but vital, that a new relation-ship be established.
>
> Listen to the sounds of nature whenever you have the chance. They are true sounds, coming from Me within each, and can lead you into My world and into the world of the sound devas. When you are close to Me, you are tuning yourself into worlds of growth and forces which are always present, and have a tremendous effect on humans uncon-sciously. When you are conscious of them, they open up and reveal how you are linked. Do not worry if you get no specific message; as

you tune into them, the link with them grows and may bear fruit in a slightly different direction—with the devas, for example.

I believe that our inner attunement and cooperation with nature created an atmosphere, a powerful note that attracted many on inner levels. We were asked to have no publicity and invite no-one here, yet people kept arriving. The strong inner energy field drew people from all over the planet, and they had incredible stories to tell of how they had found themselves here. Some felt they had come to a paradise, or had come home; some felt that the split between the kingdoms had been repaired; some felt a spirit of joy, an energy of love, wisdom and/or healing. People still describe an atmosphere that permeates the place, special qualities, and a sense of personal homecoming. Perhaps some of you have felt some of that. Perhaps here you come home to a bigger part of yourself.

From the devas I was continuing to understand more about their worlds and the links to humans. One message particularly stood out. It was from the Monterey Cypress, who said:

> We are not just the little trees you see in your garden. You feel in us an almost intolerable longing to be fully ourselves. We of the plant world have our pattern and our destiny, worked out through the ages, and we feel it quite wrong that we and others like us are not allowed to be, because of humanity and its encroachment. Trees are not so much Doers of the Word as Be-ers. We have our portion of the plan to fulfil; we have been nurtured for this very reason and now, in this day and age, many of us can only dream of the spaces where we can fulfil ourselves. The planet needs the likes of us in our full maturity. We are not a mistake on the part of nature; we have our work to do.
>
> Humanity is now becoming controller of the world forests and is beginning to realize that these are needed, but you use silly economic reasons for your selection, with no awareness of the planet's needs. You should not cover acres with one quick-growing species which, though admittedly better than none, shows utter ignorance of the purpose of trees and their channelling of diverse forces. The world needs us on a large scale.
>
> We have been vehement.... We have rather dumped this on you and you feel unable to help. You are only looking at it from a limited level. We know that a truth once in human consciousness then percolates around and does its work.

This particular message carried a sense of tremendous urgency. It was as if this Cypress was shouting, so that the whole world would realize the need for trees throughout the planet.

The Leyland Cypress expanded on this theme:

Great forests must flourish, and humanity must see to this if you wish to continue to live on this planet. The knowledge of this necessity must become part of your consciousness, as much accepted as your need for water. You need trees just as much; the two are linked. We are indeed the skin of the earth, and a skin not only covers and protects, but passes through it the forces of life. Nothing could be more vital to life as a whole than trees, trees and more trees. Spread this truth, and know that the forces of the angelic world and all the worlds in which truth reigns, are behind you.

Some of these ideas are now common knowledge, but forty years ago they were new, at least to me. The issues of global deforestation and the detrimental effect of certain forestry practices, were not generally recognized then. The devas were talking to me about things that science is just catching up with now.

Other devas had their input to offer. For example, the Lily Deva said:

We feel it is high time for you humans to branch out and include in your horizons the different forms of life which are part of your world. You have been forcing your own creations and vibrations on the world, ones which are more than strange and not at all pleasant to us and to others, without taking into consideration that all living things are part of the whole, as you are, put there by divine plan and purpose. Just as each soul has its own contribution to make to the whole, so has each plant, each mineral. No longer should you consider us as lower forms of life, with no intelligence with which to communicate.

As always, the Landscape Angel guided us, as in the following:

The angelic world is poised with great love towards humans. The energies that flow through us and all of life are purposeful, forceful and to the point. Love is a firm reality which forms a bridge over which all can walk. Gooey sentiment is not love and does not exist with us. When we step towards you, we do it energetically; you can do the same. Though you cannot see or hear us, touch, smell or taste us, still we are a tremendous force. We stand here in love, a whole dynamic world reaching for an intelligent relationship with a humanity that will wield all its God-given forces for the whole. You need us and we are ready, awaiting the recognition, love and just treatment that you give to your own kin. We wait in love for your love.

This is still true now and the initiative to make it a reality has to come from us.

In the midst of these messages and as the community was becoming known in certain circles, we were joined by another facet of nature, the elementals, when Ogilivie Crombie (often referred to simply as ROC) visited us and began actually to see nature spirits. He first encountered the delightful faun Kurmos, and later Pan, the god of the woodlands. And so you glimpse yet another strand of the story, one not for the telling now.

Cooperation between the 'nature' and 'human' parts of us, is not just partnering with nature. It is more than just getting messages or instructions. It's more than just hanging out with fairies and gnomes. Or even with Pan! It is opening and holding a connection through which a vital energy—nature's forces—can flow into the human world. This is a spiritual force which helps us cultivate what might be called a planetary consciousness, the capacity to 'think' like a planet. That is more than awareness of global events or cultures; it is a way of entering and living in a Gaian consciousness.

We are all part of a story—the story of humanity. The conventional version of that story says we are about ten thousand years old. We all know that humans have been around much longer than that.

One perspective on humanity's story that I came across recently puts forward the idea that at a pivotal point, funnily enough about ten thousand years ago, some humans decided that food, and the land that produced it, was in fact a commodity that could be owned. Controlling the food supply meant power. Farming had begun! The story of so many civilizations is built around that premise. When the ability to control the stockpiling and/ or the distribution of those commodities broke down, civilizations toppled. Other civilizations replaced them—but the premise that nature was a commodity remained. Evidence indicates that we, as the subset of humans who could be referred to as takers, are on the verge of creating global collapse.

Collectively we have taken more than we have given, and the earth is running out of new places for us to pull into the story of a humanity that treats nature, land, and food as commodities. The books of Daniel Quinn explore this perspective in detail. We have entered that longer story of humanity at another pivotal point. The outcome, the ending of the story, is as yet unwritten.

James Lovelock has said that it is too late to save the world. I disagree! Certainly we have reached a crisis point. We stand on the brink, and may well topple into global collapse. Or we can birth a new consciousness, and work to offset the destructive forces rampaging on our planet. Findhorn didn't start as an intentional community, nor was it designed as a response to peak oil or to climate change. It is an outgrowth of the dedication of a small group of people to following a spiritual path. I know that the lessons learned here can act as a template for creative responses to current crises.

And so, I wonder which community we shall focus on? Which community will respond to the current crisis? After all, we are all part of so many communities. There is the community of me, myself and I. A bit solitary I admit, but a community of sorts nonetheless. There is the community of me and my family, or me and my work mates. There is the community of my town or village, my country. There is the community of me and the whole rest of the world. The term global community is one that has come into our language fairly recently, though I suspect we have very different understandings of what it really means. Of course for us mystic types, there is also the community of me and God. Someone once said to me that 'With God, one is in the majority'. Whatever! I think we are all mystics, it's just that some of you might not know that yet.

Another of the delightful catch phrases that has emerged fairly recently is 'Think Globally, Act Locally'. I know there are many ways to understand the phrase and the sentiment behind it. Even so, I should like to offer an alternative, 'Be Global, Act Here'. Or maybe, 'Be Global, Act Local'. Even if the latter is bad grammar!

The word Gaia is used to refer to the living system that is the planet. I also use it to denote the creative and intelligent presence, the beingness, of which the planet is composed. That being is sentient and creative. Like the devas and angels I have been talking about, I believe it is available to us as a direct ally in what we collectively face on the planet. We can embody both human consciousness and Gaian consciousness, and the unique consciousness that may emerge from the engagement of these two. We can give birth to a new kind of consciousness, one that will actually make us more, not less human in our wholeness, and offset the destructive forces on the planet.

I try to be a positive person, having been trained both on the inner and on the outer to look for the highest and best in everyone, in all situations. But I must confess that as I look out into the world, as I listen to the news, read the papers, hear the concerns and worries of so many people, it's as if I am watching a plague race round the world. A plague of death that values money over love, a plague that values personal gain and comfort over the good of the whole. Of course there are many antidotes to this plague being experimented with, and new solutions are being sought.

Einstein said, You can never solve a problem on the level on which it was created. Yet it seems to me that that is just what we are trying to do. Most of the solutions are being created by the very thing that catalyzed the plague in the first place. We seek with our minds, to understand the workings of the finely-tuned systems of nature, systems evolved over millions of years. Then, with all good intent, we set out to recreate them, to restore them. All this we do from the limited understanding that our minds can bring to bear. What if we were to listen beyond the mind to the allies awaiting our invocation? What if we were to create on a planetary scale, the same level of cooperation and co-creation demonstrated in the early days of this community? Here, sand dunes were turned into gardens, some even say Eden was re-created. The success of the early garden at Findhorn remains a demonstration of the potency of cooperating and co-creating with nature. As Sir George Trevelyan noted, 'One garden can save a world'.

The early garden was undeniable proof of the principles. I have every reason to believe that the microcosm of this one garden can be replicated in the macrocosm of the planet. What if the scientists, rather than spending years in laboratories, spent a few months in nature honing their connection to the Divine, to the devic realms, and then asked their questions of those non-physical, non-human realms that I have been talking about?

Nature is so much more than a source of renewal and regeneration for our jagged exhausted selves. It is so much more than a treasure to be kept safe in selected places. We ignore the subtler aspects, the unseen dimensions, at our peril.

And let's face it, the peril on our planet is great. My request is that as we remember that we are not alone in trying to find new ways forward. We have potent allies, ready to lend their untold resources to the cause. We need only make room for them, believing that they are there, ready and willing to lend their aid. We need only welcome their input and they will reply, in ways undreamed of, in ways beyond our comprehension.

I should like to end by sharing with you a message from the Landscape Angel. It speaks of what they know about us. Afterwards I should like to ask all of you a question.

We call to you, humans, from the highest of our realms, and you are there. We call to you from densest Earth and you are there. We call from other worlds across space, and still you are there. We are inwardly still and attuned, and you share our oneness. If there are worlds we cannot reach, no doubt you are there. 'Man, know thyself.'

We talk to you from the kingdom of Nature. Do not limit the wisdom of that kingdom, which is the Divine in manifestation and includes obscure worlds that you disregard at your own peril. All around you, in every bit of matter, is what has come from, is, and leads to the only One, and within you is the consciousness that can know and express this. You are all things to all worlds. You incorporate life itself, bound to earth and bound to heaven, tiny specks on one small planet in a limitless universe, the image of it all. That is what you are.

But what do you think you are? We know what we and you are, but you, what do you think? Your thoughts tell you: they are your range of expression and you might just as well let them reflect what you really are. Are they negative or trivial? Then change them, turn them the other way. Use the mighty gift of the pairs of opposites to find Oneness, to rise and turn to what you are. Enjoy what you are; give thanks for it, give thanks to creation and its servers for making you possible. Slot in to what you are; stay put to your immensity. For this we have wielded power through the ages, but now we can know one another and come together for the glory of God. We need call you no longer; as one we can express wholeness.

And now my question for you is this:

What if what they say is all true? How will you respond?

A FATHER'S PLACE

Nikki Mackay

AS WE find ourselves at the beginning of the Twenty-First Century, the way that we see and define who we are has changed considerably from this same point in the Twentieth Century. Who we are and our sense of ourselves is very much defined by ourselves as individuals today, and by what we do to earn our living. When we are asked to describe ourselves, it is commonplace to give a description based on where we live, how we make a living, if we are in a relationship and if we have any children.

Very rarely do we think of ourselves in terms of the family and ancestors that we belong to. There is also an interesting upsurge in what we could loosely term the 'new age movement', with people generally seeking or actively embracing a more spiritual approach to life and the quandaries it throws up. Traditional religions are being bypassed, by some but not all, by those who are looking for themselves and seeking to find it through healing, Spiritualism or psychical roots.

Over the latter half of the Twentieth Century, leading up to the point we find ourselves now, there has also been a gradual shift in the perception of the relationship between the masculine and feminine roles in our

Nikki Mackay is a family constellator, sound therapist, Reiki master and an experienced pyschic medium. As a medical physicist she has researched the effects of energy healing on the nervous system and published her findings within the scientific and New Age community. An experienced intuitive and teacher, she established a holistic retreat centre in Scotland and developed the centre for three years. She is now the editor of *The WitchHiker's Guide* magazine, a guide to all things alternative in Scotland. She also teaches seminars and works with individuals exploring family and ancestral patterns. Her first book, THE SCIENCE OF FAMILY: EXPLORING ANCESTRAL AND FAMILY PATTERNS is being published by O Books and will be available from June 2009.

society. Great change occurred from the birth of feminism in the 1960s in Western society, which looked for equal rights for women in terms of the workplace, pay, education, law, and the right to choose when they have a family, to the present day. These changes have impacted on the defined roles of men and women and subsequently on the role of family. The incidences and occurrences of mental health issues such as depression and addictive, destructive behaviours such as alcoholism and drug addiction are also increasing. Major depression is the most common psychological disorder in the Western world. It is growing in all age groups, in virtually every community, and the growth is seen most in the young, especially teens. At the current rate of increase, it will be the second most disabling condition in the world by 2020, behind heart disease. Ten times more people suffer from major depression now than in 1945.† 'Me' decades generate depression: individualism erodes commitment to others.§ This increase is more prevalent in males than in females.¶ I believe there is a common denominator throughout all of this and I don't believe that I am alone in my thoughts.

Who we are and where we come from, our place in our family, has a huge impact not only on how we feel about ourselves and the relationships that we have, but also the choices that we make in our lives. As a general observation, we don't spend much time thinking about our ancestors and where we come from in our modern Western society. We don't often think about why we are the way we are, we are generally just quite busy getting on with the everyday. We perhaps accept that the immediate family that we have grown up with, our family of origin, will have an effect in making us who we are, but what about the generations before our parents, what about our ancestors, our family line? It is quite common to have some knowledge of who your grandparents were but very often our awareness stops there. It is very easy to see the people in our family only in reference to the role they provide to our family or to us as individuals. We start this behaviour with our parents, seeing them as only existing as

* Seligman, M. E. P. (1990) LEARNED OPTIMISM

†Seligman, M. E. P., in J. Buie (1988)

§APA Monitor, 19, 18

¶Leon, D A; McCambridge, J: *Liver cirrhosis mortality rates in Britain from 1950 to 2002: an analysis of routine data.*

our parents and with no lives before we were born. There is potential for reconnection through more distant ancestors, who may be easier to view as 'whole' people.

This disconnected view of our roots and our lineage is an extrapolation of our own relatively rootless lives. Because the way in which the material and financial worlds have changed, with people working for large companies that extend throughout the globe or moving to another part of the country or even another country for work, there is not the same influence from generation to generation within family. Very rarely do we now live in the house that we grew up in as children, or live in the same area close to other family members. It is easy to lose our family identity and not think of ourselves in terms of the history that we belong to.

However the rich experiences of the lives of our parents and their parents' lives before them are influencing us whether we like it or not. Their patterns can and sometimes do become our patterns, their strengths our strengths. Our choices can unconsciously mimic their choices, and very often we try to carry forward that which they started. Sometimes we carry forward their mistakes and their guilt, or things that are too heavy for them to bear themselves. It is also commonly accepted that you can inherit genetic/biological predispositions from your family and is anecdotally accepted that you inherit to some degree your talents, gifts and foibles from that same family line. So it is not that great a stretch to consider that perhaps we carry some of the burdens and baggage from those who have gone before us. That we perhaps carry forward and perpetuate patterns of behaviour, physical conditions and emotional responses.

As we explore some of our personal family and ancestral patterns, we can start to illuminate the reasons behind why we are the way we are and why we choose the things we choose. The unearthed discoveries will not only shed light on the dynamics and entanglements of our family of origin and, if appropriate, our subsequent created family, but can also have a significant impact on our emotional and physical state. However, we can also apply the theory of family and ancestral patterns and family constellation theory (Family Constellations and systemic constellations are therapeutic methods, developed by Bert Hellinger, exploring the ancestral patterns inherent upon individuals) on a wider scale and analyze the trends of society as a whole.

*Reviewed in Roy, Nielson, Rylander et al., 2000

There has been research investigating certain behavioural patterns within families such as family histories of suicide, alcoholism and drug addiction. It is now well established that a family history of suicide indicates that an individual is at raised risk for suicidal behaviour. In fact a family history of suicidal behaviour has been noted to be associated with suicidal behaviour at all stages of the life cycle, including those over 60, and across psychiatric diagnoses. This is also the case for those that self-harm and suffer from mood disorders, mental health issues or depression. 'The development of alcoholism among individuals with a family history of alcoholism is about four to eight times more common than it is among individuals with no such family history', said William R. Lovallo, Director of the Behavioural Sciences Laboratories at the Veterans Affairs Medical Centre, Oklahoma City and corresponding author for the study. 'Although the definition of 'family history' is different according to different researchers, we define it as when either or both of the person's parents have had an alcohol problem.'* Researchers in to both fields of study (suicide and substance abuse) agree that there is scientific evidence that alcoholism/ suicide/addiction has a family component, but the actual gene that may cause it has yet to be identified. Perhaps the pattern is not a genetic one but instead an ancestral one. Males are twice as likely as females to abuse or become dependent on substances except for the population of ages 12 to 17, when the abuse rates are nearly equal. The highest rate of substance abuse is in the age 18 to 25 population.† According to the observations of Bert Hellinger in his constellation work the incidents of depression, behavioural addictions such as alcoholism and drug abuse as well as suicide are linked to an event or pattern in the family, namely, when someone is missing or excluded from the family system. In the particular case of depression or addictive behaviours the missing or excluded person tends to be male or connected with the father's line in the individual's family. Men are also more likely to be excluded by external factors such as work requirements and roles within society. The effect of war on the male line is an ongoing, heavy burden that is far-reaching. If we revisit the fact that ten times more

*William R. Lovallo et al., May 2006

†'Addiction: Alcohol and Addiction Trends'. Reviewed in NASW Office of Social Work Specialty Practice Staff

§Bert Hellinger, Jutta Ten Herkel, INSIGHTS

people suffer from major depression now than in 1945,* with males being affected more than females we can perhaps begin to understand the effect that the missing males, be they husbands, fathers or sons have on family and society in general.

How would you define today's modern family? Is there any such thing as a traditional family structure or unit any more? There is no longer a social stigma attached to divorce or the creation of a family 'out of wedlock' as it were. There is also a very different attitude to working, with the 'stay-at-home Mother' and 'breadwinning Father' something of a rarity. If you think of a definition of the modern family, you would perhaps instinctively include a Mother but would you also instinctively include a Father? Given the general global increase of depression, alcoholism and drug addiction hand in hand with the continued gradual exclusion of the male role in terms of the family perhaps there is a link here which should be explored further.

The traditional role of the male in Western society has shifted hugely over the last century. The feminist movement and the search for equality for women has impacted all aspects of our modern Western lives. Women now have a place alongside, and in some cases in place of, their male counterparts. Is there any real place where the role of the male is truly left standing proud? In saying this I am in no way denigrating the emancipation of women or the feminist movement. In the much needed push to re-balance the feminine, the unique and valuable qualities and contributions of the masculine have been devalued and rendered invisible. There is now a need to acknowledge value and respect the place of both the feminine and masculine roles within society and within our own individual families. In particular the role of the Father and the role of the Mother, both have an equal right to belong.

Part of the work that I am involved in is to facilitate group and individual constellation sessions exploring the impact of family and ancestral patterns. Exploring these patterns through techniques such as energy healing or Family Constellation work enables us to bring clarity to some of the threads running through our lives and the lines within the family. Issues surrounding physical symptoms, chronic illnesses and attitudes towards our body can be looked at within the context of our family, our history, and the influences around us, helping us to see the deeper level at the root

*Seligman, M. E. P., in J. Buie (1988)

of it all. This awareness helps illuminate the purpose of the symptom or pattern of behaviour, allowing us to see our situation as it truly is. Once we have this information we then have the freedom to do something about it. Above all everyone has his or her own place in their family system and it is important to be acknowledged within that place. Very often there is at least one member of the family who is unconsciously not seen by other family members, and this is where the problems start and the root of many patterns. The 'system', or what is known as the 'family field', wants the family to remember the forgotten member. This entanglement can be highlighted through family and ancestral working and then brought back to a state of balance. Events or situations which can have an impact on the family system, which can cause members of the family to be excluded or to not be seen, are many and far-reaching. The acknowledgment of how things are, how they really are, and the repercussions of the event is really the key issue. The vast majority of participants on my group constellation sessions are women. Again, the issues they are drawn to work on are many and far-reaching, but an underlying element to many aspects of the work is the dynamic between the masculine and the feminine. I have observed a great reluctance within some women to look to the Father's line and the male line and a great surprise at what they experience when they choose to look and connect. What they experience is the quiet sacrifice and sense of service that flows through the masculine line that often isn't seen or acknowledged. This reluctance to look to the men is extended to the dynamic between men and women in personal relationships. There is an inability to acknowledge the sacrifice of the male line and an inability to say 'Thank you'. (It is important to note here that I am talking in general terms about a particular trend that I have observed, and I am not commenting on individual cases where there would be particular issues affecting the masculine/feminine dynamic.)

There is something happening to the role of men or to the perception of the role of men. It has become more socially acceptable to be a single parent; it has become more socially acceptable to become a single mother, and it is more socially acceptable to be a working Mother. It is commonplace for women to work in fields that were previously thought of as 'male dominated'. It is also possible to become pregnant via artificial insemination. In May 2008, UK MPs voted to remove the requirement that fertility clinics consider a child's need for a father.

I believe that the role of the Father is equally important to the role of the Mother. Both deserve and should hold an equal place in our hearts. When one is excluded, be it the Mother or the Father, then it impacts on the children and the subsequent generations of children that follow. When a member of the family field is excluded other members of the family, be it that generation or future generations, will unconsciously attempt to re-dress the balance. This 'attempt' can take many different forms, but the ob-servations of people such as Bert Hellinger show that the effects can be far-reaching and very serious. Eating disorders such as Bulimia and Anorexia can occur in young children where they are torn between their loyalties to their Mother and their Father.* The absence or the exclusion of the Father very often will result in issues around addictive behaviour, whether that is smoking, alcoholism or drug abuse. Depression too is a strong indicator of the effect of one who is missing from the family.

The fundamental basis of Bert Hellinger's constellation work and of working with ancestral patterns in general is to acknowledge and see 'what is' as opposed to imagining what is and rejecting reality. It is quite comfort-ing to think of our ancestors as something very far away and out of reach, something that lies dormant until we choose to think of them. As the popularity of the New Age movement increases, different types of ritual becomes commonplace among those who seek to work with it. Many of these rituals and traditions are associated with honouring our place in our family line and our ancestors. The Japanese system of Reiki is one that has a strong lineage element, where those teachers and elders that have gone before and paved the way are remembered and honoured. Traditional ritu-als such as the Native Americans' sweat lodges are now openly accepted, at least in a new age workshop context. In the sweat lodge, where both physical ancestry and energetic ancestry are remembered, the spirits and ancestors are honoured and aligned with.

The truth is that the link to our ancestors and the roots of our being starts much closer to home. It starts with our parents. They are the start of our ancestral line; for many people the relationship with their parents is the stumbling block or the root of the issue that holds them back in their life. Hellinger likens the Mother in some ways to be representative of a 'spirit mind' and therefore a rejection of the Mother, as of the Father, is

*Bert Hellinger, Colleen Beaumont, TO THE HEART OF THE MATTER

a rejection of life itself. To say that you want different parents, that they weren't good enough, and that you didn't receive enough from them is to say that you want a different life; your life isn't good enough, it is not enough for you. To say to your child that their Father or Mother is not good enough is to essentially say to your child that aspects of the child are not good enough and in effect sets them on a journey of self destructive behaviours. Again I emphasize that I am talking in general terms and individual cases have individual circumstances to be dealt with. However, if there are issues between parents, be it emotional or physical in origin, then those issues should be dealt with by the parents.

You cannot change your parents, they are who they are. They are the only parents for you, and therefore they are the best parents for you—just as you cannot change who the Mother or Father of your children is. If this can be acknowledged with love, then the children become free with nothing to hold them back in life. If this cannot be acknowledged or accepted as it is, then the children continue to perpetuate the same patterns within their life and pass them on to their own children. Their children will treat them as they treated their own parents. And so it goes on.

Obviously this is presented here in a simplistic fashion without any other dynamics that may be present in an individual's life, but this does not take away from the profound effect of simply acknowledging and honouring both the Mother and the Father within Family and within society as a whole. For some the revelation of the sacrifices and energy required to be a parent cannot be fully comprehended until they themselves become a parent. When you create a child with someone, an unbreakable bond is created between the Mother and the Father. They will share forever the joy and the burden of the child. To attempt to break or exclude this sacred bond between the Mother and the Father impacts the child, it is that simple. For society as a whole to exclude or to lessen the importance of the role of the Father will impact society as a whole and the subsequent generations that follow. The solution is to look to your roots, your own family.

The whole purpose and focus of working with your ancestors and family lines is to allow you to reconnect with who you are and to take your place. By seeing and acknowledging who has gone before, you can pave the way for those that will follow in your footsteps and importantly allow you to see it all as it really is.

Working with the energy of the family field within a Family Constellation allows us to see who is missing and who needs brought in and acknowledged. Work can then be done to find the point of resolution and balance for the family and the ancestors. Sound can be incorporated in to this work, either in the form of affirmations and words that heal, or chant exercises to release energy. An individual can also work with a simple ritual or exercise to acknowledge further what they have uncovered. This can often include a simple acknowledgement ritual for family members that need to be brought back in to the family field as well as into the individual's heart. It can involve a ritual of acknowledgement such as lighting a candle in someone's honour, planting a tree or evergreen plant/herb in the earth as a way of acknowledging a child or sibling that has been lost or excluded (this is not of course limited to children/siblings). When an individual is struggling with letting go the past or accepting the situation they are in as it truly is, then some visualization exercises where they imagine the ancestor/family member before them and allow themselves to feel the connection as it truly exists, is a useful way of paving the way for healing and further work. Again the responsibility always lies with the individual to take each step forward.

See your Father and your Mother as they actually are. You cannot change them, they are who they are and without them you would not have your life. Being able to accept your parents, your Mother and your Father and to give thanks for your life is to be able to accept yourself and take your place. When you can do this your children will follow.

References

'Addiction: Alcohol and Addiction Trends'. Reviewed in NASW Office of Social Work Specialty Practice Staff

Hellinger, Bert, and Ten Herkel. Jutta, INSIGHTS: LECTURES AND STORIES. Heidelberg: Carl Auer (2002)

—, and Beaumont, Colleen, TO THE HEART OF THE MATTER: BRIEF THERAPIES. Heidelberg: Carl Auer (2003)

Leon, D A; McCambridge, J, 'Liver cirrhosis mortality rates in Britain from 1950 to 2002: an analysis of routine data'. *The Lancet* 2006; 367: 52-56

Lovallo, William R. et al. May 2006

Roy, Nielson, Rylander et al., 2000

Seligman, M. E. P. (1990) LEARNED OPTIMISM

—, in J. Buie (1988) '"Me" decades generate depression: individualism erodes commitment to others'. *APA Monitor*, 19, 18.

DON'T PUSH THE RIVER

Drew Pryde

IN JULY 2002, I boarded a plane at Dallas airport bound for Vancouver to attend a wedding. As I sat in my seat there was expectancy in the air. A coloured gentleman sat down alongside me with his wife and two children sitting on the other side of the aisle. Nothing was said, but he began to read from the Book of Psalms printed in Spanish. After take-off, he closed the book and introduced himself. His name was Alfred Bullen, a US citizen working as a chaplain in Nicaragua.

In conversation, he enigmatically recommended that I should read the Gospel of St John, and that at a crucial turning point in my life St John Chapter 3 would have a special significance for me.

Around that time I had been seriously thinking about where to focus my energy and spend my time. After four decades working as a business executive in the UK and internationally I was keen to 'put something back' that would 'make a difference'. As a business coach I had become aware of a growing need from directors who both appreciated support and felt that 'there has to be a better way of doing business than this.' Events such as the collapse of Enron only strengthened this feeling, and the more recent global crisis in the financial world and consequent economic recession has only underlined the need for change and a new sort of leadership at all levels.

On return from the Vancouver holiday and, however tenuous the conversation with Alfred Bullen, I then knew the direction in which I was

Drew Pryde is an experienced businessman working at Board level in a variety of industries in the UK and abroad (USA and Brussels). In recent years, Drew has focused on executive coaching. He is passionate about encouraging spirituality in business and in 2003 founded the Scottish Institute for Business Leaders (SIBL). On a personal level, Drew has experienced the privilege of a 'miracle' healing and believes that 'everything is possible'.

headed. I began putting steps in place which led to the foundation of The Scottish Institute for Business Leaders (SIBL) in August 2003. This created a secure and confidential forum for the business and personal development of members. Much of what has transpired since then has been the sharing of my own continuing business and personal journey with forward-looking leaders.

The organization has grown from strength to strength and provides space and time for busy executives in both the private and public sectors to take a day a day out each month to work on the business rather than in it. It provides both the opportunity to learn both right- and left-brain cutting-edge concepts and processes from keynote speakers. There is also the chance to raise and resolve current work and life-balance issues in a confidential forum. It is about helping businessmen (and women) become more aware of themselves, and other people, and the significance of recognizing the need for authenticity as leaders. It is also about increasing an understanding of the environment around them and the possibilities that are open to them.

We have been fortunate in being helped on our way by visionary speakers and writers like Neale Donald Walsch, author of the 'Conversations with God' series. Although many business people can be 'lonely at the top', they are not necessarily consciously aware of their spirituality and will rarely openly articulate at that level. However, the positive feedback from many business people, and their willingness to explore softer topics, suggests an inherent desire to connect more fully both within themselves and with the world around them.

It has been recognized for a long time that there are many challenges in the world today in the form of environmental issues, poverty, diversity, sustainability and managing technology. The consequences of being economically manipulated by some sectors in the global financial community with mega bonuses, incentives and personal greed are plain to see. What has come more sharply into focus with the current economic recession is that not only are we all connected, but we have a collective responsibility for creating economic systems and decision-making based on moral values.

The concern is that many of those claiming to be solving the current problems came out of the same school as those that created it. If there was ever a time for new leadership in individual organizations and countries it is now. There are great expectations of President Obama in the United

States as he takes on the mantle of figurehead of new thinking and offering a new way forward when times are tough.

Business people are human beings and are subject to their feelings, stresses and strains, relationships, genetics and health the same as anyone else. In October 2004 I experienced seeing double on the golf course, and was fortunate to have a prompt diagnosis that this was an early symptom of a comparatively rare but severe disease called myasthenia gravis. It is a breakdown of the immune system which is triggered by antibodies in the bloodstream and is conventionally considered incurable. Initially it was controlled by medication but after some nine months the disease became immune to the medication and so I sought to explore the possibilities of alternative therapy and specifically vibrational medicine. In late October 2005, I went on a two-day educational vibrational medicine workshop in Nairn in the north of Scotland.

At the end of the second day my condition was extremely acute. My eyelids dropped, I was seeing double and I couldn't move my jaws, so couldn't speak or eat or swallow, and then the myasthenia started to close down my lungs. A doctor came up to me and said, 'Drew, I'm afraid you are too ill to travel. You will have to come home with me and stay with my family and I will treat you.'

At this stage of the condition the only orthodox treatment available to me was steroids or blood transfusion. In traditional medicine there is no known cause or cure for myasthenia. However, I started to receive three or four vibrational medicine treatments per week from this same doctor, Dr Helen Petrow, with no medication. The treatment is holistic and the diagnosis seeks to identify and then treat the cause of the disease rather than simply to suppress the symptoms. This means that as different patients may have different causes of disease then so they require differing treatments. In the ensuing weeks I also used regular visualization by imagining being at an airgun stall at a fairground and shooting ducks (antibodies) off a moving conveyor belt.

All atoms are vibrational and are pure vibrations of energy. Although vibrational frequencies are recognized by mainstream science in laboratory analysis the concept of vibrational medicine administering frequencies to neutralize disease has yet to be incorporated into conventional medicine.

My room in the doctor's family home overlooked the Moray Firth. I would get up each morning and ask myself if this was the day that my eyesight would recover and would I be able to move my jaws freely and speak and eat properly. But each day by late afternoon the winter sun would go down and no—this was not to be the day.

This process occurred for fifty days during which time I lost about sixty pounds through being unable to chew and swallow. Then on Christmas Eve 2005, I attended an afternoon service at Pluscarden Abbey near Forres. The monks were conducting a service in Gregorian chant, which is in itself a form of ancient vibration. And as I sat in a pew I listened to the singing and suddenly my eyelids lifted. I could see and also move my jaw freely and, hey, I could speak! All my symptoms just fell away! They returned shortly afterwards but at that point I knew that I would be healed.

My healing and recovery continued over the next few weeks and I was able to return to my family in Fife in February 2006. Throughout all of my three months in healing I had total faith in my doctor, the treatment, the visualization and that one day I could and would be well.

Between that February 2006 and the following January I had eleven months of blood, muscle and eye tests as an outpatient before being fully discharged by the Head of Neurology at Ninewells Hospital in Dundee.

My case has subsequently appeared in Dr David Hamilton's latest book HOW YOUR MIND CAN HEAL YOUR BODY, published in November 2008. As part of his explanation David writes 'Considering that myasthenia is considered incurable, this (Drew's case) demonstrates the power of faith to profoundly affect the body. Faith such as this is a state often associated with miracles of healing.'

I have no doubts at all about the effectiveness of the vibrational medicine treatment. As far as my absolute faith is concerned, I have no idea where it came from, but I have no doubts about the power of the mind being a major contributory factor in the healing of the body. I had a very ordinary upbringing with spells of churchgoing and with a child's keen interest in the Bible as a story book, but as far as religion was concerned I simply kept an open mind. I came out of my healing process feeling that from my personal perspective God is certainly not denominational. Throughout my illness, and despite losing so many faculties, I remained totally at peace within myself. Looking back it was a rare gift of sanctuary in which I had the time, space, care and support to come to understand and accept myself. It was also an opportunity to be conscious of healing as I could feel my body slowly but steadily recovering and healing.

After the experience at Pluscarden, and having made the breakthrough with my health, I wanted to read and asked if I could borrow the doctor's family bible. When I opened the bible it fell open precisely at St John, Chapter 3, and I remembered my conversation with the chaplain on that trip to Vancouver back in 2002. St John Chapter 3 tells the story of Nicodemus. He asks Jesus what it is that he has to do in order to enter the Kingdom of Heaven. To Nicodemus's bewilderment Christ tells him that only by being reborn can he enter the Kingdom of Heaven.

I do not know if Alfred Bullen, the American chaplain, had simply given his message to me as he would do to all men or whether he had a more specific and personal message in mind. I mention it now because what came with my experience of healing from an 'incurable' disease was a deeper inner understanding of myself. On returning home friends felt that I was quite different in some profound way and in that sense I had indeed been 'reborn'. I don't mean this in an evangelical way but it did leave me asking myself the questions why me? And what now?

It would be remiss to relate the whole healing experience as if this was something that involved only my doctor and me as the patient. When in October 2005 I became too ill to travel home from the workshop in Nairn, the news came as a terrible shock to my wife and family; particularly as I had always been such a healthy, active and physically strong person for so many years. Whereas I instinctively understood that vibrational medicine was the right course of treatment for me, many of my family come from a 'scientific' background and were accustomed to orthodox medicine. Understandably their reaction was one of shock, incredulity and even anger. They simply wanted me to be transferred back into the traditional medical system presumably to be treated by steroids or perhaps even blood transfusion. There was no way my family could accept my chosen path of treatment and this lead to a major confrontation and impasse with my doctor in Nairn. I became largely isolated from my family during the three months of my healing. This stress on personal relationships was compounded by the fact that I seemed to be a different person on returning home, compared with the person who had left home to attend a two-day workshop three months earlier. My recovery was in itself a challenge to their deeply-held belief-systems.

On the other hand, there were many messages of good wishes and support from friends and acquaintances during the period of my healing in Nairn. One friend, a family man with three children, whose wife had terminal cancer, contacted me to let me know that he was praying for me. Given his own circumstances, the fact that he should make that time for me was a humbling experience. I have no doubt that all this support made a practical and positive contribution to my recovery.

In July 2007 I was invited to attend an art exhibition by Colin Clayton, the Head of Art at Kilgraston Girls School near Bridge of Earn. This was part of the end-of-term festivities for parents and guests. Colin, a young Australian artist, was about to return home with his wife and family the following weekend and was selling off his large collection of paintings.

Unfortunately I arrived after the exhibition had closed, but was met by Colin. He had had a very successful sale and indeed only had one large painting left. Colin described this painting as being the best painting that he had created in the past seven years and therefore was very surprised that this particular painting hadn't sold.

He took me down a long corridor to see it. It was painted in a primitive aboriginal style and I asked Colin if he could explain what it depicted? He explained that the rough boat in the middle of the cloth represented a man's journey and the dark trees at the bottom right were indicative of the man experiencing trust in Winter that one day there would be the light of Spring.

I asked Colin why the oar was not in the boat but floating free and loose. He explained that the man had learnt to let go and had stopped trying to be in control. Next to the oar was a white cross and Colin explained that in letting go the man had had found peace and spirituality. He went on to explain the last part of the painting which was a red and orange burning ball. Having learnt to trust and let go, and having found spirituality, the man eventually discovered his passion in the burning ball. The title of the painting was 'Don't Push the River'.

I turned to Colin and simply said, 'I think that you painted this for me'.

I now rejoice in my good health and focus my energies on my passion for personal learning and encouraging the continuous quest towards new leadership that will make a real difference in an increasingly complex, challenging and wonderful world.

EMBRACING CONFLICT/
TRANSCENDING CONFLICT

Darrell Mann

There is a mysterious cycle in human events.
To some generations much is given.
Of other generations much is expected.
This generation has a rendezvous with destiny.
> Franklin D. Roosevelt, 1936

EVERYTHING is connected to everything else. Changes in one place may deliver unexpected outcomes in another. Does the unusual 2012 planetary alignment calculated by the Mayans, then, signify the end of the world as we know it? A major shift? Or the mere flapping of a butterfly's wings? Most likely the latter, in the opinion of this author. Why? Because the society we live in is defined by the humans that inhabit it. And future evolution of society is first and foremost determined by the first-order effects that we humans inflict on the system.

In theory, of course, the flapping of those now clichéd butterfly wings in Rio can cause a hurricane in London. In any complex system, highly non-linear effects are always possible. But if I had to put my money on the most likely cause of a hurricane in London, it will come from a high-altitude strongly-sheared environment formed around a parent Polar Front jet core interacting with a distortion of a pre-existing eastward-moving

---

Following a fifteen year spell working in aerospace R&D, since 1995, Darrell Mann has researched, taught and consulted in the field of innovation With over six hundred systematic innovation-related papers, patents and articles to his name he is now one of the most widely published authors on the innovation subject in the world.

baroclinic zone.*

The societal equivalent of the Polar Front jet core interacting with the baroclinic—i.e., the first-order effects that will determine whether we see the societal equivalent of a hurricane in the coming years—appears in the form of three big driving forces.

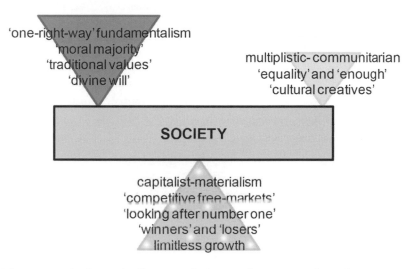

These aren't the only forces, of course, but given that close to 90% of the global population is centred around one of these three basic views of the world, they will tend to have the biggest effect on our future.† Aside from being the biggest driving forces, the other reason they will tend to determine the future of society is that each of the three views contains strong conflicts with the other two. As suggested in the figure, the biggest single set of conflicts centre around the tension between individual freedom (capitalist materialism) acting in one direction and collective responsibility, in the form of either one-right-way fundamentalism or multiplistic communitarianism, acting in the other.

As the various tensions play out, there are a number of potential

---

*The actual cause of the hurricane winds that struck the south of England in 1987.

†Readers familiar with the work of psychologist, Dr Clare Graves, will recognize these three forces as the DQ, ER and FS thinking models respectively. For those more familiar with 'Spiral Dynamics', they are the Blue 'Order', Orange 'Scientific' and Green 'Communitarian' thinking modes.

outcomes we might expect to see in the coming years. According to the Generational Cycles that will also inevitably play a part in the story, it seems highly likely that the conflict-driven tensions are building to levels that are unsustainable. Somehow, they will need to be released. Most likely this 'release' will occur around the period 2020 to 2025.* The same generational research suggests that society passes through these phases of gradual building of tensions followed by sudden release every four generations, or around every eighty to ninety years. The last big tension build up commenced with the collapse of the US banks in 1929, and the last release came as the Second World War reached its climax.

If the omens from the last generational cycle don't look good, we now have the additional pressures arising from the fact that, as a total population, we are living (thanks mainly to the capitalist-materialist 'limitless growth' worldview that has come to dominate over the last hundred years) unsustainably. Put simply, we live on the brink of environmental catastrophe. And if that wasn't bad enough, we seem to be on a runaway train that we barely know how to stop.

The environment factor serves further to increase the tension between the capitalists driving the train, and the two groups of 'collective responsibility' worldviews. Not that these two views are the same. Their only similarity is that the capitalist worldview with MNCs that are all too willing to 'externalize' inconvenient environmental costs cannot be allowed to continue. Aside from that, the overwhelming fundamentalist view is that our future will be determined by 'divine will'. God, in other words, is the only entity who can decide whether we survive or die. The multiplistic communitarian view, on the other hand, is that the future is in our hands, and that all we have to do is re-focus our energies onto the 'right' things. Although, at around fifteen- to twenty-percent of the population, the smallest of the three driving forces, this 'cultural creative' (horrible term since, paradoxically, they tend to be some of the least creative people) worldview is probably the only one that will see society emerge from the tension release in any kind of intact manner.

That the communitarian view prevails is but one of a number of dif-

---

*The pioneering social history research of William Strauss and Neil Howe, most notably described in their book THE FOURTH TURNING, is the source of this part of the story.

ferent scenarios that could pan out in the next fifteen or so years. The most likely one, if we stay on the same track we're currently riding, will be the one where the driving tensions and conflicts result in a fragmented society:

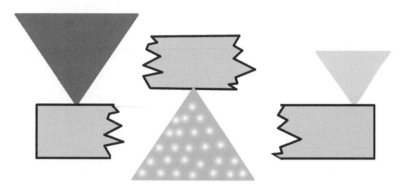

Alas, this outcome has almost zero chance of solving our environmental problems, and hence, when the dust settles, we are likely to be looking around and seeing a lot less than six billion people still living on the planet. The start along this road most likely began with the events of 9/11. In this sense, the tragedy of that terrorist attack is analogous to our flapping butterfly wings again. One event starting a chain of others that inexorably lead towards global-scale disaster.

If 2012 has any significance at all in this story, it is most likely that it will serve as the focus for another 'tipping point' event like 9/11. In theory, the tipping point that will determine how the 2020–25 tension release is manifest could happen at any point in time between today and then. In practice, however, because 2012, and particularly the winter solstice date of December 21st, 2012 is there for all to see, and because our technical capabilities have now reached such an extent that a very small number of people (read: fanatics) can create a very non-linear amount of damage, the real worry must be that someone takes it upon him or herself to 'make history' for themselves on or around this date.

In this sense, we find ourselves heading towards a self-fulfilling prophecy. A bunch of astronomers make a prediction; a bunch of terrorists decide it would be 'amusing' to make this prediction come true.

Fortunately, it is extremely unlikely that any group of individuals, no matter how fanatical, have quite the power to create a doomsday scenario. The real fear should be that they do just enough damage to create the aforementioned tipping point that leads to the real doomsday scenario ten years later.

If this all sounds pretty depressing, it probably is. But that is not to say that it is a fait accompli. There are things we can do to dig ourselves out of the problem—to save ourselves from environmental meltdown, and to emerge as a still-coherent society.

The key lies in diffusion of the tensions that currently surround us. Crucially here, 'diffusion' explicitly does not mean trying to find trade-off and compromise solutions to our problems. In a black-and-white world, choosing the best shade of grey is never the best way of doing things. Smart leaders find ways to challenge trade-offs and dilemmas to create outcomes where one plus one is significantly greater than two. Successfully challenging and transcending conflict is one of the key roles we now all have to play.

Einstein is famously quoted as saying that no tough problem can be resolved with the same level of thinking that caused it. In order to solve the assorted right-versus-right dilemmas confronting leaders, therefore, there needs to be a shift in perspective. Alas, leaders are more likely to use the KISS principle when dealing with tough problems than to act upon Einstein's words. Keep It Simple Stupid—never in the history of humanity has such an apparently common-sense acronym caused so much downstream damage. To quote another famous scientist, this time Nils Bohr, 'every complex problem has a simple wrong answer'. In today's world, there are no simple problems anymore.

Talk of one-plus-one adding to more than two—or 'win-win' to use another cliché—is common. It sounds wonderful in theory, but when it comes to practice … well, let's say the cupboard tends to be bare.

But is it just our cupboard that is empty? According to a sixty-year programme of research investigating how engineers, politicians and business leaders transcend either/or dilemmas, the clear evidence is that someone, somewhere has already found a breakthrough solution to any and all the conflicts we may be experiencing. The research, having now studied over three million case studies, has further shown that there are just a small number of possible strategies that will successfully transcend such conflicts and dilemmas. At its root, the research has been an investigation to find the DNA of breakthrough problem-solving.

Strand number one in the resulting DNA picture of the world is that job number one is about learning to embrace conflict. Strand number two is about transcending those conflicts, to move away from either/or and to achieve both/and solutions.

Both strands, according to the research and through a long list of proof-of-the-pudding clients around the world gathered over the course of the last ten years, are achievable in a systematic and repeatable manner. And so let this be my 'vital message' for 2012. Everything is connected to everything else. The spark that lit the three million data-point research, that now gives us the systematic win-win capability, came from a Russian engineer, Genrich Altshuller. Altshuller was a great studier of how mankind's finest solved problems, and one of his great role models was Conan Doyle's Sherlock Holmes character. What Altshuller learned from Conan Doyle and from close to forty years of personal scientific study was the need to embrace as opposed to ignore or run away from conflict. By embracing conflict we open the possibility that the changes we make to a system in one place will deliver positive outcomes in other places. Embrace conflict, in other words, for therein lies our future. Transcend conflict, for therein lies our salvation. The tools to do the job already exist. The only thing we need to do now is pick them up and use them.

LETTERS TO A YOUNG(ER) CONSULTANT
Inspired by Rilke's 'Letters to a Young Poet'

Verna Allee

Part I

I KNOW you were very disappointed in the meeting with the project leader today, and what essentially feels like a dismissal. According to our customer, nobody likes the ideas and methods we have introduced; she can't find anyone who feels positive about the work; it is too hard; it isn't valuable; it doesn't help them think through what is important; they aren't using it; they think it is a waste of their time—so she wants us to stop everything we are doing and if it were her decision alone we would clearly drop completely off the radar screen. Her message was thanks anyway, but this is too hard and it is time for you to go away now.

It is very frustrating to be marginalized in any circumstances and always painful to be dismissed from a project before people have really given it a chance. It certainly is not the first time for me, indeed for the type of work that we do—and being outside the power circles and dominant decision-making centres of the world as consultants are—it is all too common. It can be very difficult, but it just goes with the work. Try not to take it personally because it really isn't about us, or the quality or importance of our work. It is about all of us and about the underlying work we are engaged in as a society, which is the transformation of consciousness on the planet. For people like us this work is much larger than a job. It is a calling.

Verna Allee, M.A., is CEO of Value Networks LLC, (www.valuenetworks.com), the leading provider of value network visualization and analysis applications. She is a pioneer in value networks, intangibles, knowledge management, and new business models and is on a number of Advisory and Editorial Boards including Hazel Henderson's Ethical Markets television series.

It comes from a deep and passionate desire to help make the world a better place by demonstrating how business can be conducted in ways that are good for people, good for business, and good for the planet.

The real work we do is transformation work—transformation of human consciousness into another way of seeing the world and believing our way into what might be possible. We are moving people out of their comfort zone and presenting a challenge to what they think, what they believe, their values, how they work, who they are in terms of their role in the company and society and how they behave. So it is no surprise that sometimes people just don't want to deal with it.

People ask me sometimes what I do to get people to see the world 'this way'. I reply that it is not my job to sell or persuade or convert anyone. Tilting at windmills only gets me a bloody nose. If people are asking certain kinds of questions (like other people we know in the same company and in other quarters) then they are not only ready but eager for what we are offering. My task is to be absolutely clear about what it is I understand and believe and to communicate that as simply, clearly and effectively as I possibly can—and to not back off from the message. There is no way to make these new ideas about real partnership, collaboration, transparency, systems thinking, intangible assets, dynamic relationships, knowledge sharing, social responsibility, sustainability, ethics and self-organization 'safe' or 'easy.' As Marianne Williamson wrote in 'Our Deepest Fear',

> It is our light, not our darkness that most frightens us…
> Your playing small does not serve the world.
> There's nothing enlightened about shrinking so that
> Other people won't feel insecure around you.

On a few rare occasions your work makes a significant difference by fostering better relationships, encouraging people to play a more compassionate and positive role in the world, sparking a return to deeper human values and supporting healthier behaviours as individuals, as organizations and as nations. And in a thousand little ways and little moments you connect to people along the way, touching each other with shared hope and vision. Those moments are luminous points, like lanterns lighting a sometimes dark path. These little successes and heart-connections are great gifts. They bring a deep inner joy that reminds you that the real reason you do this is simply because it is your path—it is just what you are here to do.

Part II

Shifting people's worldview is some of the hardest work there is, I think, because if you do it really well people will almost always react by saying, 'Oh yeah, we knew that already—we just hadn't put it together quite that way'. In fact, that response is actually the best response of all and the only way you know you have really accomplished your goal of helping to shift consciousness.

Why do I say that is really the best response? Think back on break-through moments you have had. Don't they always feel like a blinding flash of the obvious? Your inner response is 'Oh, of course! How could I have not seen that? It all makes perfect sense'. Followed by a little voice that pops in there with, 'I guess I really knew it all along'. That reaction says that you now totally and completely 'own' the insight and the expanded worldview it is part of. In other words it is now part of your consciousness, where it was not before. But we don't knowingly experience it as a change of worldview or consciousness—it simply feels like the next logical step in our own thinking.

You now have taken this new idea completely within your psyche as your own understanding. You don't refer to the idea as someone else's understanding—as Joe's way of thinking or Mary's, or whoever. You may reference their work or their ideas, quote them, even critique them and disagree with them, but you will do so in a way that affirms the underlying idea as essentially correct because, of course, it is the way you have understood it all along!

This is an important point. As long as the idea somehow stays 'outside' your own understanding then that idea has not entered your consciousness as a basic pattern of understanding or belief that informs your worldview. Yet, now that you have expanded beyond the box of your more limited understanding, you can't go back inside.

We do of course recognize transforming moments in our lives. We can all name times that our sense of personal identity shifted or we had an experience that 'changed my life'. Once in a while we might acknowledge a guru or teacher that was instrumental in that life-changing experience. The older we become, however, the more difficult it is for us to acknowledge the instrumentality of another in those life-changing moments or significant shifts of consciousness or understanding. We become more and more the agents of our own transformation and perceive that transformation comes from within us more than from outside influences. So transformation no longer happens 'to' us, it happens because we ourselves are pursuing a question, seeking knowledge or are growing in our understanding.

I believe this is why as a consultant you will rarely get an acknowledgment that you had anything to do with their breakthrough. A few people over the course of your career might understand what it is you really do and appreciate it. But for the most part consultants are right behind lawyers in terms of respect.

Part III

Max Boisot reminds us that whenever there is a powerful new worldview or consciousness emerging there are a number of reactions to the new thinking. First of all it is ignored. If it still won't go away, then it is laughed at or denigrated in some way. In the consulting world this means whatever we do is dismissed as the 'flavour of the month' and shows up in Dilbert comic strips and jokes about 'consulting jargon'. If that doesn't work and it still won't go away, then two things begin to happen, almost at the same time. The first thing that happens is that it will get attacked outright, as our work was today. The academics will pick it apart, other consultants will attack it, popular business journals will 'objectively' present a totally opposite view or critique, and our customers will say it is just too hard, we are not ready for this and it won't work here.

However, the attacks become particularly intense just at the point when people are really starting to take it very seriously—and are beginning to accept and even embrace it. So in your work in the same company you will find those who love what you are bringing in and those who obviously hate it. Some people will love your books; others will use them to prop the furniture. Recently I spoke at a conference where I had one of the most positive responses I have ever experienced. At that same event someone literally shouted back from the audience that what I was saying was just wrong! Both reactions, hand in hand. Love it—hate it. This of course can be hard on a personal level as it can be quite a roller-coaster ride. But it is not nearly as hard as being ignored completely. It is actually a sign of great progress.

The important thing to remember is that whatever reaction people have it is probably more about them than it is about you. Listen carefully to the feedback, learn from it, polish your craft, try doing things a little differently next time. When you begin to have an impact some people will think you are wonderful and treat you like a guru; others might drag your name and your work through the mud. If you buy into either one of those ideas about who you are … you're sunk. As a change agent you are a moving target for whatever people want to project onto you from their own inner experiences.

Just plant your feet in what you believe, do the work that has heart and meaning for you and do the next thing in front of you. It's like dropping pebbles into a pond. It isn't your job to know where the ripples spread. Your work is to pay very close attention to the quality of the pebbles you are dropping into the pond.

DEVELOP A HEART-CENTRED BUSINESS

Jan H Stringer

WISDOM comes in the most interesting ways—like when a child points out something that is so obvious, yet filled with simple truth. In this case, the simple truth came from one of our customers.

Marty was filled with emotion at the end of the weekend training as he confessed how he hadn't wanted to attend this business retreat in the first place. He said he had only come because one of his friends had encouraged him to. Marty told his friend he would attend with the caveat 'if they ask me to take my shoes off, I am leaving'. He wasn't comfortable about what the retreat might entail. Now at the closing ceremony of the retreat, four days after his arrival, he recounted the story with the whole group while laughing and crying at the same time. He shared that his life had been forever changed out of the experience of being at the retreat. Marty shared that he was so glad that he had not left on that first day even though he was asked to remove his shoes before entering the training room.

After returning home, his partner asked him what the retreat was all about. Marty answered, 'Love'. His partner looked bewildered by his answer and said, 'What does LOVE have to do with business and marketing?'. Marty replied 'Everything!' Marty's answer summed up that love is everything when it comes to business—it is at the heart of marketing and building a business; it's a simple truth.

When people are asked about their definition of marketing, they usu-

Jan H Stringer, Founder and President, PerfectCustomers, Inc. Jan resides in Santa Fe, NM, with her business partner and husband, Alan Hickman. Together they work, live and teach their message through books, speaking engagements, workshops, and trainings. www.perfectcustomers.com. This chapter is excerpted from their book, BEE-ING ATTRACTION: WHAT LOVE HAS TO DO WITH IT!

ally share that it is about getting the word out or other traditional methods such as advertising or promotion. In the past few years of working with business owners, the common language that each person spoke was that they wanted to do something that they loved for a living. When a business owner loves what they are doing for a living, you know it. You receive the warmth of their enthusiasm, the attractiveness of their passion, and the glow of their desire to share their gifts of understandings. As a consumer, we want to do business with people because it feels good to us to be in the presence of someone who loves what they do.

If you are reading this and have studied in traditional schools, no doubt there were no business courses offered in your college about following your heart in business. More than likely you were told that you had to work hard to earn a living. It is our belief that people are attracted to heart-centred businesses which radiate love and heartfelt feelings to their customers through their service, products and programmes more than their hard work ethic. When you are the recipient of a heart-centred business, you know that the owner(s) are directly connected to their own heart and their passion. The contrast is also true—it becomes apparent when you are working with someone who is not heart-centred. Their business expression comes through as hype, pressure, easy money, too good to be true—which bring up uncomfortable feelings of being taken advantage of or being ripped off.

Now the times have changed and it signals new opportunities to be creative. Perhaps you might recognize this as a time to seek personal freedom and creative licence to apply your heartfelt unique skills and talents rather than attempting to conform to the old business models which were centred on chasing money.

A steady change has started to occur in the United States and the world, the results of which have yet to be seen as of the time of this writing. You and everyone else are having to shift in your own personal ways to embrace the massive changes taking place. In the face of new economic outcomes, the fall of systems, the failures in the mortgage industries, uncertainty in auto industries, and the unpredictable effects of the stock market, you can rise above it all as effective and successful business owners. As the owner of a business that you love, you can succeed in any economy when you allow your heart to open. You will need to incorporate your innate business instincts, of course, yet you may also want to consider extensive personal healing, and energy clearing to release past patterns and to make way for a new beginning. What you have learned in your previous experience of creating business may need to be forgotten! To become successful, you may need to let go of knowledge that you spent years mastering with great success.

For example, if your business was created to be a moneymaking machine, you may need to let go of working at all costs at the expense of health and relationships. In these days and times, the old driven mentality is obsolete. In other words, ways of being that were so effective for you before just won't produce the same results. It's time to implement a new way of being to allow for a brand new day in your current business perspective. The best place to create a new being starts with developing what is in your heart and that's what the Bee-ing Attraction Plan is designed to accomplish.

The Bee-ing Attraction process (from the book BEE-ING ATTRACTION: WHAT LOVE HAS TO DO WITH IT!) is a simple strategic planning tool that will give you a new perspective and an immediate practice to apply to your business. It will help you develop a heart-centred business and enjoy the changes that are upon you. The planning process steps you through a heart and soul thought process that involves the following steps:

Step One: Describe the qualities, characteristics and attributes of your perfect customers, employees or other stakeholders.
Step Two: Identify what makes you and your perfect customers (or other relationships) tick.
Step Three: Define what you want your perfect customers (or other relationships) to expect of you.
Step Four: Declare who you have to BEE to attract what you say you want.

Here are some of the qualities, characteristics and attributes that might be present in your Bee-ing Attraction Plan of someone who is developing a heart-centred business:

- Being present in the moment
- Follows their intuition; trusts their gut
- Uses imagination

- Expresses creativity through business
- Courageous enough to stand for loving our self and each other
- Radiates inner peace
- Steps out in faith
- Trusts their own process
- Their business, relationships and communities are centred around love and harmony
- Walks their talk every moment
- Hangs out with other like-minded people who bring the best out in others
- Makes choices from their heart
- Stands by their friends, partners, and associates

As you design and work with your Bee-ing Attraction Plan, you will start an elimination process of the previous ways that are not in alignment with your heartfelt values. It takes courage to express what you truly want from a deep connection and to believe that you can have anything that you truly desire. You can attract anything that you are willing to declare that you want to have in life and the Bee-ing Attraction Plan is a great springboard from which to gain clarity about what is perfect for you. Most of the people that have experienced the benefits of working with their Bee-ing Attraction plan say that it was the permission they needed to create from a heart place rather than from what they thought was expected of them, which is a mental place. It was also a way for them to connect with their heart and soul and to make it a priority in building their business and in forming their relationship when they identified what makes them tick.

The Bee-ing Attraction Plan is a basic introduction to our concept of building heart-centred business. If you are just starting to implement this planning process for the first time, you will be learning how to attract business relationships that you would call a perfect fit for your business, as well as, to give you a deeper understanding of your inner desires. The purpose of the creating your Bee-ing Attraction Plan is threefold:

1. To gain clarity about who and what is a perfect fit for you and your business.
2. To gain focus about what is the perfect next action to take to forward your business.

3.   To develop a deeper understanding about yourself so that your business is a true match for what is most important to you in life—therefore, is a business that is in alignment with your heart and soul.

After committing to developing a heart-centred business and using this planning process, you may never perceive business, or any relationship or situation in quite the same way. It says that you believe business is very personal and it is your way of expressing what is most important to you, or as we say it, 'what is most perfect for me!'. In this time of extreme change, it is your opportunity to activate your business spirit, initiate your imagination and use creativity to design a business that is worthy of your devotion.

THE ECONOMIC CASE FOR CLIMATE ACTION*

L Hunter Lovins

Overview[1]

This paper describes how investing in climate protection is good for business. It describes ways that intelligent uses of market mechanisms can solve the climate crisis not at a cost but as an investment in a far better future for all of the world's people. The paper describes how this future is rapidly emerging despite restrictions at every turn.

Introduction

Climate change represents a unique challenge for economics: it is the greatest and widest-ranging market failure ever seen
Sir Nicholas Stern[2]

Creating the low-carbon economy will lead to the greatest economic boom in the U.S. since we mobilized for World War II
Former President Bill Clinton[3]

Sir Nicholas Stern and Bill Clinton both have it right. Global climate change has been our greatest market failure. Now it is our greatest market opportunity. There is a strong business case for solving climate change.

Mitigating greenhouse gas (GHG) emissions worldwide will require a crash programme to use energy more efficiently, and to switch to renew-

*In this substantial article, notes have been numbered and placed at the end (p. 258)

Millennium TIME Magazine Hero of the Planet, Hunter Lovins was named 2008 Sustainability Pioneer. In demand as an inspirational speaker, Hunter consults to large corporations, small businesses, communities, and dozens of nations around the world. She is President of Natural Capitalism Solutions and a founding professor at Presidio MBA.

able energy sources. Sir Nicholas Stern, less than a year after releasing his report, stated that climate change is happening faster than had previously been thought, and that emissions need to be reduced sharply and rapidly.[4] The good news is that more efficient use of energy and renewable energy is growing rapidly, and that transforming our economy to reduce carbon emissions in line with what scientists say is needed,[5] will cut costs, drive competitiveness, create jobs and stimulate prosperity.

The Opportunity of the New Energy Economy

As economic conditions drive companies to cut costs, smart managers are realizing that energy efficiency is one of the best places to start. Historically, energy costs were believed to be small, fixed expenses. One client company instituted a simple policy: across their twenty-six facilities, employees were asked to shut off their seven thousand computers and monitors when the equipment was not in use. That one measure saved $683,000 the first year. No-one had asked just how much energy the devices were using. The 2009 PC Energy report found that shutting off unused American PCs would save $2.8 billion a year.[6] Such measures have no capital cost. The savings can then be banked to capitalize progressively more ambitious efficiency measures. Not only can investments in energy savings deliver some of the highest rates of return in the entire economy, but this stream of savings can be leveraged to achieve ongoing savings.

—Twenty U.S. states, over two-thirds of the United States economy and population, are implementing comprehensive, multi-sector greenhouse gas reduction plans. Such programmes will expand employment, income and investment, contribute to national economic recovery, while achieving net savings of at least $85 billion in 2020; and from 2009 to 2020 cumulative savings of $535.5 billion. The programmes will also deliver such co-benefits as energy independence, enhanced health and environmental protection.[7]

—Renewable energy and energy efficiency industries currently generate about 8.5 million green collar jobs and almost $1 trillion in revenue. The number could increase to forty million jobs and $4.5 trillion in revenues 'with the appropriate public policy, including a renewable portfolio standard, renewable energy incentives, public education and research and development'.[8] In the week that these numbers were released, General Electric Power Generation announced it would invest $39 million and hire

500 workers for a renewable energy division expansion in upstate New York.[9] In 2008, renewable energy and energy efficiency (RE&EE) industries generated $10.3 billion in sales and over 91,000 jobs in Colorado.[10]

—In 2008, over a seven-month period, the City of San Francisco created a hundred and eighty new jobs by enabling six hundred and forty residents and enterprises to install 2 MW in small rooftop solar electric systems. Workforce trainees filled 83% of the jobs. The City's SF Energy Watch helped 1,500 businesses and multifamily properties save over $5.7 million in energy bills, delivering six megawatts of energy efficiency savings.[11]

—The opportunity is even larger in developing countries. More than $300 billion will be needed worldwide over the next twenty years to provide low-carbon electric power and equipment to the billion people who now do not yet have access to electricity.[12] The World Bank estimates that an investment of up to $40 billion annually will be needed worldwide to adapt to climate change. Meeting those needs with renewable energy and energy efficiency will create ten times more jobs than building fossil fuel power plants.[13] Doing this will also better enhance national economies and strengthen poverty alleviation efforts.[14]

—Renewables are the fastest growing energy supply worldwide, and are, in many cases, even cheaper than conventional supply. Solar thermal is leading the charge, outpacing all conventional energy supply technologies. Modern wind machines come second, delivering over eight gigawatts of new power to the U.S. in 2008,[15] or more new power than nuclear added worldwide each year at its peak in the 1970s. Estimates by the U.S. Secretary of Interior show that offshore wind potential could more than meet all U.S. demands for electricity.[16] The third fast-growing technology is solar electric, adding almost six gigawatts of new capacity in 2008 worldwide.[17]

—Clean technology investments set another record in 2008, despite the economic collapse. In North America, Europe, China and India lean technology venture investments totalled a record $8.4 billion, up 38% from $6.1 billion in 2007, the seventh consecutive year of growth in venture investing.[18] A 2007 survey of nineteen venture capitalists investing in fifty-seven European clean-tech firms showed average annual returns since 1999 of almost 87%.[19] Returns dropped precipitously in the 2008 crash, but are expected to rebound as financing becomes available. Calling climate change 'one of the most pressing global challenges', venture capitalist John Doerr predicted that the resulting demand for innovation would create the 'mother of all markets'.[20] Investment in renewable energy projects market could reach $50 billion by 2011, with double-digit annual growth rates.[21] The United Nations described 'A gold rush of new investment into renewable power.' concluding that clean energy could provide almost a quarter of the world's electricity by 2030.[22] The European Renewable Energy Council (EREC) was even more optimistic, claiming that 50% of the world's energy supply can come from renewable energy sources by 2040.[23]

—In 2007, the U.S renewable energy and energy efficiency industries generated over a trillion dollars in sales and created over nine million jobs, representing substantially more than the combined 2007 sales of the three largest U.S. corporations—Wal-Mart, ExxonMobil, and GM ($905 billion). If the federal stimulus policies are implemented, these industries could generate over 37 million jobs per year in the U.S. by 2030.[24]

—Investing in new transit infrastructure to help Americans achieve the access that they seek without having to rely on private automobiles will cut carbon emissions, create jobs, and foster urban revitalization. There were seven hundred million 'light duty vehicles' worldwide in 2000, expected to increase to 1.3 billion in 2030 and more than two billion by 2050.[25] Better urban design, mass transit and vehicle efficiency are all needed to prevent massive increases in transport-related carbon emissions and urban gridlock. Transportation America estimates that building needed transit systems in seventy-eight U.S. metro areas will generate 6.7 million jobs and save citizens billions of dollars annually. The typical American family spends 19% of household income on transportation. Effective mass transit could return 1-15% of this income to citizens. Portland, Oregon estimates that its recent mass transit investments save its citizens $2.6 billion annually.[26]

—In December 2006, Mayor Michael Bloomberg announced PLANYC 2030 to create affordable and sustainable homes for nearly one million New Yorkers, ensure that all residents live near a park, add public transit capacity for millions more commuters, upgrade energy infrastructure and achieve 'the cleanest air of any big city in America'—all while reducing the city's greenhouse gas emissions by 30%.[27]

—Replacing the eighty-five million barrels of petroleum the world consumes each day, the three hundred and eighty-five million gallons of gasoline burned daily in the United States,[28] and the much higher fuel consumption projected for the future will require whole new industries. Between 2000 and 2005 production of biofuels grew globally by 95% and should account for 5% of transport fuels by 2020. By 2015, this could create more than two hundred thousand new U.S jobs in ethanol production alone.[29] In contrast, the high oil prices of mid-2008 represented one of the biggest transfers of wealth in history, redistributing 1% of world GDP each year. Oil consumers paid $5 billion more for oil every day than they did 5 years before. In 2007, $2 trillion flowed from customers to the oil companies and oil-producing nations.[30]

For years, the United States led the world in development of 'green' technologies including solar technologies and wind turbines. Today, such countries as Japan, Germany, Spain and Denmark lead in solar and wind power. In Germany, renewables generate more new jobs than any other in-dustry,[31] creating 250,000 jobs in the renewable energy sector and 1.8 mil-lion jobs in environmental protection. The number of jobs in renewables is projected to more than triple by 2020, hitting 900,000 by 2030. The Ger-man Deputy Environment Minister stated, 'Investments in climate protec-tion can help us get out of this crisis faster'. The German government aims to reduce its emissions of carbon dioxide by 40% from 1990 levels by 2020. The renewable energy sector aims to triple its share of power generation to 47% by 2020, from 15.1% in 2008.[32]

The Germans are not alone. Denmark aims to get 60% of its energy from renewables by 2010. Japan was first-to-market with hybrid vehicles, enabling Toyota to surpass General Motors as the world largest car com-pany in 2008. It expects hybrid vehicles to rise from 6% of its U.S. vehicle sales in 2005 to 20% by 2012.[33]

If United States wishes to retain its position as world leader it will put a priority on developing the goods and services needed for low-carbon economic development worldwide.

The Economics of Climate Protection

The 2007 McKinsey study (See Figure 1, opposite) is one of a growing number of studies finding that climate challenge can be met at little or even negative cost.

The McKinsey study found it cost-effective to cut greenhouse gas emis-sions on the scale that scientists say will be necessary to protect the climate. Importantly, the study finds that this can be achieved at less than the world spends on defence or insurance, and approximately a third of the collec-tive impact of 2007 oil price rises.[35] Although individual assumptions can

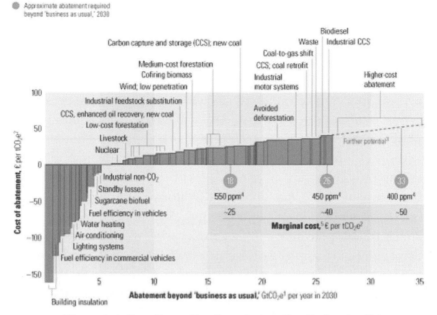

Figure 1 A Cost Curve For Greenhouse Gas Reduction[34]

be questioned (McKinsey uses historic nuclear costs, not the much higher marginal costs of building new plants, it assumes that carbon capture and sequestration of emissions from new coal plants will be cheap, while it is more likely that it will double the cost of coal) the shape of the graph is roughly correct. The savings from energy efficiency, which can cut energy use by at least half, will roughly pay for the additional supply needed to offset carbon emissions.

'This is a hugely important message to policy makers everywhere, not least those in the United States Congress,' the *New York Times* editorialized in May 2007. 'Many of them have been paralyzed by fears ... that a full-scale attack on climate change could cripple the economy.'[36]

The truth is quite the contrary, having already suffered a 'full-scale at-tack on the economy', the only way out of the current mess seems to be precisely to implement the measures that will protect the climate.

Community leaders agree. Over nine hundred American mayors pledged their cities to meet the goals set forth in the Kyoto Protocol or reduce their emissions of greenhouse gasses by at least 7% by 2012.[37] Some have already met even more aggressive targets, ranging from a goal of 20% reduction by Portland to a goal of 42% reduction over the same time frame by Sebastopol,

California.[38] Communities and companies that are implementing climate protection programmes are finding that smart, comprehensive approaches to climate planning make them more competitive and put hundreds of billions of dollars back into the economy from savings.

In the world's sixth largest economy, Californians have held their energy consumption to zero growth since 1974 while national per capita energy consumption grew 50%. This has enabled the average family there to pay about $800 less for energy each year than had the state not pursued energy efficiency.[39] In 2004, California ranked twelfth in the nation in energy prices, but only forty-fifth in energy costs per person.[40] A 2008 Study by the University of California found that California's programmes to reduce energy dependence and increase energy productivity three decades ago directed a greater percentage of its consumption to in-state, employment-intensive goods and services whose supply chains largely reside within the state. This created a strong 'multiplier' effect of job creation, generating 1.5 million FTE jobs with a total payroll of over $45 billion, saving California consumers over $56 billion in energy costs. Going forward, achieving 100% of the greenhouse gas emission reduction targets mandated by California's AB 32, a cap on emissions by 2020, would increase the Gross State Product by $76 billion, increase real household incomes by $48 million, and create as many as 403,000 new efficiency and climate-action jobs.[41]

Programmes to help buildings use less energy and encourage the use of efficient cars, appliances and machines stimulate new manufacturing ventures, increase farm income, and generate increased community income. A local government Commissioner from Portland, Oregon, stated, 'We've found that our climate change policies have been the best economic development strategy we've ever had. Not only are we saving billions of dollars on energy, we are also generating hundreds of new sustainable enterprises as a result'. A 2003 study of the impact of energy efficiency and renewables in Oregon found that one average megawatt saved increases:

—annual economic output in Oregon by $2,230,572
—wage income in Oregon by $684,536 and
—business income by $125,882.

Each average megawatt saved creates twenty-two new jobs in Oregon. The study found that over twelve megawatts were saved as a result of Energy Trust programme activities in 2002, with the number growing to a hnudred and twenty-five average megawatts by 2006.[42]

The Business Role In Climate Protection
Many corporations understand that climate protection will enhance their bottom line. DuPont, GE, Alcoa, Caterpillar, PG&E, Chrysler, Johnson & Johnson, PepsiCo and others, acting as members of the U.S. Climate Action Partnership, or USCAP,[43] have called for national legislation to cap carbon emissions, stating, 'In our view, the climate change challenge will create more economic opportunities than risks for the U.S. economy'.[44]

DuPont pledged in 1999 to reduce its emissions of greenhouse gases 6565% below its 1990 levels by 2010, and to get 10% of its energy and 25% of its feedstocks from renewables, making this announcement in the name of increasing shareholder value. DuPont delivered on that promise: the value of DuPont stock increased 340% as the company reduced global emission reductions 67% for a savings between 2000 and 2005 of $3 billion.[45] DuPont's climate protection programme demonstrated that it costs less to implement the energy savings measures than it does to buy and burn the fuel. In 1999, the Company estimated that every ton of carbon it displaced saved it $6. In 2007 DuPont's efforts to squeeze out waste were saving the company $2.2 billion a year. The company's profits were $2.2 billion a year.[46]

ST Microelectronics pledged to become carbon neutral (zero net CO2 emissions) by 2010 with a forty-fold increase in production. Figuring out how to do this drove the company's innovation, taking it from the No. 12 microchip manufacturer in the world to the No. 6. ST gained market share, won awards and reckons it will save almost a billion dollars by the time it meets its goal.

In December 2004, Chicago Climate Exchange (CCX) the world's biggest and the U.S.'s only voluntary cap-and-trade system, began trading carbon in a country where no law mandated it. Inaugural members DuPont, ST, Baxter Health Care, the City of Chicago and thirteen other businesses who voluntarily contracted to reduce their emissions by 2% a year. If they reduced emissions even further, they created tradable Carbon Financial Instruments (CFI's), which they could sell to such members as World Resources Institute or Natural Capitalism who wished to become carbon neutral. CCX's forty-four members' collective baseline is now over six hundred million metric tons (mmt), larger than the emissions from Germany in the mandatory EU program. CCX members, have already cut their emissions eight percent. CCX members represent 17% of U.S. stationary emissions, 20% of the power sector, and 20% of the Dow Jones industrials.

Partnering with the China National Petroleum Corporation (Petro China) and the city of Tianjin, CCX opened the Tianjin Climate Exchange in Tianjin, China in fall 2008. The India Climate Exchange has gathered 20 members to establish a private cap-and-trade in India. CCX also is partnered with the European Climate Exchange, which now trades 85% of the European Trading System (ETS) futures market.

In 2006, the world's largest retailer, Wal-Mart, announced goals to reduce energy use at its stores 30% over three years, double the fleet efficiency of its vehicle fleet, build hybrid-electric long-haul trucks, and ultimately become carbon neutral, 100% powered by renewable energy. The company calculates that its campaign to sell one hundred million CFLs in 2007 saved its customers as much at $3 billion.[47] Wal-Mart realized that replacing the incandescent bulbs in its own ceiling fan displays with compact fluorescent blubs throughout its 3,230 stores (ten models of ceiling fans on display, each with four bulbs. Forty bulbs per store, 3,230 stores) could save the company $6 million a year. Chuck Kerby, the Wal-Mart employee who did the math, reflected, 'That, for me, was an "I got it" moment'.[48]

Maximizing the Integrated Bottom Line

Businesses that reduce their carbon emissions strengthen every aspect of shareholder value. Shareholder value is enhanced when a company cuts its costs, grows top-line sales, better manages its risks, enhances labour productivity, drives innovation, better manages its supply chains and stakeholders, etc. This Integrated Bottom Line approach[49] shows that companies that implement climate protection programmes not only reduce expenses ow, but also position themselves for long-term performance.[50] Over time, climate protection programmes enhance core business value by delivering sector performance leadership and first-mover advantage. Companies gain greater access to capital, improve corporate governance, strengthen their ability to drive innovation, and improve government relations. Ultimately, the business enhances its reputation and brand equity. This increases a company's ability to attract and retain the best talent, increase employee productivity and health, improve communication, creativity, and morale in the workplace, and strengthen stakeholder relations.

These conclusions are borne out by the 2007 report from Goldman Sachs, showing that companies that are leaders in environmental, social and good governance policies outperformed the MSCI world index of stocks by 25% since 2005. 72% of the companies on the list outperformed industry peers,[51] were financially healthier and achieved enduring value.[52]

Regardless of how severe the economic collapse proves to be, companies that make a serious commitment to behave in more sustainable ways will emerge as leaders. Green Winners, an AT Kearney analysis, tracked the 2008 stock price performance over six months of ninety-nine firms on Dow Jones Sustainability Index and the Goldman Sachs list of green companies. In sixteen of eighteen industries, businesses deemed 'sustainability focused' outperformed industry peers over three- and six-month periods and were 'well protected from value erosion.' From September through November the performance differential across the ninety-nine firms tracked was 10%; over six months, it was 15%. 'This performance differential', the Report stated, 'translates to an average of $650 million in market capitalization per company'.[53]

Risk Management

Tolerating wasteful energy use and carbon emissions is a high-risk strategy for a company. Volatility of energy supply and increasing prices, geopolitical volatility, threats to business from extreme weather events, the risk of liability claims for failing to manage carbon all make carbon reduction simply better business.

The FTSE Index, the British equivalent of Dow Jones, states, 'The impact of climate change is likely to have an increasing influence on the economic value of companies, both directly, and through new regulatory frameworks. Investors, governments and society in general expect companies to identify and reduce their climate change risks and impacts, and also to identify and develop related business opportunities'.[54]

Insurance

In 2003 the Wall Street Journal reported that the second largest re-insurance firm, Swiss Re, 'has announced that it is considering denying coverage, starting with directors and officers liability policies, to companies it decides aren't managing their output of greenhouse gases'.[55] The prescience of this statement came clear as claims from weather related disasters rose twice as fast as those from all other mishaps.[56] 2008 was the third worse year on record for loss-producing events, with losses jumping from $82 billion in 2007 to over $200 billion, with more than 220,000 dead. The all time record remains 2005 with $232 billion in insured losses, with costs now growing 10 times faster than premiums, the population, or economic growth.[57]

In 2007, the Washington Post reported that, 'Nervous investors have begun asking similar questions of the insurers, asking them to disclose their strategies for dealing with global warming. At a meeting of the National Association of Insurance Commissioners, Andrew Logan, insurance director of the investor coalition, representing $4 trillion in market capital, warned that 'insurance as we know it is threatened by a perfect storm of rising weather losses, rising global temperatures and more Americans living in harm's way'.[58] John Dutton, Dean Emeritus of Penn State's College of Earth and Mineral Sciences, estimated that $2.7 trillion of the $10-trillion-a-year US economy is susceptible to weather-related loss of revenue, increasing companies' off balance sheet risks.[59]

Property owners are suffering price shocks and reduced availability of coverage. Highly vulnerable properties such as offshore oil platforms have seen insurance rates rise 400% in one year.[60] Homeowner premiums have risen 20–40% in many areas, if they can be obtained at all.[61] Insurers have withdrawn coverage for hundreds of thousands of homeowners in Florida, Louisiana, Mississippi, New York, Massachusetts, Rhode Island, and South Carolina.[62]

Access to capital

Investors have begun evaluating the corporate role in climate change. Large institutional investors are conducting shareholder campaigns that urge companies to disclose climate risk and implement mitigation programmes.[63]

The Investor Network on Climate Risk[64] includes over fifty institutional investors collectively managing more than $3 trillion in assets. A group of twenty-eight leading institutional investors from the United States and Europe,[65] managing over $3 trillion in assets, announced a ten-point action plan that calls on investors, leading financial institutions, businesses, and governments to address climate risk and seize investment opportunities. U.S. companies, Wall Street firms, and the Securities and Exchange Commission (SEC) are asked to provide investors with comprehensive analysis and disclosure about the financial risks presented by climate change. The group pledged to invest $1 billion in prudent business opportunities emerging from the drive to reduce GHG emissions.

In the United States, the Sarbanes–Oxley Act[66] makes it a criminal offence for the Board of Directors of a company to fail to disclose information, including such environmental liabilities as carbon emissions that
could alter a reasonable investor's view of the organization. In France,
Holland, Germany[67] and Norway, companies are already required to report their GHG emissions.

Even as early as 2005, such investor intervention and persuasion contributed to decisions by a number of large companies (Anadarko Petroleum, Apache, Chevron, Cinergy, DTE Energy, Duke Energy, First Energy,
Ford Motor Company, General Electric, JP Morgan Chase, and Progress
Energy) to make new commitments such as supporting mandatory limits
on green house gasses, voluntarily reducing their emissions, or disclosing
climate risk information to investors.[68]

Since 2002, the British NGO, the Carbon Disclosure Project has sur-
veyed the Financial Times 500, the largest companies in the world. Initially, only 10% of the recipients answered. In 2005, 60% did so. In 2007,
77% completed the survey. Ford Motor Company produced a major report
detailing its emissions. Why the change? The threat of Sarbanes Oxley liability clearly played a role. But perhaps more significantly, the Carbon
Disclosure Project represents institutional investors with assets of over $50
trillion, now representing almost a third of all global institutional investor
assets. A company that might want to go to the capital markets would be
advised to answer the survey.

The 2007 CDP report found that the world's major companies are increasingly focused on climate change and that many see it as an opportunity for profit. Nearly 80% of respondents around the world considered
climate change a commercial risk, citing extreme weather events and tight-
ening government regulations. Some 82% said that they recognized commercial opportunities for existing or new products, such as investments in
renewable energy. Globally, 76% said they had instituted targets and plans
to reduce emissions. But only 29% of U.S. respondents had implemented
greenhouse gas reduction programmes with timelines and specific targets.

The banking industry is reducing its own carbon footprint. In 2006,
HSBC won the Financial Times' first Sustainable Banking Award by
becoming carbon neutral. It provided financing for renewable energy
companies, and purchased renewable energy to cover its operations.[69] In

2007, JPMorgan Chase and the Socially Responsible Investment advisors, Innovest, announced the creation of the JPMorgan Environmental Index— Carbon Beta (JENI-Carbon Beta), the first high-grade corporate bond index designed to address the risks of global warming by tracking carbon footprint of companies. 'Taking into account environmental and social issues isn't just about good corporate citizenship, its becoming an essential part of risk management for investors'.[70] In addition to reducing its own carbon emissions, the firm raised $1.5 billion of equity for the wind power market in 2006, making investments in renewable energy totalling $1 billion. Citigroup Inc., Deutsche Bank AG, UBS AG, and ABN Amro also committed $1 billion to finance the energy savings measures in municipal buildings in such cities as New York, Chicago, Houston, Toronto, Mexico City, London, Berlin, Tokyo, Rome, Delhi, Karachi, Seoul, Bangkok, Melbourne, Sao Paolo, and Johannesburg.

Goldman Sachs, Credit Suisse, Citigroup and others created clean-energy investment funds, and pledged to purchase more products locally. 'Wall Street is waking up to climate change risks and opportunities,' stated Carbon Disclosure Project Chair, James Cameron. 'Considerably more of the world's largest corporations are getting a handle on what climate change means for their business and what they need to do to capture opportunities and mitigate risks. This all points to a continued elevation of climate change as a critical shareholder value issue.'[73]

Managing the Supply Chains
In a global marketplace the threat of more frequent and more violent storms is a challenge to companies that depend on products shipped from around the world. Wal-Mart is measuring the amount of energy that it takes various suppliers to make and transport the products sold in its stores. Wal-Mart has changed its business model to work with suppliers of such products as DVDs, toothpaste, soap, milk, beer, vacuum cleaners, and soda to help them reduce their carbon footprint.[74] Wal-Mart hired the Carbon Disclosure Project to survey factories in China that are manufacturing products for the company. 'This is an opportunity to spur innovation and efficiency throughout our supply chain that will not only help protect the environment but save people money at the same time', said Wal-Mart's Chief Merchandising Officer John Fleming.[75]

Labour Productivity

Inefficient use of energy in buildings causes most of American greenhouse gas emissions, but it also costs companies lost productivity. Bad air quality from inefficient air handling causes what is called 'sick building syndrome,' affecting 2% of workers nationwide, at a cost of almost $60 billion.[76]

Energy efficiency measures like better lighting that helps workers see better, can cut electricity use four-fold and increase labour productivity by 6 to 16%.[77] Labour costs are typically a hundred times greater than energy cost, so even a one percent increase in labour productivity will dwarf the energy savings, but attention to meeting energy needs in smarter ways makes possible the enhanced productivity. Improved worker productivity from these green building features could deliver savings of $20 to $200 billion a year.[78]

Lockheed's Building 157 in Sunnyvale, CA, achieved a 75% reduction in lighting energy, saving $500,000 a year worth of energy, with a four-year payback. The better lighting and the other green features led to a 15% drop in employee absenteeism, and a productivity increase of the same amount. This enabled the company to win a new contract, the profits of which paid for the costs of the entire building.

Boeing implemented a lighting retrofit that cut lighting energy costs by 90% with less than two-year payback (a 70% return on investment). Because the workers could see better, the error rate went down by 20%—very good news for everyone who flies around on aeroplanes. It also increased on-time delivery and customer satisfaction.

Small Businesses and Climate Protection

Small businesses are the economic engine of the country, generating more than half of non-farm private gross domestic product. They represent 99.7% of all employer firms, employing nearly sixty million workers, about half of all private employees. For the past decade they have generated 60–80% of net new jobs each year.[79]

Business Week pointed out that the twenty-five million small businesses in the United States stand to be among the hardest-hit victims of climate change.[80] According to the Institute for Business and Home Safety, at least one-fourth of the small businesses closed by natural disasters never re-open.[81] Small businesses will be least prepared to deal with increased government regulation if a mandatory programme to reduce greenhouse gas emissions is implemented.

Small businesses consume half the electricity in the country, but only about a third have invested in energy efficiency. Natural Capitalism's web-based learning platform, Solutions at the Speed of Business, shows companies how they can enhance profitability by cutting carbon emissions, cutting their costs, and increasing sales to others who are implementing emissions-reduction programmes.[82] As *Business Week* noted, 'reducing energy waste in U.S. homes, shops, offices, and other buildings must, of necessity, rely on tens of thousands of small concerns that design, make, sell, install, and service energy-efficient appliances, lighting products, heating, air-conditioning, and other equipment. Small businesses can also save as much as 20-30% on their own energy bills by making their own workplace more energy-efficient'.[83]

Energy efficiency and renewable energy can enable small businesses to become more energy self-reliant. Every year, American businesses lose billions of dollars when blackouts, power surges and other interruptions force them to shut down. In August, 2003, a tree branch fell across a power line in Ohio, setting off a cascading failure that blacked out the Northeast for thirty hours. The Wall Street Journal estimated the cost to the region at $6 billion. Two-thirds of business lost at least a day of operation with a quarter losing more than $50,000 an hour.

Harbec Plastics, a small upstate New York injection-moulding company, had recently completed a comprehensive energy efficiency program, including a lighting retrofit, and installation of more efficient motors to avoid periodic power surges and outages that lost production time, wasted materials and impacted customer relations. Harbec added renewable energy, including a wind turbine and photovoltaics, as well as a combined heat and power system to cut its soaring energy bill.

Even before the 2003 blackout, Harbec's energy efficiency and new power supply cut its costs and dramatically reduced temperatures on the shop floor, improving working conditions. Being able to operate throughout the blackout, generated profits that paid off the capital cost of the new energy investment. The company took the lessons to heart and now produces its own biodiesel and uses fuel-efficient vehicles. By reducing energy costs, the leading reason that businesses are fleeing New York, Harbec preserved jobs in an economic downturn and created new business opportunities.[84]

Conclusion

Climate protection has been presented as a moral argument. Business leader Ray Anderson[85] asks:

> When you meet your Maker, what will your conversation be about?
>
> Will you describe your rate of return? Or how you enhanced shareholder value?
>
> Or will you discuss what you did to leave a legacy for future generations?

The way most companies do business, the way that most communities operate, and the way that most of us live is leaving a legacy of an environmentally and financially impoverished planet.

We can, we must do better.

If we fail to act, there will come a time when the children who are young today will ask us, 'You were there then when there was still time to act. What did you do?' How will you answer?

There is also a very strong business case for acting now, and acting aggressively to cut carbon emissions and unleash the new energy economy. As the world economy hovers between depression and opportunity, doubters argue that we can't afford climate protection. Tom Friedman, *New York Times* columnist, stated, 'When I hear people say we can't afford to be green, that's utter lunacy. We can't afford not to be green. Because the next great pool of manufacturing jobs are going to be green smart jobs. Mom, Dad, tell your kids, anything green is going to have a good upper middle class job associated with it'.

The shift from fossil energy to low-carbon fuels will leave a fine legacy for future generations. But it will also drive wealth creation and stimulate the economy today. Companies and communities are cutting their costs, creating jobs, increasing profits and strengthening shareholder value by implementing new energy strategies. Unleashing the new energy economy will require capital, but dramatically less investment than any other way of meeting our energy needs. The jobs being created in our communities use the sorts of skills that Americans have. Small businesses will play an important role, as cities and households use energy more productively and turn to renewable sources. A transformation of the U.S. economy is under way.

Are you a part of it?

References

[1]This paper draws extensively on the Climate Protection Manual for Cities (http://www.climatemanual.org/Cities/Chapter1/index.htm) see, especially 'Climate Change: Why Act Now.' Grateful acknowledgement to peer reviewers Lyle Casriel, Bill Becker, Michael Northrup, Ray Anderson, David Overton and the staff of Natural Capitalism Solutions.

[2]'The Stern Review' on economics of climate change, www.hm-treasury.gov.uk/media/4/3/Executive_Summary.pdf October 2006 - Sir Nicholas Stern, once the Chief Economist and Senior Vice-President of the World Bank (2000 to 2003) released a report commissioned by the UK government, stating that that inaction on climate change will result in a depressed economy worse the Great Depression of the 1930s, with financial cost higher than the Depression combined with the two world wars. In human terms, the report concluded that the resulting drought and flooding will displace 200 million people from their homes creating the largest refugee migration in history. Up to 40% of world's known species are likely to go extinct. To avert this tragedy, the report states, the world will need to spend 1% of global GDP each year to mitigate climate change, equal to the worldwide advertising budget. Failure to mitigate the crisis, the report stated, would commit the world to spend up to 20% of world GDP each year to deal with the consequences.

[3]Stated in a speech to the U.S. Conference of Mayors' Climate Protection Summit, 2 Nov 2007, Reuters

[4]Vallely, Paul, 'Stern: Global Warming Warming is Happening at Faster Rate,' *The Independent*, 30 Nov 2007, http://www.independent.co.uk/environment/climate-change/stern-global-warming-is-happening-at-faster-rate-761060.html

[5]John Holdren, (Presidential Science Advisor) 'Meeting the Climate Change Challenge'. Eighth Annual John H. Chafee Memorial Lecture on Science and the Environment. Washington, DC: National Council for Science and the Environment, 2008, http://209.85.129.132/search?q=cache:OSVewfpg5PQJ:ncseonline.org/conference/Chafee08final.pdf+Necessary+actions+to+solve+climate+-+Holdren&hl=en&ct=clnk&cd=26&client=safari

[6]1E Study: http://www.1e.com/energycampaign/index.aspx

[7]Center for Climate Strategies, 'Climate Change Policy as Economic Stimulus: Evidence and Opportunities from the States,' Nov 2008, www.climatestrategies.us, For other similar studies see: Green Recovery, Center for American Progress, http://www.americanprogress.org/issues/2008/09/pdf/green_recovery.pdf http://www.unep.org/labour_environment/PDFs/Green-Jobs-Background-paper-18-01-08.pdf,

[8]'Renewable Energy and Energy Efficiency: Economic Drivers for the 21st Century', a 2007 report from the American Solar Energy Society

[9]'Green Collar Jobs Could Top 40M by 2030': Report, GreenBiz.com, URL:

http://www.greenbiz.com/news/news_third.cfm?NewsID=36231.

[10]http://www.greenbiz.com/resources/resource/defining-estimating-and-forecasting-renewable-energy-and-energy-efficiency-indust

[11]San Francisco Gavin Newsom, http://tr.im/hPPJ

[12]'Sustainable, efficient electricity service for one billion people,' Fulkerson, Levine, Sinton and Gadgil, *Energy for Sustainable Development,* Volume IX No. 2, June 2005, p. 26-34. The International Energy Agency estimates that 1.6 billion people worldwide now have no access to electric service.

[13]Daniel Kammen, 'Putting Renewables to Work: How Many Jobs Can the Clean Energy Industry Generate?', http://www.berkeley.edu/news/media/releases/2004/04/13_kamm.shtml

[14]Sanders, Robert, 'Investment in renewable energy better for jobs as well as environment', 13 April 2004. http://www.berkeley.edu/news/media/releases/2004/04/13_kamm.shtml

[15]'Wind Energy Grows By Record 8,300 MW In 2008', http://www.awea.org/newsroom/releases/wind_energy_growth2008_27Jan09.html

[16]Timothy B. Hurst, 'Dept. of Interior: Offshore Wind Could Meet 100% of US Electricity Demand,' / April 2009, http://redgreenandblue.org/2009/04/07/dept-of-interior-offshore-wind-could-meet-100-of-us-demand/

[17]'Solarbuzz Reports World Solar Photovoltaic Market Grew to 5.95 Gigawatts in 2008', http://www.solarbuzz.com/Marketbuzz2009-intro.htm

[18]'Clean technology venture investment reaches record $8.4 billion in 2008 despite credit crisis and broadening recession, Cleantech Group, llc, 6 Jan 2009, http://cleantech.com/about/pressreleases/010609.cfm

[19]'In the Black', A report by the Climate Group, August 2007, www.theclimategroup.org/index.php/resources/

[20]Ibid.

[21]'New Report Projects $50 Billion in Renewable Energy Investment by 2011', RenewableEnergyAccess.com, November 20, 2007, http://www.renewableenergyaccess.com/rea/news/story?id=50622.

[22]Macalister, Terry, 'Renewable Revolution Is Here, Says UN Report', *The Guardian*/UK, June 21, 2007 Global Trends in Sustainable Development annual rev, http://www.commondreams.org/archive/2007/06/21/2016/.

[23]'Renewables can meet 50 per cent of energy needs by 2040, claims report' *Times Higher Education Supplement*, 1 June 2004, http://www.timeshighereducation.co.uk/story.asp?storyCode=189068&sectioncode=26

[24]http://www.greenbiz.com/resources/resource/defining-estimating-and-forecasting-renewable-energy-and-energy-efficiency-indust

[25]www.wbcsd.org/web/publications/mobility/overview.pdf

[26]Michael Northrup, 'Creating the next American economy', *Miami Herald*, 22 Oct. 2008. http://www.miamiherald.com/news/environment/v-print/

story/736349.html

[27]http://www.nyc.gov/html/planyc2030/html/plan/plan.shtml

[28]U.S. Energy Information Administration at http://www.eia.doe.gov/neic/quickfacts/quickoil.html

[29]'In the Black', Climate Group

[30]Mufson, Steven, 'Oil Price Rise Causes Global Shift in Wealth,' The Washington Post, 10 November 2007, http://www.washingtonpost.com/wp-dyn/content/article/2007/11/09/AR2007110902573.html?hpid=topnews. Americans use about 22 million barrels/day, times (say) $130/bbl. This results in around $3 billion per day spent. Based on the same usage rate, or about 7 to 8 billion barrels/year, at $130 Americans are spending about $1 trillion.

[31]'In the Black', Climate Group, p. 4

[32]'Germany says green jobs will shorten recession,' Reuters, 24 Feb 2009 http://www.reuters.com/article/environmentNews/idUSTRE51N2F920090224

[33]'In the Black', Climate Group, p. 11

[34]Enkvist, Per-Anders, Naucler, Tomas, Rosander, Jerker, 'A Cost Curve for Greenhouse Gas Reduction', The McKinsey Quarterly, 2007 #1 http://www.mckinsey.com/clientservice/ccsi/pdf/Cost_Curve_for_Greenhouse_Gas_Reduction.pdf

[35]Ibid.

[36]'The Warming Challenge', New York Times, May 5, 2007

[37]As of February 2009, http://usmayors.org/climateprotection/ClimateChange.asp

[38]'US Grassroots Tackle Climate Change,' BBC, 11 July 2007 http://news.bbc.co.uk/2/hi/americas/6288172.stm

[39]Greg Kats of Capital E, quoted in The Washington Post Feb. 17, 2007

[40]U.S. Energy Information Administration, State Energy Data 2004.

[41]Professor David Roland-Holst, 'Energy Efficiency, Innovation and Job Creation in California, 20 Oct 2008', http://www.next10.org/research/research_eeijc.html

[42]Dr Randall Pozdena and Dr Stephen Grover 'Economic Impact Analysis of Energy Trust of Oregon Program Activities,' EcoNorthwest, April 2003

[43]As of May 2007, USCAP members included Alcan Inc.; Alcoa; American International Group, Inc. (AIG); Boston Scientific Corporation; BP America Inc.; Caterpillar Inc.; ConocoPhillips; Deere & Company; The Dow Chemical Company; Duke Energy; DuPont; Environmental Defense; FPL Group, Inc.; General Electric; General Motors Corp.; Johnson & Johnson; Marsh, Inc.; National Wildlife Federation; Natural Resources Defense Council; The Nature Conservancy; PepsiCo; Pew Center on Global Climate Change; PG&E Corporation; PNM Resources; Shell; Siemens Corporation; World Resources Institute.

[44]www.us-cap.org/climatereport.pdf. The report, issued in January 2007 was, in part, an effort to relieve corporations of having to navigate the disparate regional and state-level carbon-reduction regimes now proliferating in the United States.

[45]Gary Pfeiffer, Dupont CFO, 340% increase in share value paralleling 60% reduction in environmental footprint personal communication at speech he gave at a Conference Board conference 2005.

[46]Personal communication from Andrew Winston, Eco-Strategies, andrewwinston.com

[47]Andy Ruben, Wal-Mart's Vice President of Corporate Strategy and Sustainability, 29 Oct 2006

[48]Fishman, Charles, 'How Many Lightbulbs Does it Take to Change the World? One. And You're Looking At It'. *Fast Company Magazine*, Issue 108, Sept. 2006, Pg 74 http://www.fastcompany.com/magazine/108/open_lightbulbs.html

[49]Corporate managers are increasingly realizing that value returned to the owners, the real metric of success, derives from more than just attention to next quarter's profits—indeed the Financial Accounting Standards Board (FASB) has recently announced that it will revise its definition of 'profit' away from this short-term fixation. From the article 'Sustainable Executives', http://www.natcapsolutions.org/resources.htm#ART

[50]Reilly, David, 'Profit as We Know It Could Be Lost With New Accounting Statements, *Wall Street Journal*, 12 May 2007, Page A1

[51]Alderton, Margo, 'Recent report finds corporations that lead in corporate responsibility also lead in the market', *Socially Responsible Investing* 07-11 17:57, also at http://www.csrwire.com/companyprofile?id=4489

[52]GS Sustain 22 June 2007, http://www2.goldmansachs.com/ideas/environment-and-energy/gs-sustain/index.html

[53]'Green Winners', A.T. Kearney. http://www.atkearney.com/

[54]http://www.ftse.com/Indices/FTSE4Good_Index_Series/Downloads/FTSE4Good_Climate_Change_Consultation_Aug_06.pdf

[55]Jeffrey Ball, *Wall Street Journal*, May 7, 2003,

[56]Douwe Miedema, 'Climate Change Means Big Business for Reinsurers,' Reuters, 14 Nov 2006,, http://www.planetark.com/dailynewsstory.cfm/newsid/38964/story.htm

[57]Evan Mills, Richard J. Roth, Jr., and Eugene Lecomte, 'Availability and Affordability of Insurance Under Climate Change: A Growing Challenge for the U.S.', *Ceres*, December 2005. http://www.ceres.org/pub/docs/Ceres_insure_climatechange_120105.pdf

[58]Morrison, John and Sink Alex, 'The Climate Change Peril That Insurers See' *Washington Post*, 27 Sept 2007. http://www.washingtonpost.com/wp-dyn/content/article/2007/09/26/AR2007092602070.html?nav=rss_opinions/

outlook?nav=slate

[59]Eugene Linden, 'Cloudy with a Chance of Chaos', *Fortune Magazine*, Tuesday 17 January 2006, http://money.cnn.com/2006/01/17/news/economy/climate_fortune/index.htm

[60]Estimate by John Dutton, Dean Emeritus of Penn State's College of Earth and Mineral Sciences, in Eugene Linden, 'Cloudy with a Chance of Chaos,' *Fortune Magazine*, January 17, 2006. http://money.cnn.com/2006/01/17/news/economy/climate_fortune/index.htm.

[61]Evan Mills and Eugene Lecomte, 'From Risk to Opportunity: How Insurers Can Proactively and Profitably Manage Climate Change,' August 2006, p. 2. http://www.ceres.org/pub/docs/Ceres_Insurance_Climate_%20Report_082206.pdf

[62]Ibid., p. 12.

[63]For a comprehensive list of climate-related shareholder resolutions, see website hosted by the Investor Network on Climate Risk, at http://www.incr.com/index.php?page=ia&nid=186, October 30, 2006

[64]See (http://www.incr.com).

[65]Institutional Investor Summit on Climate Risk (2005), Summary, by Investor Network on Climate Risk, website: http://www.incr.com/index.php?page=19, July 31, 2006.

[66]Francis X. Lyons, a former US EPA regional administrator now with Gardner, Carton & Douglas LLP, 'Sarbanes-Oxley and the Changing Face of Environmental Liability Disclosure Obligations', *Trends*, Volume 35 No. 2, Nov/Dec 2003. Available from www.gcd.com/db30/cgi-bin/pubs/Sarbanes2.pdf.

[67]In Germany, only 'heavy' industry is currently required to report greenhouse gas emissions.

[68]Testimony by Dr Russell Read, Chief Investment Officer, CalPERS, http://www.incr.com/NETCOMMUNITY/Document.Doc?id=204.

[69]*Financial Times*, June 13, 2006, http://news.ft.com/cms/s/c1f6fade-fafa-11da-b4d0-0000779e2340.html

[70]Brian Marchiony, JPMorgan Chase spokesperson, in an interview with Socialfunds.com, http://www.socialfunds.com/news/article.cgi/2244.html

[71]Sara Kugler, Associated Press Writer, '16 Cities to Go Green Under Clinton Plan', http://salon.com/wire/ap/archive.html?wire=D8P5FE5G0.html

[72]Marc Gunther, 'The Green Machine,' *Fortune Magazine*, July 27 2006. http://money.cnn.com/magazines/fortune/fortune_archive/2006/08/07/8382593/index.htm, http://www.planetark.com/dailynewsstory.cfm/newsid/41783/story.htm

[73]http://www.socialfunds.com/news/article.cgi/article1426.html

[74]Gogoi, Pallavi and Herbst, Moira, 'Wal-Mart: Measuring Just How Green,' *Business Week*, 25 Sept, 2007. http://www.businessweek.com/bwdaily/dnflash/

content/sep2007/db20070924_008782.htm?campaign_id=rss_daily

[75]Ibid.

[76]William J. Fisk, 'Health and Productivity Gains from Better Indoor Environments' in *The Role of Emerging Energy-Efficient Technology in Promoting Workplace Productivity and Health*, a report by Lawrence Berkeley National Laboratory, February 2002

[77]'Greening the Building and the Bottom Line', http://www.greenerbuildings.com/tool_detail.cfm?linkadvid=8527

[78]William J. Fisk, 'How IEQ Affects Health, Productivity,' *ASHRAE Journal*, May 2002.

[79]Small Business Administration, http://www.smallbusiness.com/wiki/Small_business_FAQ

[80]Byron Kennard, 'Global Warming on Main Street,' *Business Week*, June 27, 2006. http://www.greenerbuildings.com/news_detail.cfm?NewsID=34996.

[81]The Institute offers advice to small businesses on disaster prevention at http://www.ibhs.org/business_protection/

[82]Solutions at the Speed of Business, contact Toby Russell, trussell@natcapsolutions.org, www.natcapsolutions.org

[83]Anna Clark, 'Practical Advice for Greening the SME [Small and Medium-sized Enterprise]', http://www.greenerbuildings.com/news_detail.cfm?NewsID=34996.

[84]http://www.cleanair-coolplanet.org/information/pdf/Harbec_case_study.pdf

[85]Founder and Chairman of Interface, Inc, a $ billion corporation headquartered in Atlanta, GA

THE 2012 HORIZON

Ervin Laszlo

THREATENING worldwide trends build toward a threshold of irreversibility. Predictions of when such 'points of no return' will come about vary with the trends that are considered. In most cases time-estimates have shrunk from the end of the century to mid-century, then to the next twenty years—and lately to the next five to twenty years. For example, it has been predicted that the Earth's atmosphere will increase by about three degrees Celsius by the year 2100. Then it was said that this level of increase will come about by the middle of the century, and lately that it may occur within a decade. The figure for the overall warming has been increased from three to six degrees. But even a three-degree global warming would cause

Ervin Laszlo is Founder and President of The Club of Budapest, President of the WorldShift Network, Founder of the General Evolution Research Group, Co-Chair of the World Wisdom Council, Fellow of the World Academy of Arts and Sciences, Member of the International Academy of Philosophy of Science, Senator of the International Medici Academy, and Editor of the international periodical World Futures: The Journal of General Evolution. He has a PhD from the Sorbonne and is the recipient of honourary PhD's from the United States, Canada, Finland, and Hungary. Formerly Professor of Philosophy, Systems Science, and Futures Studies in various universities in the US, Europe, and the Far East, he lectures worldwide.

Laszlo received the Peace Prize of Japan, the Goi Award, in 2002, the International Mandir of Peace Prize in Assisi in 2005, and was nominated for the Nobel Peace Prize in 2004. He is the author or co-author of fifty-four books translated into as many as twenty-three languages, and serves as editor of another thirty volumes in addition to a four-volume World Encyclopedia of Peace. He lives in a converted four-hundred year-old farmhouse in Tuscany.

This chapter is excerpted from the forthcoming publication WORLDSHIFT NOW! : THE CLUB OF BUDAPEST HANDBOOK FOR REAL CHANGE.

serious disruption in human life and economic activity, while six degrees would make most of the planet unsuitable for human life and activity.

Yet most predictions take only one trend into consideration—global warming and attendant climate change; water quality and availability; food production and self-reliance; urban viability, poverty, and population pressure; air quality and minimal health standards, or others. They fail to consider cross-impacts. Yet when one trend reaches a critical point, its impact on the other trends is far from negligible. For example, if global warming creates prolonged drought in some areas and coastal flooding in others, starving and homeless masses will flood less hard-hit regions and create critical food- and water-shortages also there. If the quality of the air in urban and industrial megacomplexes drops below the minimum required for health, the resulting breakdown in public health will trigger social upheavals and give rise to epidemics that spread to vast areas. If the world's financial system reaches a point of no return, not only national economies will be affected; international production and trade flows will be paralyzed as well, creating serious problems for prosperous economies and populations and life-threatening conditions for poor people and poor states.

The impact of one trend on another makes for reduced time-horizons. We don't yet have scientific certainty, but there is a distinct probability that one or another vital trend will reach a critical phase well within five years from the time of writing. If that happens, the chain-reaction catalyzed by it will engulf not only the immediately affected region and its population, but entire continents—and ultimately all continents. The time left for averting a global breakdown may not be much more than five years from the end of 2008. This is perilously close to the famed 2012 prophecies of the end of the world.

What is it about the year 2012 that makes it a plausible point of no return for humanity's tenure on this planet? There are a wide variety of forecasts, predictions and prophecies, some esoteric, others scientific. The most widely cited comes from the Mayan calendar, and we begin with that.

The Mayan calendar has been carved by priest-astronomers into the Aztec–Mayan sun stone and was completed in the year 1479. It details immense passages of time, and includes mathematical calculations so accurate that modern astronomers are at a loss to understand how they were done. The most immediately relevant time-calculation is the so-called long count. This marks the end of the fifth sun—also known as the fifth world—on December 21st, 2012 (the date is actually October 28th, 2011, but compensating for the accumulated time-shifts, it's 2012). Although we cannot be entirely certain what the Mayans had in mind (too many of the documents they produced have been destroyed), it's reasonably certain that this was not intended as a doomsday prophecy, a prediction that the world will come to an end. It's likely to indicate a gateway or, in modern terms, a phase-shift in humanity's tenure on the planet. It could be followed by the sixth sun (or world), although that world will be radically different from the one ending in 2012.

The Mayans are not the only culture that foresaw a radical shift at the end of the year 2012. The galactic re-alignment that heralds a new phase for humanity has been foretold in many sacred traditions, including the Hopi time-keeping tradition, Vedic and Islamic astrology, Mithraism, the Jewish kabala, the cycle of yugas in Hinduism, European sacred geography, medieval Christian architecture, and a variety of hermetic metaphysics. Current calculations in astrology give an exact date. On precisely the December 21st, 2012, the centre of our galaxy will complete a 'cosmic year': a 25,920-year journey around the wheel of the zodiac. According to most astrologers another cosmic year will then begin, lasting for another 25,920 of our years.

A prediction coming from astronomy coincides with the date of these esoteric traditions. Astronomers noted that since the 1940s, and particularly since the year 2003, the Sun has become remarkably turbulent. Solar activity is predicted to peak around 2012, with storms of unprecedented intensity since they last occurred some 11,000 years ago.

A related trend concerns the behaviour of the Earth's magnetic field. It appears to diminish in intensity, and produce vast holes or gaps. A pole-shift, the reversal of the North and South magnetic poles, appears possible. It, too, could occur in a matter of years and could have serious consequences.

In addition, some geophysicists assert that our solar system has entered an interstellar energy-zone. (Many sensitives agree: they see the Earth crossing what they see as a cosmic cloud of light.) Predictions of the time when we will experience the full force of this interstellar encounter—notable disturbances in the electromagnetic field and hence in global telecommunications—range from 2010 to 2020.

The period around the end of 2012 is likely to be a turbulent one. For the esoteric traditions it will mark a major phase-change, with the optimistic intepretation speaking of the old world ending and a new one taking its place. The scientifically-based predictions foresee disturbances in the physical fields that embed the planet, causing considerable, but by no means fatal damage to telecommunications and impacting on many facets of human health and activity.

None of the prophecies and predictions is one hundred percent certain, but in their ensemble they are significant. This significance is reinforced by their coincidence with the cross-impact time-horizons of a number of critical trends. These indications we neglect only at our peril. They are not a cause for pessimism and even less for fatalism—they are a call for action. In our most immediate and vital interest, we must prepare for real change—while there is still time.

DRIVING YOUR SOUL: A CRASH COURSE

Scott Fratcher

WE HAVE all heard the dire predictions of the Mayan, Egyptians, Inca, Nostradamus, and even Terrence McKenna telling us our days are numbered. Specifically, 2012, is the predicted year of earth changes. They say we can expect earthquakes, pole shifts, mass extinction, tidal waves and even possible death of our planet. How do we know this? Because it has been predicted by many credible seers over the centuries.

Ultimately, the coming years may contain an Armageddon event, or they may not. If the days go on as usual, then we can all have a good laugh at our Y2K type reactions and get on with our lives.

On the other hand, if the earth does go through a mass die-off then we have proof the predictions were right. How would the seers of times past be able to predict such a catastrophe? Because they saw through time, thus proving once and for all we live in multidimensional reality.

This is important because proof that we live in a multidimensional reality might take place just as our souls are being released from our bodies. In other words we might see the earth change occurring and say, 'That's what they were talking about. Now what?'.

In this unlikely event we may need a crash course in driving our souls through the maze of obstacles found outside the protection of our earthly reality. This article is an emergency navigation plan to help souls find safety in the outer realms of the universal conciousness.

Driving our Soul
At first glance driving our soul might sound easy and natural. We hear

Scott Fratcher is a renowned marine engineer and served as Chief Engineer aboard *Earthrace*, the boat that that now holds the 'Round the World Speedboat Record.' See Yachtwork.com for more of Scott's writings.

from 'near-death' experiences that we simply leave our earthly body, find lost relatives, and they will lead us to a place of safety.

2012 may be different, because it is predicted that billions of souls may be released in a single moment. Our collective soul-energy may even overwhelm the standard channels that contain, and protect our souls during the cycle of life and death. In other words, a flood of souls may be able to break free of the bonds that normally contain our soul-energy.

Once we're free, a series of obstacles may cross our path. For example, if you believe the early south pacific islanders, you might find yourself confronted by a 'soul-catcher' that traps your soul-energy. Hinduism predicts this is the end of the old system of reincarnation, thus the old predictions may be instantly obsolete. If you believe some Native American tales, then 'don't go toward the light, as that is where you will be caught, recycled, and ultimately harvested.'

Harvested?

A soul can be harvested? This is the scary part, and why you might wish to practice a few out-of-body exercises before an unexpected earth change.

Some believe soul-energy is the most valuable commodity in the universe. They say soul-energy can't be made; it can only be grown through cycles of life and rebirth. If this is the case, then our souls might be a celestial equivalent of small fish swimming in a large ocean.

This means it is possible our soul must either quickly ascend, or become food for something else. Ascension is my preferred choice.

Ascension

Ascension is the breaking of the mind/body/spirit trilogy. You might say ascension is the preserving of your memories and consciousness while leaving your body behind.

In order to maintain a soul without a body we need an energy-source. Energy-sources are found inside dimensions. This is the definition of a dimension. A dimension supplies the energy so our soul can 'relax', otherwise we might find ourselves in an 'overtone'. An overtone is an area where a soul can exist, but an energy-source is not readily available.

In our dimensional reality, our body is the energy-source that supports our mind/spirit. If we find ourselves without our body, then we may have to maintain our consciousness by sheer force of will.

Remember: to ascend it may take tremendous willpower to maintain our soul's form till we find a new energy-source.

Don't be Herded

In a mass die-off we may find ourselves following the flows of soul-energy, much like sheep being herded. Some fear the end of the corral will not be a place of beauty and light. To the new soul this means the sooner you can become one of the 'runaway sheep' the better. You may wish to seek escape from the herd as soon as possible.

Escape? To where?

Seek to locate a new energy-source. Find a new dimension in which to seek shelter.

Soul Movement

Here is where we can begin to have fun. Driving a soul often means the soul goes where we think we are. In other words think about another star system and be there.

Instantly.

Conceive of a new reality and you are instantly part of that reality. Without practice beforehand the newly released soul will have a steep learning curve and intuition may play a key role.

Intuitive Decision-Making

The coming events may be part of a new reality. Without our 'old reality' for reference how will we decide what is best for our soul's future?

We must use our intuition. We must feel what is right.

Ultimately we may each find ourselves, seeking and finding our own answers. That means it will be up to each of us to make decisions that are intuitively best for the moment.

Review

Let's review. In the unlikely event we find ourselves outside our body in a flood of soul-energy we may wish to consider the following plan:

—Attempt early escape from the flow

—Seek a new energy source

—Find a new dimension in which to rest and recoup

—Use intuition to make decisions

Of course, none of this 'high strangeness' should ever come to pass. We all know nobody can accurately predict the future, don't we?

2012 AND ALL THAT

Simon Bentley

ONE THING that every astrologer learns very quickly is that nearly everyone loves a prophecy, or perhaps it would be more accurate to say, they
think they do. Clients often expect you to foretell their individual future
and, if you are unwise enough to attempt to do this in any detail, generally
turn round and ask you why (if such is the case) it didn't turn out as expected! If strange things are happening in the world, you are expected to know
why. Prophecies, however, are not necessarily made by astrologers. The
most famous prophet in history was probably Nostradamus, whose pro-
phetic gift was related to clairvoyance, not astrology. Prophets, whether
self-proclaimed or so dubbed by others, are creatures of controversy—you
have only to look at the Christian Bible to remind yourself that anyone in
such a position is given a hard time, especially if he or she tells truths that
people don't want to hear. People love prophecies—as long as they foretell
favourable things! Otherwise, people tend to block their ears and in some
cases the prophet is driven out of town, sent into exile or even imprisoned
or condemned to death. A prophet is 'not without honour save in his own
country', it is said; this is borne out by history again and again.

Not all prophecies, however, are made by individuals. Some of them
are made by many people at once, or by a group or race, or they may be
part of oral tradition that has been handed on for so long that no-one

---

Simon Bentley evinced an interest in astrology long before he went to University
and studied, among other subjects, the history of science. Graduating from
Cambridge, he trained in horticulture before taking up astrology full-time. A
student of Joan Hodgson, founder of the White Eagle School of Astrology,
he became its Principal at her death in 1995. He is currently working on
HOMES IN THE HEAVENS, a book on the astrological houses, which the White
Eagle Publishing Trust will issue in the autumn of 2009. This chapter is a
revised version of an article that first appeared in the White Eagle magazine,
Stella Polaris.

can remember who originated them. Nowadays the most frequent prophets are scientists—when a number of them say the same thing we begin to sit up and listen. The many statements about global warming and its likely results are the biggest case in point. My aim in this article, however, is to address a rather different situation which has become known as a prophecy but actually isn't in itself, although many have seized upon the facts to make prophecies concerning our planet's future, some of them apocalyptic in the extreme. I refer, of course, to the furore surrounding the so-called 'end' of the Mayan calendar which will be reached on December 21st, 2012. Strictly, it is the end of the 'Long Count' of that calendar. Before we continue to explore what it might mean, we would do well to remember the similar furore that accompanied the period before the 1999 total eclipse of the Sun in the UK, and the millennium which came only a few months later. The world has certainly not had an easy time since then, but it has not come to an end, and there is absolutely no reason to suppose that the end of the Long Count will be any different in this respect.

Let's think carefully about what this 'event' really is. It is the end of a numerical, calendric cycle, certainly—and that's all. There isn't, interestingly, any particularly striking astrological configuration to set this time apart either. Calendars are a manmade convenience to mark the passage of time. Yes, most of them were drawn up by priests, probably because they needed to know when to observe festivals, but they are still manmade, artificial. No one said that the end of the Long Count cycle would be a final 'full stop'. When the calendar was drawn up, this date, now so near, was impossibly far ahead and it was doubtless felt unnecessary to take the calendar any further than that at the time. The calendar does not cease to work on that date—it is simply the start of another Long Count cycle. As an indicator of world growth and evolution, the cycle of the Ages and the Great Year associated with them is far more significant. Interestingly, there is some correlation here; many will probably say, and I wouldn't argue with them, that this point may mark the true beginning of the Aquarian Age. Yes, it may indeed, so shouldn't we be looking forward rather than dreading this date?

In the course of preparing to write this article I looked on the internet and was staggered to find just how many sites there are devoted to 2012 prophecies. Note that these internet prophecies do not date back to the time when the Mayan priests drew up their calendar: they have been made since by others trying to interpret the meaning of the calendar 'end'. People talk of the 'Mayan prophecies', but the ones being bandied about now were made much more recently. Ironically, the more 'off the wall' they are, the more people hang on to them.

At the same time, however, we must remember and recognize the great civilization that gave birth to this calendar. They and many other civilizations share similar legends concerning their origins, past, future and eventual apotheosis. The trouble is that usually their teachings and, where relevant, any prophecies, are interpreted too literally; allegory and metaphor seem to be ignored, almost as if we have some subconscious desire to see come about literally the disasters and changes predicted. Humanity loves to dramatise, but in truth its spiritual evolution is the result of year upon year, century upon century, millennium upon millennium of steady, hard effort, not a few spectacular events. We need to look at this calendar event in a much more mature way if we are to see what it means and, above all, what opportunities are hidden within it.

It has been said that there is no such thing as a straight line—all moves in circles and spirals. A calendar is a good way of understanding this: time is regarded as linear, but calendars run on cycles. December 21st, 2012, happens to mark the end of a particularly long and complicated combination of cycles but, and this is the most important thing to remember, it equally marks the beginning of another. There is no end! A new beginning suggests not apocalypse but opportunity. What matters is not the fact of a calendric cycle ending and beginning, but what we project upon it. Judging by the internet, those projections still leave a lot to be desired! You don't need to have read much, if any, spiritual teaching to be able to predict which possibility for the world's future is the most likely: it will be what we think it will be, because it is our thoughts that will produce the results that we have to live with. If we all approach 2012 with doom and gloom, that's what we're likely to get. If, on the other hand, we embrace it as an opportunity to turn over a page and make things better, that is what it will be. That December 21st, 2012, is a turning-point, at least potentially, is not in question—it is. But what turns upon it is entirely up to us. We make our future. Let's try to get it right!

2012: A TIME OF INTENSIFIED NEW BEGINNINGS AND OLD COMPLETIONS

Errol Weiner

Introduction

Many people have been predicting numerous events for 2012, mainly due to the Mayan prediction that 2012 will be the year of the 'beginning of the New Age' and that, as such, weird and wonderful (if not exceptionally miraculous) events will occur in this year. As a 'transpersonal' astrologer of thirty years experience I prefer to deal with such issues from the viewpoint of spiritual-based astrological science, backed up by the 'esoteric' teachings for the New Age and by the practical nature of human evolution and human change. Many 'miraculous' predictions have been made by numerous individuals and groups over the past forty years or so, and none of these have yet to manifested, outside of the natural 'miracles' of great political and social changes that are indeed spiritual changes. The stories of the 'rise' of Mandela, Gorbachev and Obama are indeed miracles.

The Transits of Uranus and Neptune

Let us take a look at the transits of the planets Uranus and Neptune from 2011–12 and interpret the immense changes connected to these transits. This will enable us to take a more scientific spiritual approach to this time, notwithstanding the natural 'miracles' associated with such collective changes. In 2012 the planet Uranus moves into the first sign of the zodiac

---

Errol Weiner is a transpersonal astrologer and astro-psychologist. For the past thirty-two years he has studied, updated and expanded the Arcane Teachings of the Tibetan Master DK and Alice Bailey, with a focus on esoteric astrology. Errol (and his wife Imogen) live in the Findhorn Community in Scotland where they run monthly Full Moon Zodiacal Education and Meditation events. Errol publishes a monthly email Newsletter and runs three-month email Training Courses.

Aries, where it will remain for seven years. Uranus takes seven years to transit through each sign of the zodiac and eighty-four years to transit through the whole zodiac. This is, as such, not only the beginning of a new seven-year Uranus 'seeding' cycle of planetary and human evolution but also the beginning of a new eighty-four-year Uranus cycle. Uranus is the traditional 'objective-ruling' planet of Aquarius, and thus too of the new Aquarian Age. It is also the overall spiritual ruling planet of Aries itself, which means that its movement into Aries in 2012 will directly initiate a highly intensified and accelerated revolutionary change and transformation in humanity as a whole. Uranus is the only planet governed by the Seventh (violet) Ray of Spirit–Matter Synthesis. Its energy therefore brings about the direct manifestation on Earth (Ray Seven) of the spiritual purpose or God's will (Ray One). Aries, being the first sign of the zodiac, *is* the sign of original pioneering initiating energy, so Uranus moving through Aries *is* when the central core ideas and inspirations related to God's Will/Purpose enter human consciousness, and also manifest etherically and physically on Earth in a collective manner.

From the above astrological description it is obvious that 2012 is going to be a year of the 'seeding' of many Aquarian Age pioneering 'Ideas and Inspirations' that will revolutionize human consciousness, thought, actions and projects in every area of human life. Aries, the natural rising sign or ascendant of our solar and planetary zodiac, governs every sphere of human existence and activity. It will take seven years for the full extent of these pioneering ideas and innovations to manifest themselves at 'seed' level on earth and in collective humanity so 2012 has to be put into context with this seven-year Uranus cycle through Aries (2011–12 to March 2019). This will therefore be a magical, wonderful and miraculous cycle of vastly accelerated pioneering ideas and activities, but it is only the concentrated 'seeding' cycle of an eighty-four-year Uranus zodiacal cycle and it should be recognized as such. It will also be highly uncomfortable and stressful in its own right because all such pioneering cycles are tension-ridden. In this sense 'time' is not significant for humans might see eighty-four years as a long cycle but from the perspective of the soul and the superhuman kingdom it is but a 'flicker of an eye'.

In 2012 Neptune also moves into Pisces, the twelfth and final sign of the zodiac (Neptune moves into Pisces initially in April 2011 but it moves directly into Pisces in March 2012). Neptune governs Pisces at the soul level (with Pluto), so this is also a potent transit (as with Uranus moving through Aries). This transit will last fourteen years (2011–12 to end January 2026) as Neptune takes fourteen years to move through each sign of the zodiac, and a hundred and sixty-eight years (twelve times fourteen) to move through the zodiac. In other words, as Uranus begins its new pioneering revolutionary move into and through Aries (the first initiating archetype of the zodiac), so Neptune begins the completion of its 168-year cycle through the zodiac via its transit through Pisces, the final archetype of the zodiac. We are thus talking about a major collective death and re-birth cycle, the 'seed' rebirth lasting seven years and the accelerated death 'collapse-dissolution' of the old age (of Pisces) lasting fourteen years.

This makes this time cycle of evolution one of highly intensified 'death and rebirth'. It is thus a cycle of great crisis (in the best sense of the word) and not simply one of wonderful magic and miracles. (This polarity process is often not taken into consideration because of the idealistic urge to only have the good miraculous times, but, as always, it takes two opposites to tango, personally and collectively.)

We might therefore say that the Pisces Age and its varied and ongoing rapidly- dissolving energies will be moving out of manifestation from 2011–12 to 2026. It should be noted that Pluto will be moving through Capricorn from 2008 to 2024–25 and this transit is directly connected to the death-rebirth process of the political and economic dimension(s) of humanity. In 2008 we had the out-of-the-blue financial meltdown and economic crisis, and also the new Obama Presidency. As this highly critical and vastly accelerated death–rebirth crisis unfolds in and through humanity it will bring about a situation in which everyone will have the opportunity to 'make his–her choice' about which world to live in and serve—the old or the new. This of course includes all the nations and groupings that compose humanity, and thus all individuals, couples, families and communities.

Religious fundamentalism and old and outdated religious ideals and beliefs are connected directly to Neptune and Pisces (Neptune rules Pisces) and the final collapse and dissolution of this outdated exclusive religious idealism will occur during this time. The new visions and ideas (Uranus and Aries) of the new era will simultaneously manifest, so we can hopefully 'see' the polarity conflict and also the final climactic resolution of these opposites over this short period of time.

The Appearance of the Aquarian Age Avatar
and its Deeper Understanding

One of the major climactic repercussions of this cycle will be the so-called 'Return of the Christ' or the 'Second Coming'. For this reason it is vitally important to understand the processes and repercussions of this appearance from the 'esoteric' (teachings) standpoint, rather than from idealism and belief, no matter the belief. All the major religions are at present predicting this appearance, as are various esoteric traditions. For Christians this is the Christ, for Jews the Jewish Messiah, for Muslims the Imam Maydi, for Buddhists the Sixth Buddha, Maitreya, for Hindus, Lord Krishna or the World Avatar. Neptune in Pisces and Uranus in Aries are both associated with the 'End of Days' (Pisces) and the 'Beginning of Days' (Aries), and this mixture of abstract idealism, belief, hope, fear, trepidation, revelation, 'being saved' and so on brings in its wake a great deal of confusion and conflict. The religious perspective of this Second Coming or the appearance of the Messiah is based upon naive idealism and belief and not upon deep esoteric knowledge and understanding. It is important to understand the difference, and not simply to take a 'yes' or 'no' stand on this subject. In fact esoteric astrology and the larger dimension of the esoteric teachings cannot be separated because they are directly interlinked. Traditional and even spiritual-based astrologers do not actually create this linkage, but it is spiritual common sense to do so.

Many people, including many pioneers of the new era, do not associate the beginning of the Aquarian Age with the appearance of the Aquarian Age Avatar. This is rather strange because all previous astrological ages have been initiated and inaugurated by a spiritual initiate. The Arcane Teachings for the new age (transmitted by the Tibetan Master DK, the 'executive' Master of the superhuman kingdom of the Earth) state quite clearly that the Aquarian Age will be inaugurated by the Avatar of the Aquarian Age. The difference between the two concepts of this Avatar, Messiah or World Teacher is that the Pisces-based concept relies upon naïve 'belief' while the 'esoteric' teachings is based upon the direct knowledge of the Masters of the Wisdom, the enlightened members of humanity. The Masters are the custodians of the divine Plan for humanity, and the astrological ages form a major part of this plan. The major new revelation connected to the Aquarian Age Avatar is that the status of this coming Avatar is different from initiates of the past because He will be the World

Avatar, the Master of Masters, the head of the superhuman kingdom of the Earth. This is because the new age will be (at last) the age of the one humanity and the one planet. In other words, whereas past historical initiates or avatars represented particular sections of humanity (Hindus, Buddhists, Jews, Christians, Muslims and so on), the Aquarian Age will represent humanity as a whole. This is why, at last, the Master of Masters (the Lord of the Seven Rays) can and will appear to guide humanity into the brotherhood–sisterhood of Humanity. This is not another belief—this is the 'esoteric' truth and it is destined.

All planetary systems have their inner spiritual government who are the custodians of the divine Plan for the planet in question. As with all governments, human or superhuman, there is a 'head' or what we could call the 'Prime Minister'. The 'head' of the earth's spiritual government is a cosmic consciousness (who has evolved through earth evolution) called the Christ in the West and the Buddha Maitreya in the East (the Imam Maydi or Lord Krishna and so on are other 'names' given to this great Consciousness). This is *not* Master Jesus, the Master of the Sixth Ray of religion, but the Christ Maitreya, the Master of all seven cosmic Rays. As St Matthew says in the New Testament 'He will appear like a thief in the night' meaning that He will 'appear' completely out of the blue (and thus symbolically 'from out of the clouds'). This will be by far the greatest event in human history because never before has the World Avatar (a seventh-degree initiate) 'appeared' (physically) to the whole of humanity. Once He appears His great presence and His one-humanity message will completely alter the consciousness of humanity. If we consider the wonderful influence that Gorbachev, Mandela and Obama (all spiritual initiates of a far lesser degree) have had on humanity can we even try to imagine the influence of the Christ Maitreya, the highest initiate possible on our planet?

According to the esoteric teachings, the Christ Maitreya was the first member of humanity to be become enlightened and liberated, and this far back in human history. His 'appearance' will be the final climax of the Neptune in Pisces (and Pluto through Capricorn) 'death' process, connected directly to the 2011–12 to 2025–26 planetary transits of Pluto, Neptune and Uranus. It should also be noted that on December 21st, 2020, and through 2021, Saturn and Jupiter will conjunct three times in Aquarius, and this will 'seed-activate' this new Aquarian Age cycle, leading into 2025–26.

We need to repeat: all astrological ages have been and are initiated and inaugurated by an appropriate spiritual initiate, and the Aquarian Age is no different. Just as a Gandhi, Mandela, Gorbachev and Obama were needed to rebirth their nations, so too does humanity require an even higher-grade Initiate to rebirth itself as one kingdom. This initiate or World Avatar is the Christ/Buddha Maitreya, the Imam Maydi, Lord Krishna, the Master of Masters, and this appearance and planetary inauguration has to be integrated (from an esoteric standpoint) with the astrological dimension of this article. 2012 is not going to be some super-miraculous year in which humanity suddenly changes forever. This should be common sense.

It is no use simply replacing old naïve beliefs with new naïve beliefs, and too many predictions about 2012 are just this. The complex polarities of light and shadow govern human evolution, collective, national and personal, and no one event is going to change this, certainly not 2012. Just as Mandela led the new Rainbow Nation South Africa into its new era, so too will the Christ Maitreya lead humanity into its new era, but it is ultimately humanity itself that has to do the work of 'saving itself', before and after this great destined appearance.

POSTSCRIPT

Dave Patrick

IN 1919, ninety years ago, Sir Arthur Conan Doyle wrote THE VITAL MESSAGE, arguing the case for Spiritualism. We have discovered that he was planting the seeds of a deeper spirituality, one based on Love and connection with the Christ consciousness.

Neale Donald Walsch and others in this book have demonstrated in simple, practical terms that we each have the ability to access the Divine, thereby enriching our own lives and the lives of others. We have the opportunity to awaken to a higher level of consciousness, and create a 'ripple effect' of love and compassion, by shifting our focus from narrow self-interest towards nurturing family and community relationships, and co-creating with nature instead of destroying it.

In Quantum-Touch energy healing work we have a saying 'Your Love Has Impact'. Quantum-Touch Founder Richard Gordon says it is not just about 'unconditional love' but 'preconditional love', an innate aspect of what makes us human. When we view our bodies as vibrational energy, the model for health and healing drastically changes; and as we raise our vibration the world around us is transformed.

Not only are our bodies made up of vibrational energy, the same applies to everything throughout the cosmos, from the planets in the solar system to the pebbles on a beach. Although we have not looked specifically at the new physics, which would probably require a book of its own, there have been several interesting developments in the field.

One new physicist whose work is well worth exploring is Nassim Haramein, Director of the Resonance Project, based in Hawaii. According to a recent presentation it would appear that he has cracked the 'unified field theory' conundrum which has defeated scientists for decades, and integrated Einstein's Theory of Relativity and Quantum Physics in the process.

Other contemporary researchers pushing beyond the boundaries of mainstream science include Callum Coats, who has been keeping alive the 'living energies' work of the late Viktor Schauberger. In addition, films like 'What the Bleep' have shown that the traditional scientific paradigm requires a radical overhaul to include consciousness.

Returning to Sir Arthur Conan Doyle's 'psychic matter', the survival of life after death and communication 'through the veil', the debate has been going on to the present day. The year after ACD's passing in 1930, Spiritualist Arthur Findlay published ON THE EDGE OF THE ETHERIC, in which he demonstrated that the physical world of our five-sense perception is only a small fraction of the spectrum of visible and invisible vibrations going on around us.

Since that era there appears to have been an aversion within mainstream science to link survival after death research with subatomic physics, except in a limited number of cases. It has taken distinguished scientists like Sir Oliver Lodge and Sir William Crookes to stand up for their principles and break this taboo, risking their reputations within the scientific and academic establishments.

In 1933 Sir Oliver Lodge published an article in The Queen's Hospital Annual (Birmingham) entitled 'The Mode of Future Existence', where he stated that we have to look beyond the world of matter, into the dynamics of energy, to gain a more comprehensive understanding of reality. Yet, although these same issues are confronting us now, this little-known article has largely been left to fade into obscurity.

Given that the 1930s were already a time when Einstein's Theory of Relativity was competing with the more recent Quantum Mechanics breakthroughs of Nils Bohr et al, it is little wonder that Sir Oliver Lodge felt so frustrated that his science-led research into survival after death was not being taken seriously by the scientific establishment of his day.

At the end of that decade, in the first year of World War II, Air Chief Marshal Hugh Dowding (later Lord Dowding), Head of the Royal Air Force Fighter Command, used his brilliant strategic mind to win the Battle of Britain in 1940. He was also a pioneer in the field of Spiritualism, writing two books, MANY MANSIONS and LYCHGATE.

According to Campaign for Philosophical Freedom (cfpf.org.uk) Founder Michael Roll, the reason why there has been a reluctance to research the 'afterlife' field in any meaningful manner is that it poses a perceived threat to the axioms of traditional science and religious institutions alike, and therefore we should not be surprised by vested interests within the establishment and mainstream media attempting to downplay this aspect of scientific research.

However, as with Crookes and Lodge before them, there are scientific investigators continuing to make progress, including Ronald Pearson, Professor Brian Josephson and Gary Schwartz. Australian lawyer Victor Zammit has also carried out a considerable amount of research in the field, to the extent that he concludes that the amount of evidence proving the existence of the afterlife is irrefutable.

* * *

Nowhere is the need for change more urgent than in the way business and the economy operates. In 1996 I interviewed Body Shop Founder Anita Roddick and asked her what she thought the world would look like in the year 2010. She foresaw two starkly contrasting potential scenarios.

Her nightmare vision was of a world run by a handful of transnational corporations with no corporate code of behaviour, huge social alienation developing alongside a violent drug-based urban economy and a proliferation of fundamentalist thinking. Rapid depletion of resources would diminish the availability of consumer goods.

Being the optimist that she was, she felt there was a better chance of her positive scenario being played out, of a brave new world where a more caring paradigm of business thinking would be embraced, with a greater sense of cooperation and adventure, more concentration on supporting the grass roots, local enterprise initiatives and keeping families and communities together.

In 2004 a book and associated film, 'The Corporation', was released. In the film the corporation, a separate legal entity in its own right, was examined as if it were a person. The remarkable conclusion drawn from the research was that the corporation would be considered a 'psychopath' when looked at from a psychological perspective.

Another important question we must ask is why the global monetary system is considered such a 'sacred cow', when we know that the system only works by keeping the majority of the population in debt? In the film 'Zeitgeist Addendum', the question is posed as to why have a monetary system at all, and puts forward some interesting alternatives to consider.

Although it may be a simplistic perspective, do we really want to entrust the future of the world and the human race to a collection of 'psychopaths' operating in, and controlling, a highly dubious global monetary system? This sounds very much like Anita Roddick's nightmare scenario for 2010 mentioned earlier.

In that same interview, Roddick said: 'We know, we really know, who controls what now. We really know the institutions that are passive and moribund, and those that work. We know there is something incredibly wrong with our economic order. We know that there are secrecies going on.'

This was a profound insight at that time. Since then more people are beginning to distrust what the mainstream media is feeding them, preferring to uncover their own truths from alternative information sources such as Edge Media TV, Conscious Media Network, Project Camelot, Rumor Mill News Radio and Coast to Coast AM, all freely available on the Internet, and all doing excellent research to expose these 'secrecies' and to disseminate the truth about what is really going on in the world today.

One encouraging trend which has been evolving over the last decade or so has been the development of the Lifestyles of Health and Sustainability (LOHAS) market sector, with its five main sub-sectors of Sustainable Economy, Ecological Lifestyles, Healthy Living, Alternative Healthcare and Personal Development. Allied to this is the growth of the Social Enterprise sector, where achieving the social purpose of the organization is the most important factor, as distinct from simply making a profit. There is no doubt that Anita Roddick was a champion and pioneer of both these strands of business evolution.

★ ★ ★

From a number of perspectives, this is an exciting and challenging time for humanity to be living on this planet. Where we go over the next few years, up to and beyond the year 2012, is open to speculation, and prophecies abound. We have considered the significance of the year 2012 from several viewpoints here—but what now?

In seeking to find a way to bring this Postscript to an end, especially as 2012 is such a huge topic in its own right, I decided to meditate on it to see if any flashes of inspiration might fire my imagination. Very quickly I became conscious of a Mayan spirit guide directing me to watch the interview by Drunvalo Melchizedek on Conscious Media Network. I was also given a name, 'Amaris', which meant absolutely nothing to me.

As I viewed the interview, which I had already seen some time before, I realized that Drunvalo was giving the precise 'vital message' on which I wished to end this book.

Out of curiosity, I later Googled 'Amaris', thinking it must have some Mayan connection, instead finding it was a rare Hebrew female name meaning 'God has said' or 'promised by God'. Any implied significance could of course have been a complete coincidence or 'just my imagination'; however, I remembered that a couple of years before, also in meditation, I had been given the name of a Tibetan spirit guide, Chung-Li, which turned out to mean 'President' in Chinese. Another 'coincidence'? I prefer to think that we should learn to pay attention to these inner promptings, otherwise a lot of potentially useful information might just pass us by. Carl Jung coined the word 'synchronicity', meaning 'meaningful coincidence'; we should think carefully before dismissing coincidences as unimportant, especially in these times.

In the interview Drunvalo commented on the significance of the year 2012 from the Mayan and Hopi Indian standpoint; he believes strongly that we have the opportunity to change our consciousness, and that things will get easier as everything accelerates spiritually into an unstoppable force.

The Mayan prophecies are linked in with the mystery of the crystal skulls, believed to be thirteen in total, and each containing knowledge and wisdom from certain time periods. From the Mayan tribes spread throughout Guatemala, Belize and Mexico, there is a Council of 440 Mayan Elders, who will be writing this knowledge and message to the world into a book between now and 2012; they will be rewriting over five hundred years of Mayan history, information which they believe has been wrongly interpreted and recorded within Western historical perspectives of events.

In the prophecies the Mayans predict that the earth will undergo a magnetic pole shift followed by a physical pole shift, sometime around 2012. This could happen very suddenly, the geography of the world changing dramatically, with mountains going up and down and continents breaking off in pieces.

These predictions are uncannily similar to Sir Arthur Conan Doyle's warnings from the 1930s as channelled through Grace Cooke.* ACD foresaw physical catastrophes on earth, that there would emerge a great continent where now exists ocean, and there would follow the equivalent subsidence of land. Around the same time 'sleeping prophet', Edgar Cayce,

---

*What White Eagle has said about the 'changes' is that they are more to do with upheavals at an inner level—in other words, complete shifts of consciousness

also predicted apocalyptic world events, a period of purification involving natural disasters that would dramatically alter the surface of the Earth.

What the Mayans are saying is that they were part of the Atlantean civilization during the last pole shift thirteen thousand years ago, when the legendary continent of Atlantis was devastated by floods and earthquakes. Having experienced this catastrophe in the past, they want to offer the world the wisdom of what to do when these earth changes take place, because in Atlantis millions died as they did not know a few simple things.

Drunvalo says there are certain things we need to change within ourselves; and that if we do, not only will we not die, but we will go up in awareness and consciousness. He believes that those who want to listen can change the outcome of what happens during these times, and that we are starting to access some of this information intuitively. The Mayan philosophy is for us to be calm and balanced, and if we understood what awaits us after the transition people would be jumping up and down with joy; they anticipate a time of great celebration, when we become more than human.

The fall of Atlantis thirteen thousand years ago was caused by people moving from their heart to their head, reckons Drunvalo. Now they need to move from head to heart, and everyone who does this will survive.

As the old ways dissolve, this might be disconcerting as new ways start to replace them. The banking systems, governments and religions are all unstable and will break apart, he says. In its place will be a brand new way of being, a way we haven't seen for thousands of years, where fear goes away.

To sum up, the most vital message for these times seems to be loud and clear—it is for us to choose to get into our hearts rather than our minds. If there are to be earth changes, the best way to survive and move through them is through being in our hearts. Alternatively, if enough people move into their hearts, choosing love over fear, the resultant shift in consciousness may be enough to dissipate or eliminate these earth changes altogether.

Either way, doesn't it make sense for you to choose to go into your heart?

When the power of love overcomes the love of
power, the world will know peace.
Jimi Hendrix

ACKNOWLEDGMENTS

THIS BOOK could not have been written without the people who have contributed to it, sharing their stories with great humility; to them all I offer my heartfelt gratitude.

Although the writing and publication has happened over an unbelievably short period—a little over six months—its incubation period has been considerably longer. I thank my children, Fionn and Fiona, from the bottom of my heart for showing great love and tolerance as I wrestled with the disruptions caused by shifting from corporate executive to writer and healer, attempting to live a life more in alignment with my soul's purpose.

Another special person who has shared my spiritual journey in recent years and taught me so much in so many ways is Wendy Springett, whose encouragement has been a vital ingredient in my creative endeavours.

Others who have provided welcome support at critical times along the way include Rhod and Sue MacLennan, Philip Andrews, Kate Clark, Will Bower, Alan Massey, Aileen and John Ross, Jeanne Ames, Jean Bell, Pip and Jose Harper, June Woods, Carin Schwartz, Dee Ryan, Carole Gray, Dee Buchanan, Tracey Houe, Sheila Pollock, Karen Fraser, Kathleen Murray, Bridget Pemberton, Dave Macdermid, David Munro, George Gray, Susan Stewart, Stephen Liggett, John Abdey, Frances Robbe, Miriam and John Galt, Tony and Lizzie Hodgson, Frances Tait, Jayne Owen, Liz Hoskin, Mike Scott and Bob Keillor.

Writing requires confidence and clarity, and for their invaluable feedback and expertise I would like to thank Joycebelle Edelbrock of the Enlightened Wealth Institute, Gabriele Rico, author of WRITING THE NATURAL WAY, and author Sue-Ellen Welfonder; thanks also to Moira Bergman for setting up the Findhorn Creative Writing Group, which helped spur me into writing action.

For opening my eyes to new health and healing paradigms I am grateful to members of my Quantum-Touch® network, Richard Gordon, Jennifer Taylor, Mervyn Foster, Di Wilson, Tiffany Primrose Stephens and Jan Collinson; also to Derek Talbot and Bob Edwards, practitioners and trainers in Vibrational Medicine with Dr Helen Petrow.

A big thanks also to the leader of my Spiritual Development Circle, Karen Collesso, and other members of the Inverness Spiritualist Church; also the Nairn Spiritualist Group, and the many mediums who have given me messages over the last four years.

Elizabeth McIntyre and the White Eagle Lodge Deeside Group, Alice Provan and the White Eagle Glasgow Daughter Lodge, and Ranald Godfrey and the White Eagle Edinburgh Daughter Lodge, for welcoming me into White Eagle Lodge activities.

Bill Henderson and Kate O'Connell, leaders of the Forres Big Choir, and fellow members; singing with this wonderful group helped me 'find my voice'.

Alastair Cunningham and the Anam Cara community and men's group in Inverness, for the uplifting and inspirational spiritual energy provided by the place and the people.

Fellow spiritual travellers Milena Fiore, Robert and Gloria Zadek, and others in the 'H Team' in Half Moon Bay and the San Francisco Bay Area in Northern California; Gwynne Rogers and Steve French of the Natural Marketing Institute, and Ted Ning of Conscious Media, for the great work they are doing in developing the Lifestyles of Health and Sustainability (LOHAS) market sector, which has had a major impact on the evolution of socially responsible business, from its roots in Colorado and California.

Silva Method UK Director Ian Pollock and Phyllis Pollock, for teaching me the Silva Method, my first formal introduction to meditation practice and the power of the mind.

The late Anita Roddick, who taught me the importance of trust, and who led by her example as a radical activist to help drive business, social and environmental change.

Colum Hayward, Chief Editor of Polair Publishing, who over the last few months has become not just a new acquaintance and business colleague, but a valued friend.

The Spirit of Sir Arthur Conan Doyle, and other helpers from the invisible realms operating in Absolute Truth, for guidance throughout this project.

Dave Patrick
Nairn, Scotland
April 2009